AF292509

The Scottish Rebellion
against Robert the Bruce

The Scottish Rebellion against Robert the Bruce

Exiles and Traitors

James Turner

Pen & Sword
MILITARY

First published in Great Britain in 2026 by
Pen & Sword Military
An imprint of Pen & Sword Books Limited
Yorkshire – Philadelphia

ISBN 978 1 03614 623 8

A CIP catalogue record for this book is
available from the British Library.

Typeset by Mac Style
Printed in the UK by CPI Group (UK) Ltd, Croydon, CR0 4YY.

The Publisher's authorised representative in the EU for product
safety is Authorised Rep Compliance Ltd., Ground Floor,
71 Lower Baggot Street, Dublin D02 P593, Ireland.
www.arccompliance.com

For a complete list of Pen & Sword titles please contact:

PEN & SWORD BOOKS LIMITED
47 Church Street, Barnsley, South Yorkshire, S70 2AS, England
E-mail: enquiries@pen-and-sword.co.uk
Website: www.pen-and-sword.co.uk
or
PEN AND SWORD BOOKS
1950 Lawrence Road, Havertown, PA 19083, USA
E-mail: uspen-and-sword@casematepublishers.com
Website: www.penandswordbooks.com

Contents

Introduction

July of 1331 saw the gathering of a most unusual army, its billets scattered across the modest ports of Yorkshire's eastern coast. Its purpose, the invasion of Scotland and the overthrow of the yet inchoate line of Bruce kings. This was a task monumentally disproportionate in scale to the tiny army that sought to undertake it, which was barley 1,500 men strong. It was also a goal that they would ultimately fail to realise, though not before experiencing some spectacular successes and forever changing the balance of power within Scottish politics. The most notable of these triumphs were the opening battle of the campaign, fought on Dupplin Moor, shortly after the army's arrival in Scotland, and the relatively better-known Battle of Halidon Hill. Such unlikely victories lent credibility and cachet to their cause, igniting another decade of vicious, fundamentally internecine, warfare.

The majority of this precocious army was composed of Englishmen, although included within its ranks were soldiers drawn from cultures across Europe, such as Germany and the Lowlands. It was by no means a royal army, although its leader undoubtedly thought of himself as a king. Indeed, the King of England, Edward III, in whose domain the army mustered, had given the planned invasion only the most tacit and circumspect of approvals. Rather than march out from England and risk conjuring afresh memories of the all too recently thwarted imperial ambitions of the young Edward's predecessors, the army was only permitted to leave England by sea. As a result, they would arrive on Scotland's shores as a host of anonymous marauders, emerging from a trackless and primordial domain beyond the ken of man and reach of their former affiliations and associations. This narrative, while undoubtedly romantic, was as everyone involved knew, a gossamer-thin shroud of official deniability. The leadership cadre of this army, who had for years sheltered beneath the auspices of the English throne, were no strangers to Scotland. For them, the expedition was to be both invasion and homecoming.

In keeping with broad trends in contemporary European warfare that would come to a head in the next few decades, most of the of army, whatever their national origins, were soldiers of fortune and adventurers. They were part of a growing class of professional and semi-professional warmakers attracted by the promise of pay and plunder. In England, the careful negotiating system of raising soldiers through the principle of feudal obligation, while still extant, had over the last century been gradually eroded by the greater expediency, quality and centralised control offered by cash. In any case, the nature and circumstances of the army's commanders meant that their landed estates and holdings would have likely been insufficient to provide much beyond the bare bones of a functional army. This is because the army was led by the Disinherited, a clique of closely related Scottish nobles, or nobles of intimate Scottish heritage, who had lost their estates and homes because of their families' opposition to Robert the Bruce's claim to the throne of Scotland.

They were headed by Edward Balliol, royal hopeful and eldest son of deposed King, John Balliol, Alice Comyn, the heiress of the Earldom of Buchan and a member of the once powerful and influential Comyn family and her husband Henry de Beaumont, a French-born nobleman and military adventurer who was himself the grandson of an emperor. Others included David Strathbogie, the titular Earl of Atholl and a member of the extended Comyn family, and Gilbert de Umfraville, a prominent claimant to the earldom of Angus that had previously been held by his father and grandfather before being awarded to a branch of the Bruce-aligned Stewart family. Far from coincidentally, Gilbert was through his paternal grandmother, Elizabeth, yet another Comyn relative. These luminaries and figureheads were joined by dozens of retainers, affiliates and lesser members of the nobility who had also found their ancestral lands confiscated and nominally inviolate inheritance claims set aside as a result of their opposition of the Bruce monarchy.

Today, these figures are strangers to us, would be usurpers. Their presence in the historical narrative trespasses upon our commonly held assumptions about the form and character of the amorphous Wars of Scottish Independence, as well as the nation-affirming consequences of the Bruce family's eventual triumph. Yet when divested of centuries of myth making and viewed as political actors on their own terms, it is clear that the Disinherited stood at the centre of a major and era-defining cleavage in Scottish aristocratic society that predated the paradigm of Anglo-Scottish conflict with which it would become entangled. This book is about the history of these men and women and their place at the heart of contemporary Scottish politics, charting their plight during exile and their spectacular homecoming when they once more staked a claim in Scotland's future upon the battlefield.

While focusing on the Bruce's enemies and the ongoing factionalism that characterised his reign and that of his immediate successor, this book in no way aims to disparage King Robert I or undermine his achievements. Indeed, its examination of his long-running struggle with both rival Scottish aristocrats and the imperialistic ambitions of England's Edward I will, like so many other studies, reveal that he was a man of admirable ability, unflagging tenacity, and enviable vision. It merely aims, through a study of the history of the Disinherited and their later revanchist activities, to question and examine the often-seen conflation between the Bruce's faction and Scottish identity.

Despite his great success in cultivating support among members of the Scottish aristocracy, the Bruce had no special claim on Scottish identity or even for that matter the throne. His claim to the Scottish crown was of roughly comparable dynastic validity as that of his family's greatest rivals, John Balliol and his nephew John Comyn. It was from this rival faction of Scottish nobility that the Disinherited, their relatives and associates sprang; their invasion of Scotland in 1331, the latest manifestation of a multigenerational and extraordinarily bitter blood feud between neighbouring Scottish families.

The notion that history is written by the victors is a Churchillian truism that is so often repeated, it is almost as wearying to hear as it is true. The effect of this principle on our collective perceptions of history are further exacerbated by the manner in which distance and the repetition of rote learning inevitably bleed the nuance from a topic. The cracks and fractures of historical discourse are papered over with convenient or reassuring simplifications. This is doubly the case regarding intangible or deeply personal matters such as identity.

In addition to the weight and influence of carefully cultivated national myths and narratives, our modern conception of the world is, for the most part, reflective of the reality that we exist within a deeply embedded global structure in which the default unit is the nation state. Comparatively few of us spend much time pondering the nature of our cultural and political identity, precisely because it is often so manifestly obvious and tangible, secured in the bedrock of modern citizenship and all the manifold administrative apparatus and bureaucracy that accompany it.

We know we belong to one or more nations, because to do so is, usually, an unambiguous legal reality with the certificates, passports and tax returns to prove it. Within this model of nationalism, a modern child's national identity is informed by our expectations regarding the connective tissue that encompasses and merges territory, culture and government. This has not always been the case. Indeed, even now identity, nationhood and the structures we have built around them are rarely as clean cut or accommodating as the ideal.

No one in thirteenth-century Scotland was handing out paperwork saying who was Scottish and who was not. Royal authority was still almost entirely personal, rather than institutional in nature. Naturally Robert, his son David and virtually any other contemporary king would hope for and demand the loyalty of all those living within his kingdom. In practice, however, the co-operation of both the Church and nobility had to be secured through the fostering of reciprocal relationships between the monarch and individual groups of regional powerbrokers. The Bruce was therefore the head not of a united polity in the sense of a modern nation state but of a coalition of allied aristocratic families and their conjoined interests.

Of course, Scotland clearly existed within contemporary consciousness as a very real territorial and cultural unit, but one whose exact boundaries remained ill defined. Identity is a layered and multifaceted construct and within these borders there were significant cultural and regional variances. As a result of these variances and the paramount importance of the family as a structural unit within contemporary society, political affiliation and loyalty tended to be derived from regional and familial loyalties, formative ties that existed underneath a more generalised and encompassing sense of Scottish identity. In practice, royal authority extended only as far as the Bruce or one of his regional proxies were willing or able to enforce it. For the most part, kingship remained a title, a bauble, rather than an office with defined roles and powers.

It makes for a fascinating and nuanced puzzle. The Wars of Independence and Scotland's resistance to English conquest are, despite the centuries of distinctive Scottish history that precede them, commonly viewed today as the nation's premier foundation myth, the bedrock upon which Scottish identity proudly stands. Who are the Scottish? Well, that's a complex and engrossing question but thanks to the triumph at Bannockburn, we at least know they are not English. When I attended primary school, our first real introduction to Scottish history was not the formation of Dàl Riata or the Davidian Revolution but the Wars of Independence. Scotland already existed as a well-established and seemingly naturally occurring polity and culture that was suddenly endangered by the cupidity and avarice of its southern neighbour. A previously amorphous perception that was granted sharp definition by the release of a certain film. Yet despite its formative influence on our conceptions of our history and our understanding of Anglo-Scottish relations, both Wars of Independence began with disputes between rival Scottish aristocratic affinities.

Part of the Bruce's political genius was the manner in which he turned his Scottish rivals' connections with the kings of England into a poisoned chalice, presenting them as collaborators and stooges in the English invasion of Scotland. This was a particularly impressive feat because Robert, like his Balliol and Comyn rivals, had previously enjoyed extensive ties with the English monarch and had willingly engaged and co-operated with him as the Scottish nobility attempted to navigate the succession crisis brought about by the premature death of Princess Margaret, the maternal granddaughter and sole heir of King Alexander III of Scotland. The process through which English interest in Scotland escalated from that of neutral arbiter and facilitator to direct military intervention and conquest was an incremental one. The relatives of the Disinherited began by courting support for their preferred candidates in a dispute over the Scottish succession, only to see themselves slip precipitously into the role of English proxies and junior partners in a war for control of their own country. However, as we shall explore, this was far from a straightforward or simple process and the barrier between the two rival Scottish parties remained blurred and permeable right up until the conclusion of the conflict.

As is often the case with history, the blame in part lies with an ambitious Englishman. Edward I's grandfather, John I, had lost an empire. The Angevin Empire had been a patchwork of domains composed of many culturally distinctive regions and entities that had been stitched together by the dynastic claims and personal political commitments of Edward's great-grandfather, Henry II. In contrast to his father, who had been one of the greatest monarchs of western Christendom, and his often-celebrated elder brother, Richard the Lionheart, John lost almost the entirety of the family's European holdings before becoming embroiled in a drawn out and deeply destructive conflict with the English aristocracy. Similarly, the young Edward had witnessed the unsuccessful attempts of his own father, Henry III, to win back their ancestral lands and the nadir of royal power during the second Baron's Rebellion.

Previous English kings, such as Edward's ancestors Henry I and Henry II, had claimed overlordship of the entirety of the British Isles, in part supported by the overwhelming and transformative popularity of Arthurian literature. Such claims to Overlordship were often iterated but seldom applied and while Anglo-Norman and Angevin kings wielded a great deal of influence within the 'Celtic Fringe', their involvement was neither uniform nor consistent. In Ireland and Wales, the authority of the English kings was predicated upon the presence and military activity of semi-autonomous Anglo-Norman warlords. In contrast in Scotland, overlordship was advanced tentatively through close dynastic connections with consecutive Scottish kings and was often the product of extensive negotiations.

In order to secure his somewhat tenuous claim to the throne of England, Henry I had leapt into action upon the death of his elder brother in 1100 to claim England's two most important resources. The first of these was the royal treasury at Winchester, the second was a young nun in training, Matilda of Scotland. Matilda was the daughter of King Malcolm III of Scotland and his wife Margaret, a descendant of the royal house of Wessex and the line of native kings that had first unified England. Henry's subsequent marriage to Matilda, therefore, not only brought him the potential support of the Scottish king but greatly enhanced his legitimacy and right to rule in the eyes of his English subjects. This connection was further strengthened by the marriage of one of Henry's illegitimate daughters, Sybil, to Malcolm's son and successor, Alexander I.

This familial connection defined Anglo-Scottish relations every bit as much as the contrivances of English kings to exert seniority. Alexander's younger brother and successor, David I, remodelled the royal court and the administrative structures of Scotland on those of his Anglo-Norman relatives, a process that involved the settlement of a number of Anglo-Norman aristocrats and adventurers within Scotland. When David invaded England in 1138, he did so in support of the claim of his niece, Empress Matilda, the daughter of Henry I and Matilda of Scotland, to the English throne. Likewise, David's grandson, Malcolm IV and his successor, William the Lion, co-operated amicably with Henry II of England to resolve the succession disputes and infighting that had consumed their mutual Gallovidian relatives.

The first break in the largely convivial relationship between the Scottish and English royal families was heralded by William the Lion's invasion of England in 1173. William's father, Prince Henry of Scotland, had held two English earldoms, Huntingdon and Northumbria. Generations earlier, David I had been able to secure the Scottish annexation of Cumbria, while William through his mother, Ada de Warenne, possessed a potentially convincing claim to the Earldom of Surrey. Henry II, perhaps understandably, alarmed by the King of Scotland's growing hold over northern England had confiscated all of William's English lands with the sole exception of the Earldom of Huntingdon.

After diplomatic efforts to reclaim his lost English inheritance proved to be fruitless, William eventually threw his support behind the rebellion launched in 1173 by King Henry's eldest legitimate sons. This revolt, fundamentally caused by Henry's unwillingness to share power or secede territory to his sons, also enjoyed the support of the King of France and large sections of the aristocracy. Unfortunately for King William, his invasion of England was defeated and he himself captured at the Battle of Alnwick the following year. He was forced to sign the Treaty of Falaise in which he acknowledged a formalised and far more heavy-handed form of English overlordship, while many of Scotland's most strategically important castles were garrisoned by Henry's troops.

Within Henry's grand hegemonic strategy, the kings of Scotland were to continue to be treated as junior allies and colleagues. However, the English king's overlordship of Scotland was for the first time articulated in terms of legal absolutes, rather than deliberately vague allusions to seniority that were almost always filtered through personal and familial contexts. Should William be inclined to withhold his co-operation or once again throw his lot in with Henry's enemies, he would now have to reckon with the mercenaries that Henry had placed within Berwick, Stirling, Edinburgh, Jedburgh and Roxburgh. These forfeitures and the Scottish monarch's tangible loss of status not only made William incredibly vulnerable to aggressive intervention from his southern neighbour but also had a very real detrimental effect on his ability to project royal authority within Scotland. The decade following the signing of the Treaty of Falaise saw Scottish control over the relatively recently annexed Galloway become increasingly tenuous, while William faced mounting dissent from members of the Scottish nobility, although his continued co-operation with Henry did secure him the return of the earldom of Huntingdon which he passed on to his younger brother David.

The effects of the treaty, while dramatic, were ultimately short-lived. When Henry II died in 1189, he was succeeded by his eldest remaining son, Richard, who was determined to take part in the impending third crusade, alongside the King of France and the Holy Roman Emperor. Lion and Lionhearted swiftly came to an agreement in which the Treaty of Falaise was dissolved in return for a substantial cash payment of 10,000 marks. While William's canny bargaining saw the restoration of the traditional paradigm between English and Scottish monarchs, he and his immediate successors would not quickly forget the boot that had been pressed upon their necks.

The loss of his family's prestigious pseudo-imperial status, alongside the cultural impact of adapting the myths and pseudo history of Britain to reflect the sensibilities and customs of contemporary European aristocratic society, inspired Edward I to attempt to assert the English crown's overlordship once again over the entirety of the British Isles. In Wales, parts of which had been under the effective rule of an invasive Norman minority since the immediate aftermath of the Conquest, these ambitions manifested themselves as direct military intervention. Between 1277 and 1283, Edward launched a series of sustained and substantive military campaigns to support the Norman marcher lords and annex the lands of the remaining independent Welsh princes. These territorial gains were subsequently protected and English royal authority within the region cemented by the undertaking of a ruinously expensive programme of castle building. In Scotland, Edward sought to project authority and overlordship by presenting himself as a neutral arbiter of the succession dispute that arose following the death of Alexander III in 1286. Edward's success in the early stages of these negotiations and the obviously large levels of political cachet he enjoyed within Scotland appear somewhat incongruous to those aware of the decades of bloodshed that were to follow.

The English king not only reconciled the Scottish nobility to the candidacy of Alexander III's granddaughter, Margaret of Norway, but had actually managed to secure an engagement between the young queen to be and his son and heir, Prince Edward. While the various factions and rival claimants of the Scottish nobility had been prevailed upon to support or at least reluctantly acquiesce to both Margaret's claim and engagement, they were cognisant of the danger the marriage presented to Scotland's continued independence. In the second Treaty of Birgham in 1290, the collective voices of the Scottish nobility asserted the continued independence of the kingdom and its institutions, specifying that Margaret was to be crowned without Prince Edward and that Scotland would not simply default into the possession of her husband. However, the English were able to carve enough exceptions into the treaty to successfully muddle this crucial delineation. Regardless of the exact provisions or wording of the treaty, in practical terms, Margaret and Prince Edward's marriage unavoidably left open the strong possibility that one day either he or one of their potential children would rule both England and Scotland.

Even considering the obvious trepidation felt by elements of the Scottish nobility and their insistence on the statutes and restrictions imposed upon the marriage by the treaty, the fact that so many of Scotland's leading magnates were willing to accept a marriage between their monarch and the future English king is significant. As strange as this arrangement may seem through the lens of modern nationalism, at this point in the Middle Ages, power remained principally a personal rather than national or institutional resource. Titles and territory were acquired and retained through familial ties and carefully maintained internal lines of inheritance that frequently, even routinely, cut across cultural and political borders. Royal authority was highly personal in nature and the political integrity of any given kingdom predicated upon the willingness and ability of a monarch to cultivate relationships with their vassals, whoever they happened to be. The exact nature and parameters of such relationships and their mutual obligations were by their very nature varied and flexible.

In this sense, the Treaty of Birgham, in which members of the Scottish nobility came together to collectively bargain over the remit and potential applications of royal authority, was far from atypical. Indeed, among the nobility, the distinction between Scottish and English is not always immediately apparent and of limited critical use. Generations of intermarriage and ongoing political affiliations meant that many nobles had family and therefore potentially inheritable landed and financial interests on either side of the border. A not inconsiderable number of Scottish nobles, such as John Balliol and Robert Bruce, already possessed estates in both England and Scotland and therefore owed fealty in one form or another to both thrones. In addition, a large number of the Scottish nobility were, like their English equivalents, partially or even primarily of Norman descent.

Further, regardless of the exact details of their ancestry, all member of the nobility of Christian Europe at this time shared certain traits and cultural touchstones. The most important and obvious of these were the overwhelming use of French as a shared first language and a dedication to the tenets and trapping of the cult of Chivalry that provided the nobility of Europe with a shared culture and martial ethos. The members of the tightly interconnected Scottish and English nobility consequently had far more in common with one another than they did with the lower orders of their respective host cultures.

When King Edward's plans were disrupted by the tragic death of Margaret, the Maid of Norway on Orkney, having fallen ill on her long-delayed journey to her coronation at Scone, he quickly revised his strategy. In 1291, Edward and the other auditors of the council he convened and chaired elected John Balliol, the father of Edward Balliol, the future leader of the Disinherited and victor of Dupplin Moor and Halidon Hill, as King of Scotland. John's election was accepted without major incident or co-ordinated dissent from his rivals, and he was soon crowned at Scone. Edward was able to inhabit such a crucial role in Scottish politics because he was the ruler of a powerful neighbouring kingdom and because it suited the various claimants and factions of the Scottish aristocracy to have a prestigious neutral party overseeing what was a largely unprecedented process.

Edward's influence and authority within Scotland was primarily personal in nature, predicated upon his prestige as a monarch and working relationship with the principal members of the Scottish aristocracy. His attempt to convert this personal influence into institutional authority by formalising the powers and remit of the previously largely nominal and amorphous position of overlord provoked a powerful backlash among members of the Scottish nobility. Edward's insistence upon his rights and dignity as overlord, combined with the continuation of his supervisory role in Scottish politics, fuelled the perception that John Balliol was nothing more than a puppet king.

When a faction of the disenfranchised Scottish nobility seized power for themselves, Edward mobilised the resources he possessed as the King of England to defend his claim to the overlordship of Scotland. This invasion, as we shall discuss later in greater detail, resulted in the abdication and exile of John Balliol and the formation of a keen rivalry between Balliol's Bruce rivals and Comyn relatives. This complex and multifaceted conflict eventually resulted in a deep-seated shift in contemporary conceptions of Scottish identity and the historically misleading relegation of the Disinherited to the position of mere adjutants within a broader fundamentally Anglo-Scottish conflict.

In actuality, as extraordinary as it was, the Disinherited's ambitious invasion of Scotland and renewed bid for the Scottish throne was first and foremost a private and personal enterprise undertaken by members of a single extended family and supported by a handful of opportunistic adventurers. The English king, Edward III, was young, inexperienced and had already suffered a humiliating defeat while prematurely pursuing military action within Scotland. As such he and his advisors were disinclined to give the Disinherited much beyond circumspect support by tacitly ignoring the presence of the small army mustering on the north-east coast of his kingdom. The arrival of the Disinherited in Perth and their apparent willingness to court the support of the Scottish king's allies and deputies, struck decisively at political fault lines within the Bruce regime.

In part, thanks to the sudden death of one of King David's premier military commanders, the Disinherited won an astounding and decisive victory at the Battle of Dupplin Moor. This victory paved the way for their leader, Edward Balliol to push forward and have himself crowned King of Scotland at Scone, just as his father had been. While the Bruce faction rallied decisively, eventually compelling the Disinherited to solicit English military support, it is worth emphasising that the conflict began and, in some senses, continued as a re-initialising of hostilities between two distantly related and rival factions of the Scottish nobility. The Battle of Dupplin Moor and the campaign of the Disinherited is a little commented on but fascinating tale of a motley crew of exiles and underdogs risking life and limb to return home and reclaim their ancestral lands. For members of the fourteenth-century nobility, for whom politics was unavoidably personal and whose legacy was conceived of primarily through the transition of landed interests between family members, there could be no higher calling or spur to action. On top of this engaging human aspect, close study of the Disinherited and their attempts to reclaim the Scottish throne provides an invaluable and unique insight into both the form and character of fourteenth-century aristocratic affinities and the evolving interplay between Scottish cultural and political identity at a pivotal stage in their development.

This book is the first full-length scholarly account of the history of the Disinherited, the origins and circumstances of their rivalry with the Bruce monarchy and their audacious attempt to turn back the clock and regain their former position of dominance at the heart of Scottish politics. As previously discussed above, the conflict known as the First War of Scottish Independence has come to occupy a place of singular importance within modern conceptions of Scottish history. Despite occurring several hundreds of years after the actual foundation of the kingdom, victory over the English invaders is an integral part of the nation's creation myth and a cornerstone of Scottish identity. One does not have to look far for signs of this legacy. 'Flower of Scotland', the anthem sung by both Scotland's international football and rugby teams, composed in the mid-1960s, celebrates the Scottish victory at Bannockburn; implicitly framing the battle through its resistance to the English king as a central component of Scottish identity. The role of this conflict within the nation's collective imagination is further reflected in the great number of works of history, both scholarly and populist, that concern themselves with Robert the Bruce's bid for the Scottish throne and the cut and thrust of the tenacious struggle to thwart the imperial ambitions of consecutive English kings.

In comparison, awareness of the Second War of Scottish Independence is relatively muted within popular historical narratives. Relatively little of the war's historical context or the events of this complex and long-running conflict have penetrated deeply into the public consciousness or discourse on the history of Scottish identity and Anglo-Scottish relations. A possible explanation for this lack of traction is that the rapidly seesawing military fortunes of its combatants and the war's staggered, somewhat inconclusive resolution, fails to deliver the clear-cut narrative of perseverance and eventual triumph against the odds that the campaigns of Robert the Bruce did. Were it a movie, critics would say that as a sequel, the Second War of Independence was overly complex and perhaps unnecessary. Bruce appears to us now as a natural hero and protagonist; generations of cumulative mythmaking have enlarged Robert the Bruce to fill the roles of founder, saviour and revolutionary hero. Meanwhile, awareness of David II has to a certain extent been subsumed into the long shadow of his father's legacy; his personal reputation tarnished and diminished by his uneven martial record, capture and failure to perpetuate the dynasty.

As was the case with many great rivals throughout history, the shared enmity that existed between the Bruce and Balliol families owed as much to their similarities as to their differences. They were first and foremost neighbours, the rulers of contiguous and historically connected regional affinities. Both families were essentially Anglo-Scottish in origin, descended from Norman or English adventurers. Both families had reached the positions of prominence they enjoyed within the Scottish aristocracy because of marriage into an existing native dynasty. As it happened, the Bruces and the Balliols married into two different branches of the same dynasty.

Even the primary point of contention between the two families, their rival claims for the Scottish throne, originated from the same source, descent from a daughter of the Scottish prince, Earl David of Huntingdon. These similarities and elements of shared heritage contributed to the fierce nature of the rivalry and eventual conflict between the two families. In a strange coincidence a generation before the onset of the Succession Crisis and failure of the Dunkeld royal line, the Bruces and Balliols had both married into the competing branches of a family descended from the old Princes of Galloway. We will delve into the origins and ramifications of this joint connection in more detail imminently but in short, Galloway had been divided into the Earldom of Carrick and the Lordship of Galloway in 1186.[1] This was done at the behest of King Henry II of England, who colluded with King William the Lion of Scotland in an attempt to end a succession dispute being fought by his cousins, the grandsons of Prince Fergus of Galloway.

It was in the remains of this formerly autonomous region that both families would come to true prominence within Scottish politics. There they formed an inherited regional rivalry that was later compounded by the great difficulty of untangling their competing dynastic claims. It was a rivalry that did much to shape the boundaries and often overlooked tragically internecine character of the Wars of Scottish Independence. Happily, for our purposes, delving into the history of Galloway and its partition not only illuminates the shared familial history of the Bruce and Balliol families but allows us to further examine the changing nature of Anglo-Scottish relations and shuck off the last of the preconceptions that twentieth-century nationalism has imposed upon our understanding of medieval polities. We will come to the reign of David II and the momentous events of the Second War of Independence in due course, but first we must turn our attention to the shared origins of the two families.

Chapter One

Neighbours and Rivals

Located upon the coast of what is now south-western Scotland, Galloway was an independent marcher region that supported a layered, multifaceted cultural identity. For much of its existence as an autonomous entity, Galloway found itself suspended precariously between the fraying seaward-facing world of the Norse-Gaels, the waxing power and ambition of an increasingly Normanised Scotland and the looming shadow of English overlordship. Galloway has been progressively associated by historians and archaeologists with the elusive sub-Roman kingdom of Rheged; recent archaeological evidence has even led some to speculate that the charmingly named Trusty's Hill on the southern coast of Galloway may have been the site of a major Brythonic royal centre in the sixth and early seventh centuries.[1]

Following the forcible consolidation of the northern Saxon kingdoms, the region became the frontier between Northumbria and the Brittonic Kingdom of Strathclyde.[2] It is somewhat unclear whether or not following the conquest of Northumbria by the Danes if Galloway was ever claimed by the kings of Strathclyde or Scotland. This was the fate of much of the fallen kingdom's north-eastern holdings, which had once stretched as far as Edinburgh and the Firth of Forth. However, if this was ever the case, the disruption caused by Norse and later Norse-Gael settlement of the region during the ninth century effectively preserved the area from annexation.[3]

The name Galloway itself is derived from the phrase 'among the Stranger-Gael', demonstrating the extent to which the hybrid culture created within the area came to be regarded as distinct and separate from its Scottish neighbours.[4] Galloway, particularly in the west, where Scandinavian settlement was most pronounced, was politically and culturally orientated towards the Norse-Gaelic settlements of the Irish and North Seas, interacting extensively with the Norse-dominated Kingdom of the Isles and Kingdom of Dublin. In

1098, as part of a grand campaign to bring the widely dispersed Norwegian settlements within the region under his direct control, King Magnus Barefoot of Norway invaded the Kingdom of the Isles, sacking the Isle of Man and it seems bringing neighbouring Galloway under his direct control.[5] However, Galloway's absorption into Magnus' thalassocratic Norwegian empire proved to be short-lived. When in 1103, Magnus died while attempting to bring the kingdoms of Ireland's eastern coast to heel, the local Norse-Gaelic aristocracy capitalised upon the resulting power vacuum to reassert their independence and authority. Throughout this period, there is little evidence regarding the political organisation and coherency of Galloway, although its continued existence as a geographical and cultural entity suggests that the region's networks of aristocratic families had some capacity for co-operation and concerted action. This makes it difficult to determine the extent to which Fergus of Galloway's rise, to the dominance of the region by the 1120s, marked a departure from the political norm or what the parameters and pre-conditions of his authority were.

Given the testament of Scottish sources that Fergus was relatively elderly at the time of his death in 1161, it seems probable that he was born sometime in the late 1090s or early 1100s and grew up amidst the dramatic collapse of Magnus Barefoot's authority over the Norse-Gael population of the British Isles.[6] Frustratingly, as with so much else concerning the history of Galloway prior to its incorporation within the Kingdom of Scotland, there is little to no information about Fergus' origins or family circumstances, beyond the fact that he was almost certainly a Gallovidian of Norse-Gaelic extraction. There is some evidence that Fergus' original holdings were concentrated within central Galloway and that his rise to prominence may have come through a policy of opportunistic westward expansion into Norse-Gael affinities that had fallen foul of the chaos and infighting that had engulfed the Kingdom of the Isles.[7] Fergus' first definite appearance within the historical record comes in 1134 when he can be found, alongside his son Uhtred, in Glasgow witnessing a charter of King David I of Scotland.[8] Fergus' appearance within the witness lists of the Scottish king in which he is identified with the toponym 'of Galloway' strongly suggests that Fergus had already established himself in a position of pre-eminence within the region.

For all their ubiquity, kings and kingdoms were terminologies that were neither inert nor inviolate. Rather than a precise classification defined by strict parameters, they were broad concepts that have been applied to a wide variety of different institutions and polities possessed of variable levels of power, sovereignty and internal coherency. Frustratingly, how Fergus styled himself within his own charters and the title he used within Galloway itself are unknown, perhaps because of circumstances that led him to being deposed. Throughout his tenure as ruler of Galloway, Fergus made frequent appearances within the witness lists of David I, the great reformer of Scottish kingship. His appearances within the court of his more powerful neighbour and participation within the essential business of Scottish kingship does not necessarily amount to an unqualified recognition of Scottish sovereignty. Although on balance it seems probable that Fergus recognised, whether implicitly or explicitly, some form of Scottish overlordship or seniority. Compellingly, the Chronicle of Holyrood, even while describing his eventual fall from grace and clash with their Scottish royal patrons, refers to Fergus as 'princeps' or prince, a clearly royal title traditionally used to refer to independent rulers.[9]

In 1128, Henry I ruled as King of the English and David I King of the Scots, yet the writ of both men ran through territory inhabited by multiple, often layered ethnolinguistic groups. Henry was a Norman, the ruler of a cross-Channel realm whose European domains had come to encompass formerly distinctive and independent regions such as the County of Maine. While very much a Norman himself, Henry attempted to cultivate a perception of continuity between his own reign and that of Edward the Confessor, while utilising and adapting the traditional institutions and powers of Anglo-Saxon kingship to strengthen his position in the struggle against Norman rivals and dissidents.[10] Individual Norman familial affinities were also heavily engaged in the piecemeal conquest and pacification of southern Wales, while the variability of Saxon influence throughout England had led to the retention of regional identities within fringe areas such as Cornwall and Cumbria.[11]

Meanwhile, in Scotland there was significant Norse-Gaelic influence in Galloway, Argyll and the Highlands, all of which were politically oriented towards the Norse-dominated Irish Sea and the Kingdom of the Isles.[12]

Almost paradoxically, in reaction to these challenges and the retention of strong regional identities and affinities throughout Scotland, David I and his immediate successors encouraged and facilitated first Norman and then Flemish settlement within southern Scotland.[13] The adaptation of Norman cultural trappings, practices and institutions by the Scottish kings was part of a rigorous programme to create a powerful and centralised monarchy, recast in the same mould as their English counterparts. Foreign settlement within Scotland further catalysed this transition, promoted economic growth, and provided the Scottish kings with a pool of allies unaffiliated with existing factions or affinities. In fact, as we shall see, it was David's active incentivising of Norman and Flemish settlement to Scotland that led to the establishment of the Bruce family within the kingdom.

As a result of the weight of our own history and political contexts, we tend to see the rise of England and Scotland as inevitable, almost as if both were entities that merely grew and settled into their preordained shapes. This is obviously not the case. Rather than the political or institutional manifestation of specific cultures, the medieval incarnations of England and Scotland were the result of great tangles of interconnected and reciprocal networks of personal, familial and regional affinities. The history of Galloway ably demonstrates the dangers inherent in seeing the emergent or newly reconstituted kingdoms of medieval Europe as indivisible and natural political units.

Fergus' status as a powerful and independent prince is attested to by his marriage to an unknown illegitimate daughter of Henry I of England. The English chronicler and court intimate, Roger of Howdon, explicitly describes Fergus' younger son, Uhtred, as a cousin of Henry II.[14] Fergus' two remaining children, Gille Brigte and Affraic, are not explicitly mentioned as part of this dynastic connection but Robert of Torigni describes Affraic's son, King Guðrøðr Óláfsson of Dublin, as a maternal relative of Henry II.[15] Repeated solicitations for protection and patronage to the Angevin kings of England by Gille Brigte and his son also strongly suggest a shared familial bond. Fergus' marriage, which probably took place sometime around the late 1110s or early 1120s, fits into the larger pattern of Anglo-Norman royal dynastic strategy. Henry I had a plethora of illegitimate children and throughout his reign he utilised this pool of auxiliary family members to offset his dearth of legitimate heirs to advance his political and dynastic strategies.[16]

The marriage between Fergus, a relatively powerful regional ruler strategically located on the Anglo-Norman periphery, and one of the king's numerous illegitimate daughters must be seen within the context of the advancement and exertion of Anglo-Norman overlordship within the British Isles. Most notably, King David's elder brother and predecessor, Alexander I, had been married to another of Henry's illegitimate daughters, Sybil.[17] While these strategic marriages were undoubtedly an attempt to enhance Henry's authority and influence within Scotland, they were not necessarily gambits intended to facilitate conquest or direct rulership. Instead, Henry's overlordship was exerted through the induction of his neighbours as junior partners in a shared dynastic enterprise. In northern France, Henry had similarly arranged for his children to marry the rulers of many of the autonomous or semi-autonomous territories that surrounded his continental domains, such as Brittany, Perche and Anjou. These marriages created buffer zones that secured Henry's borders and drew these lesser domains further into alliance and political alignment with the Anglo-Norman realm. Other facets of this strategy of exertion of overlordship and projection of influence through the creation of dynastic and political alliances can be seen in the conferring of the lordship of an enlarged Cumbria upon David, then his brother's primary heir.[18]

By the same token, participation in this network of familial alliances and obligations was, in the short term at least, immensely beneficial to Fergus of Galloway, greatly increasing his status and authority. Fergus' marriage to a daughter of Henry I secured his position of pre-eminence among the aristocracy of Galloway, allowing him and his sons to continue to consolidate their power within the region without fear of outside interference. More importantly, it imposed an equilibrium between Galloway, England and Scotland that must have seemed at the time like a formidable barrier to Scottish aggression. If the efficacy of this arrangement was compromised in any way by the early death of Alexander I in 1124, Fergus must surely have been placated by Henry I's support for David's bid to the throne and the new Scottish king's inclination towards co-operation.

Even the death of Henry I in 1135 did not have an immediately detrimental effect on Fergus' status or relationship with the Scottish kings. A strong Gallovidian contingent, perhaps led by either Fergus or one of his sons, accompanied David I in his invasion of England in 1138.[19] While this co-operation could be due to a recognition on Fergus' part of David's overlordship, it probably also reflects the fact that both rulers had a close familial relationship to King Stephen of England's primary dynastic rival, Empress Matilda. In a way, Fergus, now isolated within Scotland, was perhaps even more heavily incentivised than David to see that Matilda was restored to her father's throne. Following the resounding Scottish defeat at the Battle of the Standard, Anglo-Norman accounts of which made particular reference to the wildness of the Gallovidians, Fergus declined to participate further in the Anglo-Norman dynastic clash. Instead, he pursued a policy of broad conciliation towards the Scottish kings, while attempting to expand his own power and influence. For instance, with Gallovidian help, Óláfr of Dublin enjoyed a substantial degree of success bringing his fractious kingdom some measure of stability, providing Fergus with a powerful ally whose presence represented a significant deterrent to Scottish aggression.[20] However, Óláfr's assassination by his nephews in 1153 led to a spiralling cycle of violence that quickly destabilised the Isles and seriously damaged Gallovidian power. This process began with the massacre of the Isle of Man's substantial Gallovidian population and was followed by a pre-emptive invasion of western Galloway which had to be bloodily repulsed.[21] While Fergus' grandson Guðrøðr was able to temporarily secure his father's throne with Norwegian support, this brought only a temporary reprieve.[22] There was blood in the water and Guðrøðr's increasingly desperate and frantic wars continued to consume Gallovidian lives and martial prestige until his final ousting from power in 1158. For Fergus, this situation was further compounded by the death of David I in 1153 and the political upheaval and wrangling that followed the accession of his young grandson, Malcolm IV.

The reason for Malcolm IV's sudden and decisive invasion of Galloway in 1160 remains opaque. Fergus' authority and power were certainly at a low ebb and there is some chronicler evidence suggesting significant dissent and conflict within Galloway at this time as the weakened Fergus vied with his own sons and local rivals. In the immediate prelude to the invasion, Malcolm was engaged heavily in quelling a rebellion by Earl Ferteth of Strathearn. It is possible that Fergus was attempting to rally his flagging fortunes by either supporting the rebels directly or seizing upon the chance presented by the revolt to expand his power beyond Galloway.[23]

Alternatively, Malcolm faced with continuing aristocratic discontent, may have orchestrated the invasion of a weakened Galloway as a means of increasing his personal prestige and of uniting the bitterly divided Scottish nobility against a common enemy. Whatever the exact reason, Malcolm subdued Galloway over the course of three military expeditions that scythed through Fergus' power base and eventually compelled him to submit.[24] Galloway was subsequently divided between Fergus' sons, which may suggest they had supported the Scottish king, while the former ruler of Galloway was forced into confinement at Holyrood Abbey, where he died the following year.

While Malcolm IV succeeded in extracting acknowledgement of his overlordship from Fergus' sons, Gille Brigte and Uhtred, he did not manage to meaningfully establish royal Scottish authority within Galloway, whose affinities and institutions remained largely independent and autonomous. After a degree of wrangling, Gille Brigte came to rule over the western portions of Galloway, the heartland of its Norse-Gael culture and heritage. Meanwhile, Uhtred was left with control over the principality's eastern domains.

In 1173, provoked in a large part by Henry II's refusal to share power meaningfully, his eldest sons rose up in rebellion, supported by their mother and King Louis VII of France.[25] Early the following year, Malcolm's brother and successor, William the Lion, invaded England in response to this crisis. It appears that both Brigte and Uhtred joined William's expedition, alongside their respective military retinues. The campaign proved to be a disaster for the Scots. Following the successful capture of Carlisle, William divided his army in order to simultaneously besiege multiple English royalist strongholds. He then impetuously dispersed those forces under his direct command yet further, possibly to more thoroughly pillage the lands around the fortress of Alnwick. The bitter result of William's lack of caution was that he and his immediate retainers were ambushed by a much larger force led by Henry II's chief justiciar, Ranulf de Glanvill. Despite the king's personal valour, he was captured swiftly, effectively bringing Scottish involvement in the rebellion to an end.[26]

According to the chronicler Roger of Howden, the Gallovidians seized upon the opportunity presented by King William's defeat and capture to reassert their independence and identity.[27] Returning home, they immediately began uprooting all vestiges of Scottish royal governance in the region, expelling Scottish bailiffs and garrisons, in addition to murdering members of the imported English and French nobility.[28] However, the leadership and structure of this rebellion remains murky. Howden's account implies a degree of co-operation between Gille Brigte and Uhtred and a unity of purpose among the Gallovidians as they railed against the foreign influences that had inveigled their way into the principality. If this was ever the case though, the brothers soon found themselves at each other's throats. Subsequent events and his ruthless pursuit of control over Galloway make it seem probable that Gille Brigte was the true mastermind behind the rebellion and that his struggle against Uhtred was an integral part of the conflict from the very start. Whether the result of a premediated strategy or naked opportunism, at some point during the chaos of the uprising, Gille Brigte captured Uhtred.[29]

The now pervasive continental aristocratic culture that had been carried to Scotland by the Anglo-Normans brought with it certain expectations and taboos in regard to the treatment of noble prisoners. At the Battle of Alnwick, King William defiantly proclaimed his status and calibre as a knight as he and his bodyguards charged out to meet the numerically superior foe. He did so in the knowledge that the enemy's primary goal would be to disable and capture rather than kill them. The widespread and lucrative practice of ransoming noble prisoners unharmed back to their relatives meant that knights were both culturally and financially incentivised to avoid killing each other whenever possible. Added to this were equally strong cultural prohibitions against deliberately harming or killing members of their often convoluted and extensive familial networks. However, politics and warfare in the world of the Norse-Gaels was a far more savage and merciless affair. In keeping with the native expectations of this bloody and supremely competitive arena of politics, Gille Brigte had his brother thoroughly mutilated, removing his tongue, genitals and eyes. These were calamitous impediments by any measure and effectively removed Uhtred as a competitor for control of Galloway.

With his brother safely disposed of, Gille Brigte set about attempting to secure Galloway's freshly reasserted independence and his paramount position within it. Understanding that William's imprisonment and the consequent vacuum in Scottish royal authority that had made the Gallovidian rebellion possible was only temporary, Gille Brigte made a momentous decision. Writing to Henry II, Gille Brigte promised him a substantial cash payment of 2,000 marks and an exorbitant yearly tribute in livestock in exchange for the king's help in formally dissolving Scottish sovereignty over Galloway.[30]

Henry was certainly interested in the proposal, dispatching his courtiers Roger of Howden and Robert de Vaux north to discuss the matter further.[31] Such talks ultimately came to nothing, however, trapping Gille Brigte in a perilous position between the English and Scottish kings. Henry was less than impressed to hear about the details of Gille Brigte's brutal treatment of Uhtred, who was, after all, also a relative of the king. Worse still from a Gallovidian perspective, Henry had just signed the Treaty of Falaise with William the Lion. The terms of the treaty were frankly extortionate. Henry not only secured acknowledgment of his status as the Scottish king's overlord but also gained possession of many of the key castles of Scotland, which he garrisoned with his own troops, massively weakening William's ability to project authority within Scotland.[32]

The severity of this treaty meant that Henry had relatively little to gain from helping Gille Brigte; after all he now already possessed a measure of suzerainty over Galloway through his freshly recognised claims to the overlordship of Scotland. Meanwhile, an undertaking as drastic and dramatic as carving Galloway from Scotland would have had the serious potential of inciting further conflict with the already dissatisfied Scottish nobility. Rather than gaining autonomy or a prestigious position within Henry's hegemonic empire, Gille Brigte found himself fined and reprimanded by the English king and compelled to make peace with William the Lion. Meanwhile, his eldest son and heir, Donnchadh, was given to Henry II as a hostage for future good behaviour.[33] Despite these setbacks, Gille Brigte retained rulership of Galloway and was largely successful in preventing the re-establishment of Scottish royal authority. Indeed, the latter portion of his time as lord of Galloway in the 1180s was spent fighting a series of escalating raids and small border wars with William.[34]

Unable to outrightly subjugate Galloway, King William adopted a longer-term diplomatic strategy to regain control of the rogue former principality. Following Uhtred's capture, his son Lochlann, who also went by the name Roland, fled to William's court. There he was taken under the king's wing and furnished with an advantageous marriage to Helena, the daughter of the Constable of Scotland, Richard de Morville.[35] Evidently William hoped that he could one day capitalise upon his protégés' claim to Galloway, subsequently drawing the region further into the web of Scottish royal authority through Lochlann's newfound personal and dynastic connections. Indeed, upon Gille Brigte's death in 1185, Lochlann, supported by William, set about securing control of Galloway, fighting and defeating a coalition of Gallovidian nobles.[36] As it transpired, Henry II was less than thrilled about the displacement of his kinsmen and ward, Donnchadh. It is even possible that Henry, like William, harboured an ambition to increase his influence over Galloway by installing his own proxy ruler. When William dithered in the face of Henry's demands to bring Lochlann to heel, the English king struck northward himself, accompanied by a small army, compelling William and Lochlann to negotiate. In the end, a compromise was reached in which the two cousins, Lochlann and Donnchadh, would divide Galloway between them.[37] Lochlann retained the majority of the former principality, while its northern environ, Carrick, was broken off and given to Donnchadh. Lochlann ruled Galloway as a lord, abandoning the royal titles that his grandfather had experimented with, while Donnchadh eventually began to refer and style himself as the 'comes' or earl of Carrick.

The new Lord of Galloway remained close to the royal Scottish court, and in 1186 Lochlann was entrusted with the command of a Scottish army dispatched by William to end the rebellion of rival royal claimant Domnall mac Uilleim. Lochlann decisively crushed the rebellion at the Battle of Marna Garvia, during which, it was claimed by Roger of Howden, he personally slew the pretender.[38] Upon the death of his father-in-law in 1189, Lochlann inherited the office of Constable, alongside an extensive collection of estates within Scotland. In 1200, Lochlann took ill and died suddenly on a trip to England, during which he hoped to petition Henry II for the restoration of his wife's English estates. He was succeeded as Lord of Galloway and Constable of Scotland by his eldest son, Alan, who would transcend the title used by his father and imitate his great-grandfather, Fergus, by emerging as a great regional power, pursing a vigorous and almost wholly independent expansionary policy outside of Scotland.

Alan's first marriage was to a daughter of Roger de Lacy, whose name has been frustratingly lost to history. A powerful aristocrat and highly favoured royal official, Roger held a number of lordships located within the north of England, was the sheriff of Cumberland and Yorkshire and held the Constableship of Chester.[39] Such a union was a sound strategic marriage for Alan, increasing his influence across the Anglo-Scottish border and opening up the serious possibility of inheriting lands in England. In 1209, after the death of Alan's unfortunate and unnamed first wife, he married Margaret of Huntingdon, the eldest daughter of Earl David of Huntingdon.[40] Margaret and her father were close members of the Scottish royal family, while David was a grandson of King David I and the younger brother of William the Lion. Indeed, prior to the birth of William's daughter, Margaret of Scotland, in 1193, David had spent two and a half decades as William's primary heir. It was this marriage into the Scottish family that the Balliols' later claim to the throne was derived from. A claim that would see John Balliol sit upon the throne of Scotland and motivate his son, Edward, and his allies, the Disinherited, to once again rise against their Bruce rivals.

Following this marriage, possibly emboldened by the enhanced prestige and connections it brought him, Alan began to take a more active role within English politics and the Norse-Gael-dominated kingdoms of the Irish coast, which his father had largely neglected in favour of his close relationship with William the Lion.[41] In the early 1210s, Alan began to take an active role in the ongoing English conquest of Ireland and was soon rewarded by King John for his efforts when he was granted a large swathe of land in Ulster, composed of Antrim and the north-eastern portions of the modern county of Londonderry.[42] In 1212, Alan led a large contingent of Gallovidian troops into Wales on John's behalf, although he had a minor spat with the English king over his refusal to pay for the upkeep of these troops.[43]

He remained close to John as the king became increasingly embattled by baronial rebellion, first accompanying him during the negotiations around the signing of the Magna Carta and then supporting John in his bloody-handed attempt to repudiate the document. Alan's continued adherence to the English king had a deleterious effect upon his relationship with William the Lion's son and successor, Alexander II, who tacitly supported the rebels. However, this rift never seems to have seriously threatened Alan's control of Galloway. Following John's final defeat and death in 1216, Alan's involvement in English politics declined sharply, although he was eventually successful in securing acknowledgement of his English lands from Henry III's regents. Despite being politically isolated in both England and Scotland, Alan remained defiant and undaunted. From the 1220s until his death, Alan redirected his energies and Galloway's considerable military resources into the power struggles surrounding the Kingdom of the Isles and its surrounding Norse-Gael affinities.[44]

In 1223, John de Balliol, the urbane father of the future Scottish king of the same name, married Alan's third daughter, Dervorguilla of Galloway.[45] Upon her father's death in 1234, Dervorguilla split her inheritance, which through her grandmother included a claim on the Earldom of Chester, with her two sisters Helen and Christina, who were married to Earl Roger de Quincy of Winchester and Earl William de Forz of Albemarle respectively.[46] The Gallovidians, resenting both the increasingly apparent imposition of Scottish overlordship and the division of Galloway, rose up in revolt in 1235 and again in 1246, following the heirless Christina's death.[47] Notably, the violence on both occasions required the direct intervention of the Scottish king to subdue. The death of Christina without issue and the absence of Roger de Quincy, who was distracted by both his duties as Constable of Scotland and his numerous commitments in England, meant that the path was clear for John Balliol to consolidate his position within the fractured lordship and emerge as Galloway's most conspicuous and senior aristocrat.

It is instructive to note how the division of Alan's land between his co-heiresses and their husbands displays the extreme permeability of the border between the Kingdoms of Scotland and England in the mid-thirteenth century. All three of Alan's daughters had married English aristocrats and each of these men were able to simultaneously hold and administer landed interests in both kingdoms. To a large extent the aristocracies of the two kingdoms could be regarded as one virtually seamless community, the members of which just so happened to owe homage to one or more kings. As the husband of Alan's eldest daughter Helen, Roger de Quincy inherited from his father in-law the Constableship of Scotland, an incredibly important office that placed him near the heart of the apparatus through which royal authority was exercised throughout Scotland.[48] Occupation of this office, which had a clear and immediate military aspect, was not seen by Roger's contemporaries as incompatible with his ownership of an English Earldom. Likewise, his growing preoccupation with politics in England and his leadership role within the baronial resistance to Henry III does not seem to have meaningfully compromised his position within Scotland.[49] Upon his death in 1264, the constableship remained within the family, settling on Earl Alexander Comyn of Buchan, the husband of Roger's second daughter, Isabella (sometimes known as Elizabeth).[50]

King Alexander II of Scotland's support for the division of the Lordship of Galloway and enthusiasm for upholding the cosmopolitan cross-border claims of Alan's English sons-in-law was a clearly calculated and strategic move to absorb the region definitively into the Kingdom of Scotland. The recognition of these claims, which were embedded in the traditions and practices of an essentially European aristocratic monoculture, represented the imposition of Anglo-Franco legal and inheritance practices upon a region in which they had previously held little sway.[51] The Davidian Revolution of the early twelfth century had brought the culture and social trappings of the Scottish royal court and nobility into greater alignment with their Norman and European counterparts.[52] Since then, continued developments in aristocratic culture were reflected closely within Scotland, which had also increasingly adopted elements of continental social structure and legal practice, particularly regarding inheritance.[53]

Within Galloway, however, this transformation was partial at best and limited only to the top echelons of Gallovidian society. The Lords of Galloway seemed content to present themselves as model thirteenth-century aristocrats outside of Galloway but largely reverted to their traditional modes of behaviour and conceptions of rulership within it. Indeed, they continued to carefully cultivate one of the most idiosyncratic features of Gallovidian lordship in the form of their unusually proprietary sponsorship of the local Church.[54]

The grass root rebellions that followed Alan's death and the division of the Lordship between his daughters and their English husbands was not only the upswelling of outrage at the imposition of an alien system of inheritance. Its instigators and participants were keenly aware that they faced an existential crisis. The inevitable corollary of the scrapping of the Lordship of Galloway as a unified political entity was the diminishment and eventual extinction of their culture. While Alan was predeceased by his only legitimate son, Thomas, he was not totally bereft of alternative heirs who would have most likely been greeted with relief by the people of Galloway. Alan had an illegitimate son, somewhat confusingly also called Thomas, likely born sometime around 1207 or 1208. While Thomas' maternal heritage is unknown, it is possible that his mother was Norse-Gael in origin. Certainly, Alan was cognisant of his illegitimate son's status as a valuable dynastic resource, arranging for him to marry a daughter of the Norse-Gael King of the Isles, Rǫgnvaldr Guðrøðarson.[55]

Rǫgnvaldr was caught in the teeth of a long-running war with his younger half-brother, Óláfr the Black, who contested his possession of the throne, if not necessarily his right to it. Rognvaldr's only son, Guðrøðr, had been blinded and castrated upon being captured and defeated by his quarrelsome relatives in 1223, while Guðrøðr's own son was still an infant. This meant that if Thomas, backed by the wealth and manpower of Galloway, was able to displace the now ascendant family of Óláfr the Black, he had through his wife a strong claim to the Kingdom of the Isles. Unfortunately for Thomas, this vision of the future did not suit Alexander II in the least. The king wanted to see the power and resources of Galloway yoked once and for all to the Scottish throne by amenable local proxies. He was understandably less happy with the notion of one of his most powerful and historically independent vassals winning a separate crown for themselves. Not only would this vastly complicate the relationship between king and lord but it threatened to draw Galloway out of Scotland and into the north Atlantic world of the Norse-Gaels entirely.

In addition to his less than desirable dynastic connections, at least from the perspective of the Scottish king, Thomas' claim to the lordship was complicated by his illegitimacy. In Scotland, as with the rest of Europe, the Church reform movement of the twelfth century succeeded in establishing marriage, formerly a largely secular and political institution, as a sacrament. This imposition of the numinous into the mundane, alongside a raft of corollary reforms aimed at improving the quality of pastoral care by attacking the practice of hereditary offices within the Church, had a profound effect on contemporary conceptions of legitimacy.[56] Such reforms had the effect of more firmly and clearly delineating legitimate from illegitimate.

By the time of Alan's death in 1234, it would be incredibly unlikely for an illegitimate son like Thomas to gain recognition as his father's heir from either the Church, his peers in the nobility or the royal court. As it transpired, the Gallovidian rebellion succeeded in giving Alexander II a bloody nose but little else. After a spectacularly successful ambush in which the Gallovidians routed the royal host, sustained pressure from the Scottish and their indulgence in widespread raiding and looting eventually broke the back of the rebellion, forcing Thomas and Gille Ruadh, the leader of the revolt, into exile in Ireland.[57] While they were able to return the next year with a fresh army, a testament to the cohesion and interconnectedness of the Norse-Gael community even during its twilight, Gille Ruadh entered into a negotiated settlement with the Scottish soon afterwards, possibly as a result of some sort of disagreement or conflict with Thomas. Kept imprisoned for the next sixty years, Thomas, the Lord of Galloway that never was, was finally released in 1296 by Edward I, only to be tragically reincarcerated the following year.[58]

Another potential heir that was shunted aside in Alexander II's eagerness to bring Galloway to heel and absorb it once and for all into Scotland was Alan's nephew, Patrick. Patrick's father was Alan's younger brother and extremely able right-hand man, also named Thomas, who had been intimately involved in Alan's highly profitable Irish and English adventures.[59] His mother, Isabel, was the Countess of Atholl, a position she had inherited from her own father, Henry, upon his death in 1211.[60] Isabel's family had strong dynastic and regional ties with the ever increasingly powerful Comyn family, whose members would eventually provide so many diehard Balliol supporters and fill the ranks of the Disinherited.

Unfortunately for Patrick, this maternal inheritance almost certainly played a role in Alexander II's decision to dismiss his claim to Galloway. Alan had already been the second most powerful and influential man in Scotland, a potentially puissant rival to royal authority. Combining the Lordship of Galloway with the Earldom of Atholl and Thomas' substantive Lothian lands would have further elevated an already powerful and dangerous aristocratic affinity. In addition to these dynastic concerns, Patrick was still in his minority at the time of Alan's death. While this may have suited Alexander's goal of weakening the Gallodovians in the short term, the presence of a child lord could hardly help the king in his efforts to impose meaningful royal authority on the lordship and left the door open for a populist uprising.

Despite his relegation from the Lordship of Galloway, Patrick was still exceptionally well connected, with excellent inheritance prospects, and could in time reasonably be expected to number among the kingdom's leading aristocrats. Upon coming of age in 1236, Patrick took over control of Atholl from his mother, only to be murdered in 1241 when local rivals set his residence ablaze.[61]

Within a few decades of the tripartite division of Alan of Galloway's lands by his sons-in-law, the Balliol family had firmly established themselves as the region's pre-eminent political affinity. The blow-by-blow details through which this process was achieved are now sadly opaque and difficult to reconstruct. What seems probable and in keeping with the conventional methods of exercising personal aristocratic authority during this period was that John gradually extended his web of patronage throughout the former lordship. In supporting regional powerbrokers, John brought the continuing interests of these various familial affinities and institutions into alignment with his own, effectively co-opting them as his local proxies. This approach, however, was a broad principle, the way in which all engaged and competent thirteenth-century aristocrats were expected to behave; it was not a master plan. Balliol's eventual de facto dominion of Galloway owed much to the vagaries of fate and dynastic fortune.

As we have seen, Fergus of Galloway's immediate heirs had split the lordship into east and west. With the creation of the Earldom of Carrick, their sons had done much the same thing, splitting the lordship of Galloway from its northernmost territories. In contrast to these geographically concentrated power block partitions, Alan's daughters inherited smaller concentrations of lands or individual estates scattered throughout Galloway and intermingled with one another. The exact process through which Alan's lands were allocated to each heir is unfortunately entirely unknown to us, although it is possible that they were divided in this scattershot manner in an attempt to ensure parity between each daughter's inheritance, perhaps precisely because the process was so fraught and exhaustively negotiated. Of course, Alexander II remained the directing force behind the division. The fact that the nature of the division all but ensured that the trifecta of incoming lords would have had to co-operate with one another to overcome grassroots Gallodovian resistance, while simultaneously hampering each of their ability to establish a meaningful power base from which they could impose authority over the others, was unlikely to be entirely accidental.

In 1246, Alan's youngest daughter, Christina, died, the circumstances of her passing unclear to modern historians. Since she and her husband, the Earl of Albermarle, William de Foze, had no children, her inheritance was divided between her sisters, Helen and Dervorguilla.[62] More accurately, practical control of the lordship's composite domains was now split between their respective husbands, Roger de Quincey and John de Balliol. Following the death of his wife and subsequent loss of lands in Galloway, William went on to marry Isabel de Redvers, the daughter of the earl of Devon, after a semi-appropriate period of mourning.[63] Partial fragments of the lands inherited by Helen and her husband Roger de Quincey can be pieced together thanks to the legal proceedings that followed the death of their youngest daughter in 1296. As the eldest sister, one of Helen's most significant concentrations of landed interests surrounded and encapsulated Kirkcudbright, which had in many ways functioned as Galloway's capital during Alan's lordship.[64] In addition to this, they held lands scattered throughout the lordship with other notable concentrations in the Marchars and around Troqueer.[65]

Helen and Roger's marriage produced three daughters, Margaret, Isabella and Helen, a quirk of dynastic fortunes that ultimately led to the further fracturing and division of the Quinceys' estates in Galloway. The couple's eldest daughter, Margaret, was married to the gout-ridden Earl of Derby, William de Ferrers, in 1238.[66] The match provides a potentially entertaining example of the dense and tangled nature of the thirteenth-century aristocracy and the crucial dynastic ties that held it together. William de Ferrers had previously been married to Sybil Marshall, a daughter of the legendary knight, Earl William Marshall of Pembroke, with whom he had produced seven daughters. When Helen died in the late 1240s, in a move worthy of any guest of *The Jerry Springer Show*, Roger de Quincey married one of William and Sybil's daughters, the teenage Eleanor. The union made Margaret both Eleanor's stepmother and stepdaughter![67]

Isabella, another of Helen's daughters, made a highly advantageous match with the Kingdom of Scotland's coming man, Alexander Comyn, the Earl of Buchan.[68] This marriage was to prove to be highly fruitful as the Comyns, already a family on the rise, would greatly expand their influence throughout the latter half of the thirteenth century as Alexander became entrenched as a crucial advisor and functionary in the royal court. As we shall see in the next chapter, Alexander and Isabella's children, particularly their eldest son John, would go on to play a vital role in the careers of their Balliol cousins, aggressively opposing the Bruce family's bid for the throne of Scotland.

Roger and Helen's youngest daughter, named after her mother, was married to Alan la Zouche.[69] Alan first came to prominence in the court of Henry III when, according to the chronicler Matthew of Paris, he bid the exorbitant sum of 1,200 marks to be appointed as the justice of Chester, over twice the amount his predecessor had paid for the office.[70] The position extended to a large collection of Welsh territories that had been subordinated and administratively tethered to Chester. Alan proved to be immensely unpopular in Wales, even drawing royal censure for the inflammatory manner in which he exercised his office. Despite this blemish, Alan became close to the future Edward I and was appointed as the Justicar of Ireland in 1259 and as the Sheriff of Nottingham in 1261.[71] Alan was fatally wounded in 1270 when he was ambushed by a former rebel supporter, Earl John de Warenne of Surrey, and his retinue. Alan and Helen had a number of children, of which three sons, Roger, William and Oliver, and a daughter, Margaret, survived infancy, further dividing the inheritance of their Gallovidian maternal grandmother.

Following the death of the elder Helen, her oldest daughter, Margaret, and her husband William de Ferrers, inherited the large concentration of lands around Kirkcudbright. However, there is compelling evidence that by the 1270s these lands were now under the control of Alexander Comyn, the husband of Margaret's younger sister, Isabella. In fact, Alexander's talent and position within the Scottish royal court was such that he managed to secure the Constableship of Scotland for himself, a position that strictly speaking should have fallen to Margaret and her descendants by hereditary right. Sometime around 1274, Margaret formerly renounced her claim to the constableship and its accompanying lands and incomes, apparently designating Alexander as her successor.[72] However, it is unclear if this remarkable relinquishing of office was truly the instrument through which Alexander first came to hold the constableship or if it was merely a formal and legal acknowledgment of a pre-existing state of affairs.

Certainly, the latter seems more likely considering a reference made in the Exchequer Roll of 1264 to Alexander as the 'keeper of two parts of the lands of the late Roger de Quincy in Galloway'.[73] It seems then that by the 1260s Alexander not only held the lands his wife had inherited from her parents but had somehow come to exercise practical control over the Gallodovian portion of his sister-in-law Margaret's inheritance as well. Again, frustratingly the circumstances surrounding these acquisitions are unknown. Margaret's husband, William de Ferrers, had died in 1254, and even when alive his ability to travel had long been limited by his gout.[74] The couple's eldest son, Richard, would have only been fifteen at the time of his father's death, and would not fully assume control of his family's English estates until 1260. Galloway was relatively distant from the nucleus of the family's lands and populated by troublesome natives who had shown themselves to be prone to armed uprisings. It is possible that faced with all the challenges and limitations that accompanied an earl still in his minority, not least of which was the Kings of England's propensity for claiming guardianship over minority heirs and extracting large cash payments for the transfer of their inheritance, the family decided to abandon their already somewhat neglected lands in Galloway. More probable is the idea that they came to some arrangement with their Comyn kin, who either purchased their holdings or agreed to administrate them on their behalf. Maybe the Comyns, seeing an opportunity, simply muscled them out.

That was all reasonably dense, complicated by the handover to a new generation and the aristocracy's insistence of constantly recycling a small pool of politically resonant familial names. To summarise, Alan of Galloway's lands were split between his three daughters, Helen, Christina and Dervorguilla. Upon the death of one of these daughters, the childless Christina, her lands were divided between her sisters, leaving each with half of Alan's original territories. Helen's lands were further divided by her three daughters and their respective husbands. By the late 1260s, by hook or by crook, the Comyn family had gained not only their portion of Helen's inheritance but that of their de Ferrers relatives as well, giving the Comyns control of roughly two thirds of half of the last Lord of Galloway's lands.

Dervorguilla's husband, John de Balliol, died in 1268. His three eldest sons, Hugh, Alan and Alexander, all either predeceased him or died shortly after their father.[75] Crucially they died without having fathered heirs of their own. While undoubtedly tragic and greatly taxing for the family on a personal level, these deaths meant that John and Dervorguilla's fourth son, also called John, was able to inherit the majority of the Balliol estates, including his mother's extensive lands in Galloway after her death in 1290, relatively undiluted. These holdings were, as stated before, scattered throughout Galloway but there were notable concentrations, the most significant of which were the Lordship of Buitlle in the lower Ur valley, Lochkindeloch, and Kirkbean, in the east alongside the encompassing lordships of Kenmure or Kells, Balmaghie and Crossmichael.[76] While Alexander Comyn had succeeded in monopolising the shrievalty of Wigtownshire, the Balliols also held substantive estates in the area, particularly in Rhims and the southern reaches of the Marchars.[77]

While the lack of substantive tax records and the massive disruption that would be shortly unleashed during the Wars of Independence makes it extremely difficult to fully reconstruct the Balliol holdings, the balance of evidence suggests that the family was the centre of the most substantive network of land holdings within Galloway. The Balliols had, thanks to a quirk of dynastic fortune, kept a tight control over their Gallodovian lands, while their Quincy relatives had been compelled to further divide theirs between the ambitious husbands of a second trio of heiresses. While the Comyn family had eventually succeeded in securing the lion's share of Helen of Galloway's portion of the inheritance, they could not avoid some measure of fragmentation. Moreover, their existing commitments in Buchan and acquisition of the Constableship of Scotland required the attention of Alexander and his immediate heirs. This division in both inheritable interests and focus allowed the Balliols to emerge as the pre-eminent aristocratic affinity within Galloway.

However, this rise was a decades-long process that, as we have seen, owed more to happenstance than bold action. The Balliols had extensive lands in England, which had been further supplemented by the substantive

English portion of Dervorguilla inheritance, and were not particularly proactive in their management of Galloway, which they may have thought of primarily as a source of income. Certainly, Dervorguilla's son, John, became far more involved in the region during his bid for the Scottish throne but even then his family's pre-eminence in the region greatly benefited from his willingness to co-operate with the Comyns and their stronghold in Wigtonshire.[78] Dervorguilla's longevity and John's status as her sole male heir represented a clear and direct link between the Balliols and the traditional Lords of Galloway. The strength of this connection not only greatly helped John in establishing himself as the de facto ruler of Galloway but through Dervorguilla's royal mother, Margaret of Huntingdon, provided him with an excellent claim to the throne following the extinction of the Dunkeld line in 1290.

The Balliols' claim to the throne of Scotland would emerge triumphant from the Great Council of 1292 and would a generation later inspire their relatives and their allies within the Disinherited to take to the battlefield in a quest to overthrow the newly established Bruce regime. But who exactly was John Balliol and what was the history of his family prior to their entrance into Scottish politics? Guy de Balliol, the first member of the family to establish himself within the British Isles, was a minor noble from Picardy who entered the service of King William Rufus of England.[79] The north of England had proven to be something of a hotspot for rebellions against the newly established kings of England. Following the capture of the rebel Roger de Mowbray in 1090 and the royal confiscation of the earldom of Northumbria, Guy, alongside a number of other nobles loyal to William Rufus, were granted lands in the north of England. William's aim in this redistribution of lands was to both defend the Scottish frontier and simultaneously bring this wild hinterland more firmly under royal control. It was a duty Guy was well suited for, having previously lived upon the equally fraught and contentious border that separated Picardy from Norman-controlled Ponthieu.

Sometime before 1130, Guy was succeeded by his nephew Bernard, the great-grandfather of Dervorguilla of Galloway's husband.[80] This successful transfer of lands and authority was something of an achievement in itself. Despite the emerging ubiquity of the arrangement, holding and administrating lands on opposite sides of the Channel and potentially hundreds of miles apart was no easy feat. To do so successfully required the implementation of specific institutions and practices, as well as a great deal of trust in family and subordinates; trust that had to be continually earned and renewed through the distribution of largesse. In the years immediately following the Norman Conquest and the redistribution of land among the newly imported nobility, these administrative complexities were exacerbated by the simmering discontent of the locals and ever-present threat of rebellion. These conditions were not dissimilar to those that the husbands of Alan of Galloway's daughters found themselves in during the 1230s to mixed results. Despite the magnitude of the potential rewards, a significant proportion of the continental nobility that had taken part in the Conquest abandoned their newly acquired territories within the British Isles. The first transmission of newly acquired inheritable landed interests and authority was therefore a make-or-break moment for any ambitious aristocratic family. Bernard's importance in establishing the Balliol family within England can be seen in the naming of the family's first lordship and principal fortification, Barnard Castle, after him.[81]

In a strange twist, Bernard was involved alongside Lord Robert de Brus of Annadale in negotiations with King David of Scotland on behalf of King Stephen of England in 1138.[82] David was not only King of Scotland, but also the Earl of Huntingdon and the ruler of a greatly enlarged Cumbria. Evidently, he was also Bernard's feudal overlord. While this placed Balliol in a precarious situation, his personal stake in the matter and pre-existing relationship with its belligerents was probably why he was selected as a diplomat alongside the charismatic and talented Robert de Brus. When negotiations failed, Guy threw his lot in with King Stephen, repudiating his loyalty to David, and was almost certainly with the English army that triumphed at the ensuing Battle of the Standard. In another strange coincidence, despite emerging on what seemed like the winning side of the conflict, Guy's lands in the north of England were repeatedly ravaged when David succeeded in having his partisan William Comyn, the great-great-uncle of Isabella de Quincy's husband Alexander, installed as Bishop of Durham.[83] When Bernard died sometime between the mid-1150s and early 1160s, the lordship briefly fell to his eldest son, the childless Guy, and then to a younger son also named Bernard. This second Bernard, who remained loyal to Henry II during the Great Revolt, achieved a measure of fame for this pivotal role in the capture of King William the Lion during the Battle of Alnwick. When this Bernard died childless in 1189, he was succeeded by his cousin Eustace, the grandfather of Dervorguilla of Galloway's husband.

This might be a good time to briefly address the seeming paucity of first names across the medieval aristocracy and the sometimes confusing and frustrating tendency for families to constantly recycle the same names down the generations. Surnames would not fully develop into formalised and permanent indicators of familial identity until well after the grand gambit of the Disinherited. Balliol itself is a toponym referring to the family's origins in and continued ownership of the village of Bailleul in Picardy, its use and adoption a transitional phase in the development of modern surnames. The difference here is more than semantic, Balliol was as much a label as a name. The use of such toponyms was purely elective; its selection was underpinned or informed by no legal status or strong social convention.

Aristocratic families had a small pool of family names that they drew upon again and again. In the absence of formal surnames or a similar consistent convention, the repetition of such names by a family was an indicator of identity. Additionally, relatives, associates and neighbours looking to court the favour and patronage of a particular family would often adopt the use of these names for one or more children and in doing so cultivate a closer association. Conflated with this process was the occasionally applied custom of naming a child after their godparent. Of course, all of this meant that families' naming stocks were over the generations prone to mutation because of intermarriage and families' attempts to foster advantageous associations with various neighbours and regional powerbrokers.

Eustace, a maternal cousin of the Balliols and the Lord of Hélicourt in Picardy, appears as an aberration in a line of Bernards and Guys because his name is derived from his paternal family's naming stock. Eustace and his wife Petronilla FitzPier had four sons, Hugh, Enguerrand, Bernard and Henry.[84] Hugh was probably named after the Bishop of Durham, Hugh de Puiset, who was a major landholder in northern England and the overlord of much of the family's English lands. He was involved in negotiations with Eustace in the 1190s in regard to claims over the manors of Long Newton and

Newhouse. Enguerrand's name likely comes from either Eustace's paternal family's naming stock or those of his maternal grandparents. Bernard is, of course, drawn from the Balliols' traditional pool of names, while Henry is almost certainly named after Henry II. Hugh, Eustace's eldest son and the primary Balliol heir, likewise named his eldest son John after King John of England while his younger son was named Eustace.

While the marriage between Hugh's eldest son, John, to Dervorguilla marked the entrance of the main Balliol line into Scottish politics, his uncle, Enguerrand (or Ingram as he is sometimes referred to in Scottish sources), had already established himself within the northernly kingdom. Enguerrand, who had inherited the Lordship of Dalton in County Durham and Tours-en-Vimeu in Picardy from his father, married the Scottish heiress Agnes, the daughter of Walter de Berkeley of Redcastle.[85] The Lord of Redcastle in Montrose and Urr in Galloway, Walter had been the Great Chamberlain of Scotland, one of the most important and prestigious administrative officers within the Scottish royal court. In addition to Walter's lands, Enguerrand inherited something of his association with the royal government. Enguerrand's allegiance eventually brought him into conflict with his family during the unfolding barons' revolt in England. His brothers, Hugh and Bernard, were both diehard supporters of King John, and this led King Alexander II to briefly besiege Bernard Castle in 1216 when he attempted to invade England in support of the rebels.[86] The familial bonds of the thirteenth-century medieval aristocracy were, however, both flexible and resilient. The complicated web of reciprocal relationships and overlapping territorial claims that unpinned their society meant that such clashes and conflicts of interest were relatively common and eminently negotiable. The conflict they found themselves engaged in was limited in both terms of scope and duration, and in its aftermath both branches of the family maintained amicable relations. Certainly, the decision for John to wed one of Alan's daughters needs to be viewed within the context of his uncle's status as one of Galloway's leading landholders.

The oldest son of Hugh and his wife Cecily de Fontaines, John, was probably born sometime around 1205. By the time of John's birth, assiduous royal service down the generations, combined with a series of advantageous marriages, had swollen and fortified the family's lands. The majority of these fell within the lordships of Balliol, in France, Hitchin in Herefordshire and Bernard Castle and Gainford in County Durham.[87] John's marriage to Dervorguilla took place in 1223. John was his father's eldest son and primary heir, inheriting the vast majority of Hugh's lands upon his death in 1229. His marriage was clearly a tremendously advantageous one. Dervorguilla was of royal blood, albeit from a branch now increasingly distanced from the throne, and her father was easily the second most powerful man in Scotland in terms of both wealth and military capabilities. Both Hugh and Alan shared a loyalty and association with King John and had in the darkest most desperate days of the baronial rebellion laboured to maintain the king's authority and position within northern England. The two men therefore were almost certainly personally acquainted with one another and had probably co-operated closely through the cavalcade of crisis that constituted the latter years of King John's reign.

The potential to inherit land in Galloway was no doubt a tempting one for the Balliols, who already had family and allies within the former principality. Meanwhile, Alan would have had reason to hope that a connection with the main stem of the Balliol family could bring him closer to its Scottish branch and lessen royal Scottish influence over Galloway. It is worth bearing in mind though that by 1223 Alan was still a young man who had every chance of producing a legitimate son. Likewise, the decisive way Alexander II acted to sweep away Alan's alternative male heirs and establish royal control of Galloway would have been hard to predicate in the early 1220s when Alan was at the height of his power. Of course, through her mother Margaret, Dervorguilla had a claim to extensive estates in Chester, which would have made her an extremely desirable match for the Balliols, even discounting any possibility of inheriting land within Galloway.

As we have seen, the Balliol family inherited a great swathe of Galloway and had by the late 1250s emerged as the region's pre-eminent landowners. Dervorguilla's swelling inheritance made her and her husband exceedingly wealthy. John successfully parlayed this influx of capital into access to and influence within the English royal court, establishing himself as one of King Henry III's most prominent courtiers. Alexander II had died in 1249, leaving the throne to his eight-year-old son, Alexander III. Royal minorities tended to be turbulent and dangerous times in the medieval world as the leash that constrained the various aristocratic familial groups and rival court factions slipped. The Scottish royal court soon became dominated by the feuding of the Comyn and Durward families, as each faction attempted to monopolise crucial royal offices and seize control of the levers of power.[88]

While the Scottish nobility vied for control over the boy king, Henry III of England seized upon the opportunity to assert his overlordship of Scotland. A notion that can be slightly hard to parse through the lens of modern conceptions of statehood and national identity is that prior to Edward I's reign, the medieval kings of England's preferred instrument in the exercise of their overlordship were the kings of Scotland. While they might require a deal of cajoling or outright bullying to acquiesce to the imposition of outside authority, in general it suited the kings of England to conduct affairs in Scotland through a junior partner or powerful subordinate capable of decisive intervention within Scotland rather than risk becoming bogged down in the mire of Scottish politics. Henry III, therefore, had a vested interest not only in controlling Alexander III but in preserving his authority and suite of royal power from the fractious courtiers intent of carving up the spoils of royal administration. Therefore, taking matters into his own hands in 1251, Henry insisted on appointing two of his own courtiers, Robert de Ros and John Balliol, as Alexander III's guardians.[89]

John's appointment had presumably been informed by his loyalty to Henry III and the large financial stake he held in Scotland. Of course, Alexander III was still young, his health potentially fragile. Moreover, the king was an only child. In a society built around dynastic ties and mediation of the flow of inheritable interests, it is inconceivable that John and Henry would not have been keenly aware of Dervorguilla's excellent claim to the throne in the event of Alexander's death. As interesting as it is to speculate upon what ambitions stirred within the Balliol line during this period of guardianship, it proved to be a position to which John was ill suited. John was either incapable or unwilling to rein in the excessive corruption that his fellow guardian, Robert de Ros, gleefully engaged in. When the following year, Henry III became aware of Ros' abuse of power, he dissolved the dual guardianship and set about restructuring the Scottish royal court.[90] Despite this setback, John remained one of Henry III's principal courtiers and supporters, fighting alongside the king against the rebel forces of Simon de Montfort. John was present at the disastrous royalist defeat at the Battle of Lewes and was briefly captured by the rebel barons before rejoining the king's war effort.

John had been born and lived most of his life in the shadow of Durham Cathedral, one of the Kingdom of England's principal seats of education and learning. The chances are good then that John himself was educated to a relatively high standard compared to many of his aristocratic peers. Certainly, in later life, John displayed an interest in academic affairs, creating a scholarship for aspiring students at the University of Oxford. Upon his death in 1268, Dervorguilla greatly expanded upon this grant, establishing Balliol College as a memorial to her husband. While John's son and grandson would both go on to be crowned kings of Scotland, the establishment of Balliol College is arguably the family's greatest and certainly their most long-lived legacy.[91] John had used his wealth to win prestige and position within the English court but had been disinclined to press his highly advantageous position within Scotland, instead content merely to farm the income of those lands he already possessed.

The elder John and Dervorguilla's marriage was, in addition to being highly profitable and advantageous for the Balliols, also enormously successful in a dynastic sense. Together they produced four sons and five daughters, although one imagines that Dervorguilla did the majority of work in this regard.[92] As stated earlier, the couple's three eldest sons, Hugh, Alan and Alexander, all died within a decade of their father without issue. This string of tragedies left their youngest son, John, born sometime around the very late 1240s, as the primary heir to the amassed Balliol estates. The couple's five daughters were Ada, who married William Lindsay of Lamberton in 1266; Margaret, who married Thomas de Moulton; Cecil, who married John de Burgh; Eleanor, who married John de Comyn; and Matildia, who married Bryan FitzAlan.[93] We shall return to examine this generation of the family in more detail in subsequent chapters as the younger John pressed his claim for the throne in the midst of a succession crisis. However, it is worth noting here that, with the exception of Eleanor and Matilda, who appear to be John and Dervorguilla's youngest children, their other daughters made curiously humble matches.

The Bruce family's claim to Scotland came from a nearly identical source to that of their Balliol rivals. Sometimes around 1219, Robert de Brus, the 4th Lord of Annandale, married Isobel of Huntingdon, the daughter of Prince David, the Earl of Huntingdon, and the younger sister of Alan of Galloway's bride, Margaret.[94] Their son Robert, the 5th Lord of Annandale, known as Robert the Competitor, would be John Balliol's primary rival for the throne, pitting the legal principles of primogeniture and tanistry against one another.[95] It was the Competitor's son, Robert, the surprisingly leprosy-free father of the future king, Robert the Bruce, who married Countess Majorie of Carrick in 1271. Majorie was the eldest daughter and primary heir of Earl Nial of Carrick and his wife Margaret Stewart. Nial was the son of Donnchadh, the man for whom the Earldom of Carrick had first been created after his inheritance had been seized by his cousin Lochlann (or Roland) of Galloway and King William the Lion.[96] Majorie and her children were therefore not terribly distant relatives of Lochlann's granddaughter, Dervorguilla, and her children. Moreover, at the time of Majorie and Robert's marriage, there still existed some sense within abutting Carrick and Galloway of their shared historical and cultural connections.

From the Bruce point of view, the marriage was not necessary a great boon. Apparently, Bruce failed to ask King Alexander III for permission to marry Majorie, who as an orphaned heiress would have fallen under the nominal guardianship of the king. This bizarre omission on Robert's part led to the almost immediate confiscation of Majorie's patrimony, which was only returned to the couple following the levelling of a hefty fine. Possibly because of these unusual circumstances, a bizarre tale subsequently spread in which Robert, returning home from the Crusades, travelled to Majorie's castle to inform her of the death of her husband, Adam of Kilconquhar. Majorie, apparently not unduly distressed by the death of her husband, was so taken by the handsome and courtly messenger that she had him imprisoned, refusing to let him free until he promised to marry her.

Majorie was certainly married to Adam, their daughter Martha joining the extended Bruce household, but the evidence for Robert's participation in the Crusade in which Adam died is confused and predicated on hearsay. As dubious as this story is, it seems probable that Majorie and Robert's rush to get married, before seeking royal permission, was influenced by Majorie's reluctance to submit to a royal guardianship. Rather than place her fate at the whims of the royal court, Majorie pressed forward scandalously quickly with a legally questionable marriage to Robert, a man she had some measure of affection for or understanding with. The idea that love may have played some part in the hasty marriage is somewhat supported by the fact that Robert risked the king's wrath for a marriage that brought him no great fortune. Despite possessing the committal status denied to the Lordship of Galloway, Carrick was smaller and far less wealthy than its southernly neighbour. While Alan of Galloway had stood astride the Irish sea like a colossus, Majorie's grandfather and father had dwindled in importance and influence.[97]

While the Balliols' marriage to a granddaughter of Prince David marked the main branch of the family's entrance into Scottish politics, the Bruce family had been thriving within Scotland for several generations. In the next chapter, we turn our attention to the Great Succession Crisis, the Balliols' brief moment in the sun and the crucial role played by the Comyn family in the subsequent struggle for the Scottish throne and subsequent formation of the Disinherited. We could, of course, have begun our story here but by returning to the history of Galloway and the lands that would form the Balliols' and Bruces' principal power bases in the struggle to come, we gain a crucial insight not only into the shared history of the two families, but the mercurial nature of notions of nationality, statehood, and identity during this formative era.

Chapter Two

The Succession Crisis, Factionalism and the Path to Civil War

The monarchy of Scotland was as ancient and storied an institution as practically any other European throne. Its deep roots stretched beyond the ken of records and history into the ever-fertile realm of myths and legends. Yet it would be a mistake to equate antiquity with statis. The character, size, shape and even name of the kingdom was a thing of constant flux. It had begun life as but one of several precariously balanced rival polities that over the centuries had in a flurry of blows, adroit negotiations and simple twists of fate come to consolidate power over much of the area we now call Scotland.

It was first and foremost a political rather than a cultural construction. Like the vast majority of its contemporaries within medieval Europe, its boundaries were defined by the political and personal relationships of its ruler rather than any grand theory of statehood. Often these relationships were burdened by the expectations of history and circumstances; certain regions and communities were likely to cleave to a particular throne or line of kings based on the length of their association and history of mutually beneficial co-operation. Some were simply pinned under the superior coercive power of their neighbours and forced to participate in a larger hegemonic polity. Other relationships were more recent, their character and boundaries as yet protean and untested. All were to some extent subject to careful and continual renegotiation between the monarch, in this case the King of Scotland, and the array of regional families, aristocrats and powerbrokers through which a facsimile of control and authority could be exercised.

As we have seen in the previous chapter, the history of how the two halves of the former principality of Galloway fell broadly under the control of the Balliol and Bruce families, the establishment of overlordship and the integration of new regions into an existing polity was far from a simple process. Fergus of Galloway, the first truly powerful hegemonic of the region, was overthrown and defeated by Malcolm IV as early as 1160.[1] Yet Malcolm was unwilling or unable to displace Fergus' sons and Galloway retained its strong sense of regional identity. Indeed, even its partition through the creation of the northerly Earldom of Carrick in 1186 failed to fatally undermine the power of its native dynasty and the Gallodovian aristocracy that supported it.[2]

The Lords of Galloway alternatively served and fought against both the English and Scottish monarchies throughout the twelfth and thirteenth centuries or else busied themselves pursuing an independent agenda in the challenging arena of North Sea politics.[3] The extent to which any of the Scottish kings' military interventions into Galloway during this period succeeded in implanting Scottish royal officials into the region is unclear. Likewise, it is very difficult to ascertain if the scattered presence of such officials represented true royal oversight or if they had been co-opted into the administration of the Lords of Galloway. Certainly, the region was wracked by native populist uprisings, partly motivated by a desire to maintain the lordship of Fergus' descendants, as late as the mid-1260s, more than a century after its initial 'conquest' by the Kingdom of Scotland.[4] There was for Galloway no grand plan or inevitable march to integration with Scotland or Scottish culture. Only a sporadic series of eagerly seized upon opportunities.

Rather than a weakness, the flexibility of this approach and the elasticity of overlordship can be taken as evidence of the robustness of the Kingdom of Scotland and medieval European kingdoms in general. While fully subjecting Galloway and suppressing the regional identity of its inhabitants would have been a supremely bloody and expensive affair that quite possibly could have taxed the resources and governmental apparatus of the kingdom past the point of breaking, a succession of Scottish kings were able to negotiate a broad acknowledgement of Scottish overlordship that kept the region essentially stable and freed them to pursue their ambitions elsewhere. The kings of Scotland and their family were continually compelled during this period to renegotiate the terms upon which they held their vast estates in northern England and the ever-thorny issue of where the border lay. The distinction between the Kingdom of Scotland and adjoining lands owned by the King of Scotland in another kingdom, while ambiguous, was one that the kings of England were exceptionally eager to uphold.[5] The Norse-Gael Kingdom of the Isles, with its deep connections to both Norway and the kingdoms of Ireland's eastern seaboard, presented a severe challenge to Scotland's westward expansion and would require both tireless campaigning and the careful courting of local powerbrokers to overcome.[6]

A fell-handed and forceful alternative to the kings of Scotland's strategy to entice the Lords of Galloway into the Scottish political community was simply unnecessary. Because the kingdom was essentially formed by a network of personal bonds, of inevitably varying strength, it could encompass multiple cultural groups and regional identities with little adjustment and was gloriously unburdened by arbitrary preconceptions regarding the form these relationships or the kingdom as a whole needed to take. While a distinctive Scottish culture certainly existed, it was neither the foundation upon which the kingdom rested or universally applied within it. Instead, it was alloyed to varying extents with regional identities and other cultures throughout the kingdom. Galloway, with its large Norse-Gael population and powerful semi-autonomous lords, lay near the extreme of one end of this spectrum, while the traditional heartlands of the kingdom from which it initially expanded formed another. Between them lay regions such as Lothian that retained elements of a distinctive cultural and regional identity.

On top of this, since the early twelfth century the Scottish royal court and an ever-increasing proportion of the Scottish nobility had adopted the trappings of French culture.[7] The royally sponsored influx of Norman and Anglo-Norman fortune seekers and settlers to Scotland meant that by the time of the Succession Crisis of the 1280s, the vast majority of the Scottish aristocracy were at least partially of Norman or Anglo-Norman descent. Indeed, this mingling was part of an ongoing process, with several families such as the Balliols having only been introduced to the realm of Scottish politics a generation or two previously. Similarly, just like the Dunkeld kings of Scotland and their would-be Balliol and Bruce successors, significant amounts of the Scottish aristocracy held lands and titles outside of the Kingdom of Scotland.[8]

Such arrangements and happenstances were far from atypical and would not have been viewed as inherently problematic by Europe's royal and aristocratic inhabitants. Since the Norman Conquest in 1066, the royal family of England and its aristocracy had been composed of Normans. In addition to their English subjects, who they were distinguished from culturally and linguistically, the kingdom also incorporated areas possessed of strong regional identity such as the Celtic-speaking Cornish and Cumbrians. This is to say nothing of the Norman elite's extensive colonial efforts in Wales and Ireland.[9] In France, the French kings ruled over not only a plethora of strong regional identities, constructed around the dominance of a network of interrelated aristocratic families, but also distinctive linguistic and cultural groups such as the Occitans and Bretons. Likewise, the Holy Roman Empire was composed of Germans, Italians and Lowlanders, all of whom broke down further into a vast medley of composite cultural and regional identities upon even the most cursory of inspections.

We must be very careful, therefore, in this chapter and beyond when discussing the Scottish political community. As already stated, the king rather than the actual institutions or apparatus of royal government was the focus of this community. Over the course of the twelfth century, successive Scottish kings had sought to supplement their efforts in expanding the boundaries of their kingdom and their personal control within those boundaries by adapting, rather than adopting wholesale, many of the administrative practices of the English Monarchy.[10] Such reforms included the introduction and modification of sheriffs, justiciars, and an array of other regional offices answerable first and foremost to the royal government. The successful implementation of these offices throughout Scotland strengthened the connection between the kingdom's distinctive regional political communities and the royal centre. By the thirteenth century, a pattern or expectation had been established in England that most of these positions would be filled by a stratum of minor but well-connected aristocrats who operated as royal functionaries. In contrast, in Scotland these positions were usually awarded to the high nobility, to members of families who together exercised control over significant swathes of territory.[11] This distribution of royal patronage and positions both reflected and consciously attempted to reinforce the Scottish kings' relationships with the Scottish magnates, their tenants in chief.

Again, we need to tread carefully when discussing the role of administrative positions and the extent to which the proliferation of bureaucracy strengthened royal authority and contributed to the cohesion of the Scottish aristocracy. They almost certainly did all these things, constituting one of the kingdom's most important centripetal forces, but perhaps not quite in the way that first comes to mind. Life in the modern world unavoidably brings us into contact with vast bureaucratic monoliths, most acutely characterised by their unyielding lack of personality and inflexible nature. The same was not necessarily true of medieval bureaucracy.[12] In the highly personal world of medieval politics, more or less everything was open to negotiation. Taxes, fees and even fines were routinely levelled by the royal centre and its confederates but often the initial amounts represented a starting place for negotiations rather than a definitive and final demand. The advances in royal administrative and bureaucratic practices facilitated these negotiations between the king, his regional proxies and the localities by providing them with a framework. It did not replace the intrinsically personal nature of government. Indeed, it was this degree of flexibility that made the approach so valuable and effective in fostering mutually beneficial co-operation between the king and his leading aristocrats.

In many ways Scottish kings were, like all contemporary European monarchs to one extent or another, the first among equals within their kingdom.[13] A comparable modern analogue would be that theirs was a ministerial rather than presidential style of government. In order to rule effectively, Scottish kings had to co-operate extensively with the powerful noble families and affinities that could function as their local and regional proxies. In exchange, the dominant position of these individuals and groups among their own networks of supporters were both legitimised by royal authority and enhanced by the access to patronage and resources that royal service yielded.[14] It was therefore in some ways this mutual need, rather than the sheer power or the prestige of the Scottish throne, that secured the Scottish monarchs' place as the centre or lynchpin of the Scottish political community.[15] In fact, this political community and the kingdom itself were essentially defined by the limits of a king's network of functional and productive relationships.

The true quandary of the succession crisis that followed the extinction of the royal house – and the primary focus of this chapter – is what happened to this system, shored up with historical and personal expectations, when the centre failed. The succession crisis would not only trigger a determined English invasion, shattering the previously well-established paradigm of Anglo-Scottish relationships, but lead to a dramatic rise in factionalism among the Scottish aristocracy. With the stakes at an all-time high, the nobilities' struggle for mastery led to the parabolic arc of Balliol kingship, the resultant struggle between the Comyns and Bruces for control over the Scottish war effort and eventually the exile of those portions of the Scottish nobility that found themselves on the losing side of a civil war. It was an exile that paved the way for the Disinherited's dramatic attempt to re-enter the realm of Scottish politics and recover their ancestral lands and titles.

A final challenge that we will have to be aware of before we proceed revolves around the relatively elongated nature of this conflict and the manner in which it overlapped with, and bled into, the struggle to thwart Edward I's imperial ambitions. Alexander III, the last Dunkeld King of Scotland, died in 1286.[16] John Balliol was crowned king in 1292.[17] Bannockburn, the decisive battle that secured both the Kingdom of Scotland's independence and Robert the Bruce's place on the throne, took place in the summer of 1314.[18] The intervening decades were enough time to see the Bruces go from opportunistic rebels against the Scottish throne and English collaborators to the beating heart of the struggle for an independent Scotland. The Disinherited and their relatives on the other hand went from being the inner circle of the legitimate Scottish king to the guardians of a kingless kingdom and then, in their bid to oppose the Bruce domination of Scotland, allies of the English. The course of history is seldom straightforward. Much of the nuance and character of this process has been obscured by later sources, written to reflect the political concerns of their time in which the Bruces' Stuart relatives struggled to maintain royal prestige in the face of continued English belligerence and the increasing truculence and ambition of the now supremely independently minded Scottish nobility.

Alexander III's reign both began and ended in crisis. Alexander was born in 1241, the only child of King Alexander II of Scotland and his second wife, Queen Marie de Coucy.[19] Alexander II had previously been married to Princess Joan of England, a union that had secured Alexander's extensive estates in northern England.[20] However, the marriage also provided her English royal relatives with a degree of additional leverage in their attempts to exercise their claims of suzerainty over the Kingdom of Scotland. Joan was just nine at the time of her marriage in 1221. The marriage would therefore not have been consummated, and Joan would not have been expected to have started producing royal offspring for at least another five or six years.

Yet as the years wore on and the royal marriage remained childless, increasing concerns began to circulate through the Scottish court. Alexander II was the only legitimate son of William the Lion; he therefore had no brother to succeed him if he died childless, as had been the case with previous generations of Scottish kings. His legitimate sisters, Margaret, Isabella and Majorie, where all married to powerful English magnates. Were Alexander to die without children, then it was likely that there would be a dispute over the throne, which would either go to one of his English brothers-in-law or one of the disparate descendants of his great uncle, Prince David. Such dynastic concerns placed Alexander II in a difficult position. Were he to attempt to divorce Joan or annul their marriage, her brother, Henry III of England, to whom she was very close, was likely to declare war and use the opportunity to place the Scottish king yet more firmly under thumb. Indeed, there is some evidence to suggest that Joan, who was largely isolated and without allies in the Scottish court, spent increasing amounts of time away from Alexander in her English estates.[21]

Joan's death from illness in 1238 therefore presented Alexander II with the opportunity to both produce a sorely needed heir for Scotland and perhaps fenagle his way out of the looming shadow of English overlordship. His choice of new Queen, Marie de Coucy, reflected these mingled concerns and hopes.[22] Marie's father was Lord Enguerrand III of Coucy, one of the King of France's major vassals and a distant relative of the French royal house.[23] Her marriage therefore worked to draw Scotland closer to the French royal court, an influence that, if carefully cultivated, could help to guard against Henry III's claims to Scottish overlordship.

In 1249, Alexander died from a fever he caught while on an expedition to detach the Kingdom of the Isles from Norwegian sovereignty and formally absorb its territories, which included a large portion of the mainland's north-western coast such as Argyll, into the Kingdom of Scotland.[24] His only heir, his young namesake, Alexander III, was a mere child at the time. Clearly in a political system constructed around a single figure and that person's ability to reach an understanding with and properly incentivise multiple factions of power brokers and stakeholders, a period of minority rule was a time of acute danger. In the absence of a strong senior partner to distribute patronage and mediate between the various aristocratic factions, certain groups were liable to either attempt to shuck off their former associations and with them royal control or seek to expand their own power bases by vying for control over key offices and the apparatus of royal government.

At the time of the seven- or eight-year-old Alexander III's accession to the throne, the most powerful and influential figure within the Scottish court was probably Walter Comyn, Lord of Badenoch, and through his wife, Earl of Menteith. Under Walter's father, William, the Comyn family had become firmly entrenched within the Scottish court through their extensive contributions to the growth of royal authority within the north of Scotland.[25] Walter's brothers, John and David, were able to acquire the Earldom of Angus and the Lordship of Kilbride respectively through advantageous marriages, in part because of the depth of royal favour the family enjoyed. Their paternal half-brother, Alexander, eventually inherited the Earldom of Buchan from his mother, while their sisters, Johanna, Margaret and Elizabeth, found matches with Earl William of Ross, Sir John de Keith, the Marshall of Scotland, and Earl William of Mar.[26] The Comyns were a powerful, expansive and crucially tightly knit family whose various branches co-operated closely with one another in pursuit of their mutual interests. Naturally, this prominence combined with their multitude of close familial connections to other major families within the Scottish aristocracy made them a force to be reckoned with and something of a default choice for the provisional leadership of the Scottish political community during the king's minority.[27]

Yet the position of Walter Comyn and his family within the Scottish royal government during the minority of Alexander III was contested vigorously by Alan Durward and his allies.[28] Alan was the son of Thomas de Lundin, the royal Hostarius or doorkeeper; a coveted court position that gave him remarkable access to the king and entailed a level of responsibility for the protection of the king's person and personal property. Thomas was the maternal grandson of Earl Gille Crìst of Mar and had upon the earl's death in the early 1200s successfully launched a legal challenge that saw him secure a significant portion of the earldom's southern territories.[29] The identity of Alan's mother is unknown but his later political activities and repeated attempts to secure the earldom of Atholl strongly suggest that she was a daughter of Earl Máel Coluim of Atholl. Alan was therefore well connected to major factions within the Scottish aristocracy, but his familial situation was such that he was highly unlikely to inherit a comital title. Instead, he followed his father's example by attaching himself to the royal court and the king's great project of bringing the north and west of Scotland more firmly under royal control. By 1233, he had not only inherited his father's position as Hostarius but also been awarded control of Urquhart, near Inverness.[30]

Alan's true rise to prominence came five years before the coronation of Alexander III and strangely resulted almost directly from the intemperate actions of his future Comyn rivals. The Comyns alongside the king's cousin, Earl Patrick of Dunbar, began ravaging the lands of the Bisset family, who they held responsible for the death of their relative, Earl Patrick of Atholl.[31] The same Patrick whose case for inheriting the Lordship of Galloway from his uncle, Alan of Galloway, we examined in the previous chapter. The Bisset family soon found themselves overwhelmed and unable to resist the powerful aristocratic coalition arrayed against them. Members of the family successfully took shelter within the royal court of Alexander II.[32]

However, the Scottish crown, almost certainly acting under pressure from the Comyns and the family of Patrick of Dunbar and their allies, subsequently judged the Bissets to be responsible for the murder and ordered the confiscation of their Scottish lands and property.[33] The Bissets responded by once more striking out for the protection of a royal court and a perceived higher authority, this time that of Henry III of England. The English king, ever eager to expand his authority within Scotland, argued that Alexander had no legal right to confiscate the lands of one of his vassals without first receiving approval from his own overlord, Henry.[34] While the incident was eventually resolved, it was something of a black eye for the Comyn family and in the subsequent reshuffling of royal government, undertaken by Alexander II to consolidate his authority in the face of the English king's heavy-handed tactics, Alan Durward was appointed Justicar of Scotia.[35]

This position gave Durward near vice-regal authority and responsibility within the north of the kingdom and was accompanied by a shift in which Alan replaced Walter as Alexander II's most trusted and intimate councillor.

However, it is worth noting that Alan took the position of Justicar not from Watler but from Philip de Melville and Robert de Monte Alto, who had both proven largely ineffectual during the crisis. As noted above, Alexander II's reaction to the Bisset incident and his subsequent reforms had more to do with staving off further English intervention than attempting to curb the power of overmighty subjects. While the Comyn family did not emerge from the incident covered in glory, having inadvertently drawn the covetous eye of Henry III to Scotland, it was not damaged in any meaningful way and remained the single most powerful and influential aristocratic family within Scotland. What the crisis did mean, however, was that by the time of Alexander II's unexpected death in 1249, Alan and his allies were deeply entrenched within the Scottish royal government.

Divided as it was by internal rivalries, the minority government of Alexander III initially proved itself to be almost surprisingly effective in its efforts to preserve the integrity and independence of the Scottish throne. Henry III had seized upon Alexander III's minority as another chance to impose his personal overlordship over Scotland. In his attempts to cajole a recognition of overlordship from the young Alexander and his advisors, Henry went as far as writing to the Pope to launch an ultimately unsuccessful legal challenge to the validity of Alexander's coronation. This claim was strongly refuted by Alexander's councillors and the massed ranks of Scottish nobility, even as Henry succeeded in influencing other more limited aspects of the minority. Indeed, the Scottish royal government, at this crucial juncture, skilfully negotiated Henry's pretensions to suzerainty over the British Isles while denying him any major practical concessions. Evidently both the Comyns and Durward recognised that while there were significant short-term political advantages to be gained from co-operation with Henry III, their positions and personal security ultimately relied upon the existence of a strong Scottish-based monarchy.[36]

It was a difficult and tense balancing act. We should be careful to remember though that as severe a challenge as forced acknowledgement of English overlordship was to the independence and prestige of the Scottish throne, the threat was not an existential one. Submission, so heroically resisted, would have drastically changed the form and function of Scottish royal government but did not entail its dissolution. Henry III sought to bring Scotland and its throne firmly under his thumb rather than occupy it himself. Indeed, his later actions and attempts to impose change upon the minority government strongly suggest that the ceiling of his ambition was tapping the kingdom's military resources for his revanchist wars in Europe. This, of course, was not an inconsiderable ambition, and it is easy to see why the Scottish nobility and both factions within the royal government did all they could to refute or otherwise blunt his intervention in Scotland.

As we explored previously, while Henry III failed to extract an acknowledgement of his overlordship in 1251, he did succeed in arranging for Alexander to marry his daughter, Margaret.[37] As part of his settlement, two members of Henry's court, John Balliol and Robert de Ros, were appointed as the guardians of Alexander and his young bride. However, the members of the Scottish government demonstrated their continued independence by firmly rebuffing English attempts to extract hostages in exchange for Margaret's safety. The guardianship of these two strongly English-aligned Anglo-Scottish nobles proved to be short-lived as word of Robert de Ros' eager corruption and abuse of power soon reached Henry's ear.[38] In any case, their authority had been extremely limited, with both men appearing relatively low down the witness lists of charters issued in the name of Alexander III during this time. With the failure of this scheme, Henry changed tactics and began to cultivate a closer relationship with the Durward faction as a way of increasing his influence in Scotland. Durward and his allies were, after all, perfectly positioned to bypass the Scottish nobility and as the weaker faction within the minority government were more likely to co-operate with Henry, as long as that co-operation did not result in anything too obviously damaging to the integrity of the Scottish government.[39]

Durward attempted to use this new association to undermine the Comyns' position and further widen the rift between them and Henry III, who increasingly blamed the family's hostility and influence for his daughter's allegedly poor treatment in Scotland. Events reached a head in 1255 when Durward and his supporters made a concerted effort to oust Walter and the Comyns from the royal government. This involved the speedy relocation of the king and the royal court to Edinburgh Castle, denying the Comyns access to either. At the same time, the Comyns' aristocratic rivals, including the Bruce and Stewart families, as well as their one-time ally Patrick of

Dunbar, were given license to openly challenge them.[40] While this coup was successful in preventing the Comyns from gaining access to the king and apparatus of royal government, Durward's new allies failed to effectively disrupt Comyn authority or networks of affinity, leaving the family's core power base intact. Henry III hoped to use the change in the Scottish royal government to enact a more formal structure for the minority in which authority was to be held by a council of seven guardians who served for a fixed number of years. However, he soon found that without the support of the Comyns and their allies, such reforms could not practically be enacted. Additionally, Alexander was rapidly approaching the end of his minority, and it seems probable that many Scottish aristocrats and bishops would have seen any further retooling of the royal government as unnecessary or suspicious.

By 1257, the Comyns were both desperate and largely undiminished in terms of military capacity and political influence, a dangerous combination. A prolonged series of negotiations with Henry III proved ultimately fruitless as it became clear that the English king increasingly preferred to cultivate influence in Scotland by leveraging the position of Anglo-Scottish magnates whose divided loyalties he already had some claim over. The Comyns therefore adopted a new highly reckless solution to their problems: they kidnapped Alexander.[41] That they were able to do so, holding him at Kinross castle in the family's heartlands, is quite a feat in itself. As incredible as their success in gaining control of the king was, the strangest thing about the kidnapping incident was the anti-climactic way in which it concluded. By April 1258, the king, now sixteen, was free and presiding over his first parliament in Stirling. It is maddeningly unclear if Alexander escaped, was liberated by the efforts of his other supporters, or was simply let go after coming to some understanding with the Comyns.[42] It seems probable that the Comyns were at least able to persuade the king that they meant him no harm since the family faced little in the way of repercussions for a crime as momentous and serious as the abduction of the monarch and continued to work closely under the king for the remainder of his reign.

Just as the Comyns and Durward understood that their power and prosperity relied upon close co-operation with the Scottish throne and access to the rewards royal service brought, Alexander would surely have appreciated the collaborative nature of Scottish government. To begin his majority with a violent clash with the most powerful members of the Scottish aristocracy would clearly endanger his rule and pave the way for further English intervention. It is also possible that the death of the family's head, Walter Comyn, the following November helped to clear away any remaining royal ill feeling about the incident and presented the king and the remaining Comyns with the opportunity for a fresh start. Walter's younger half-brother, Earl Alexander of Buchan, quickly emerged as the new head of the Comyn family. He also took Alan Durward's place as the Justiciar of Scotia, reaffirming the almost vice-regal power that the family wielded in the north.[43] That the Comyns' continued to co-operate closely with one another, even as authority passed to another branch of the family, speaks to both an admirable degree of familial solidarity and a keen awareness that the family owed its ongoing power and prosperity to its engagement in royal service. The family members in the best position to participate in royal government and negotiate with the crown on their collective behalf naturally wielded enormous influence over the rest of the family.

Throughout Alexander III's reign, Alexander Comyn served as Alexander III's most trusted lieutenant and was one of the most prominent and regular witnesses to royal charters. Alan Durward and many of his allies remained in office or continued to serve Alexander in the Scottish royal government in some capacity but the king's presence and the existence of a succession of mutual enemies curtailed the worst of the infighting.[44] Freed of the hindrances Alan and aristocratic factionalism had burdened them with, the power and influence of the Comyn family's various branches continued to wax. Alexander III proved a highly capable ruler who through a series of shrewd military actions and relentless diplomatic pressure continued his father's efforts to bring the Western Isles into the Kingdom of Scotland. Alexander was opposed vigorously in this ambition by the Norwegian King Haakon IV, who was eager to reassert his role as the Kingdom of the Isles' traditional overlord.[45] Thanks in large part to Alexander's strategically minded handling of the campaign and the cultivation of productive relations with his deputies and regional proxies, the Norwegian invasion of Scotland was thwarted. Shortly after Haakon's defeat and death, his successors acknowledged Scottish control of the Western Isles in the Treaty of Perth.[46] While the presence of Henry III still loomed large over the early years of Alexander's minority, his involvement in Scotland was eventually compromised by the emergence of the extreme political difficulties in England that prefaced the Second Barons' Rebellion.[47]

The crisis that surrounded the beginning of Alexander III's reign is important to our overall subject because it prefigures, in many important ways, the succession crisis that followed his death in 1286. Alexander Comyn, one of the future Guardians of Scotland and foremost political figures during the early years of the succession crisis, had already experienced one crisis in which an opportunistic English king had attempted to leverage instability within the royal Scottish centre into a recognition of English overlordship. This example loomed large in the minds of Alexander and his peers within the Scottish aristocracy and heavily informed their negotiations with Edward I of England over the succession and the relationship between the two kingdoms. Unfortunately for them and their immediate descendants, Edward I's imperial ambitions within the British Isles were far greater and far more direct than those of any of his predecessors.

When the forty-four-year-old Alexander III died in 1286, his most likely successor was a three-year-old Norwegian princess. Alexander and his wife Margaret of England had three children, Margaret, Alexander and David. Margaret was married in 1281 to Eric II of Norway, a union that was meant to improve Norway and Scotland's recently tempestuous relationship and forestall the outbreak of another war. In 1283, Queen Margaret of Norway died shortly after giving birth to a daughter, also named Margaret in honour of her mother and maternal grandmother.[48] Queen Margaret had been predeceased by her youngest brother, Prince David of Scotland in 1281.[49] The agreement that paved the way for Margaret and Eric's marriage had explicitly stated that any children that resulted from the union were eligible to succeed to the throne of Scotland. Princess Margaret of Norway was therefore born third in line to the throne of Scotland, just behind her mother and her uncle, Prince Alexander.

At this juncture, it is possible that Alexander III and the Scottish aristocracy were not unduly concerned over the succession, despite the personal tragedies these loses represented for the king. According to the Launceston chronicle, Alexander had not been particularly lonely since the death of his wife in 1275, having eagerly sought out the company of maids, widows and even nuns.[50] It is telling, however, that he did not feel a political or dynastic imperative to remarry either then or after the deaths of his daughter and youngest son. After all, Prince Alexander was eighteen or nineteen at the time of his sister's death and presumably already attempting to father royal heirs of his own with his wife, who I regret to inform you was also called Margaret. If this was the case, Prince Alexander's sudden death in 1284, a mere week or so after his twentieth birthday, sharply alerted all involved to the reality of the looming crisis.[51]

Reacting with his customary energy and decisiveness, Alexander ordered the entirety of the Scottish aristocracy and the kingdom's bishops to gather at the kingdom's most important royal centre, Scone.[52] There, the kingdom's thirteen earls, the clan chiefs and remainder of the nobility all swore before the stone to recognise Princess Margaret, the Maid of Norway, as their heir and support her rule. Yet the situation was uncertain and the oath replete with caveats; it was not yet clear whether Prince Alexander's wife, Margaret of Flanders, was pregnant or not. The king, only in his early forties, probably also chose the occasion to make it known that he intended to re-marry. The oath therefore had to specify that the claims of either Margaret of Flander's hypothetical child or any other sons produced by the king in the future superseded that of Margaret of Norway.

Soon afterwards, Alexander married Yolande of Dreux, the daughter of Count Robert of Dreux and Countess Beatrice of Montfort.[53] Yolande was a highly placed member of the French aristocracy, further fostering positive relations between Scotland and France. They also shared a closer, slightly strange and tangled connection in that Alexander's stepfather, Jean de Brienne, had during his first marriage also been the stepfather of Yolande's mother, Beatrice. Jean was the Grand Butler of France, a middling office within the royal court.[54] His father and namesake had incredibly been in turn both the King of Jerusalem and Emperor of Constantinople. Perhaps then, the marriage was in part an attempt to consolidate this unusual family grouping and their presence within the French royal court. Surely though, such concerns came a distant second for the groom who now saw the extinction of the ancient and royal house of Dunkeld looming before him.

Alexander III died in 1286, scant months after his wedding, rather counterproductively suffering a fatal accident on an ill-advised midnight ride to meet his queen.[55] Despite the obvious strains caused by the king's death and the uncertain prospects of another long minority, the greater part of the Scottish nobility, accustomed to co-operation with the royal centre and broadly consensus-driven decision making, rallied around the empty throne. At a parliament convened shortly after the king's death, the Scottish nobility selected six of its own to serve as regents or 'Guardians' who were to protect Alexander's rightful heirs and together rule on their behalf.[56] These 'Guardians' were chosen from a cross section of Scottish powerbrokers and were composed of two bishops, two earls and two lesser barons.[57]

The selected bishops were the Bishop of St Andrews, William Fraser, who had prior to his elevation to the bishopric served as Alexander III's Chancellor, and the Bishop of Glasgow, Robert Wishart, a member of the influential Wishart family.[58] The earls were the leader of the Comyn family, Earl Alexander of Buchan, and Earl Donnchadh of Fife, who by long tradition held the right and responsibility to preside over the coronation ceremony of the Scottish monarch.[59] The lower ranks of the nobility were represented by James Stewart, the hereditary High Steward of Scotland, and John Comyn of Badenoch, the great nephew of Earl Alexander Comyn.[60] It was overall a robust selection of talented and well-connected individuals that broadly represented the balance of power among the Scottish aristocracy. The presence of two Comyns among the Guardians reflected the breadth of the family's influence and power. The appointment of the Earl of Fife and the High Steward as the other secular Guardians were also canny inclusions. Not only were both men influential members of powerful factions within the aristocracy but they also held offices that were vital to the recognition of a lawful monarch and the control of the royal household respectively.

Yet the exact identity of the rightful heir these paragons were to guard and represent was initially unclear. There was a brief period of confusion in the immediate aftermath of Alexander's death when Queen Yolande announced that she was pregnant but within a few months it became clear that this was no longer the case, the queen likely having suffered a miscarriage.[61] This left the infant Princess Margaret of Norway as her grandfather's clear successor. While her position was greatly bolstered by Alexander's shrewd decision to have the kingdom's nobility swear to uphold her claims, there were still significant issues that had to be resolved in regard to the form Scottish royal governance would take during her minority.

The first and probably most significant of these issues was that the young Margaret was not only the uncrowned Queen of Scotland but a Princess of Norway. Indeed, she was her father's only heir and a prospective Queen of Norway. Eric was therefore understandably reticent to send his only daughter and heir off to a strange country where she would be completely under the control of the Comyns and the other Scottish aristocratic affinities that clustered around the throne. One possible solution to the issue, championed by the Norwegian king, was that he would take the throne of Scotland, either on behalf of his daughter or his deceased wife.[62] It was a legally tenuous plan that stretched and then ruptured hereditary practices and the principles of Scottish inheritance law.

The practice of male aristocrats adopting and making use of their wife's titles was exceedingly common across the thirteenth century and was based on the concept that the husband was holding and discharging the duties of that position on his wife's behalf. But upon Queen Margaret's death, all her hereditary claims would have devolved not to her husband but their daughter. Moreover, Eric's wife had never been Queen of Scotland or even her father's immediate heir. Likewise, relatives regularly acted as Guardians and regents for minority heirs, but by this period, actual assumption of their titles would have been viewed as a usurpation. It was a state of affairs only complicated by the royal nature of the office in question, since at this period there existed no satisfactory or widely accepted mechanism for the removal of a reigning monarch, even through abdication.

All this, however, amounts to so much legal quibbling; ultimately the important question was would the Scottish aristocracy accept Eric as their king? The answer, of course, was that they would not. As we have seen, in Scotland the aristocracy's ability to exercise authority was largely contingent upon their relationship with the royal centre. The majority of this aristocracy were evidently content to co-operate with one another to preserve the power and authority of the throne and maintain this mutually beneficial equilibrium. What they would not brook though was the imposition of a foreign ruler. Not necessarily because of their foreignness – medieval power structures were after all highly flexible and porous with aristocratic culture providing many points of commonality – but because they would inevitably have their own followers who they may seek to further reward and patronise using the resources of the Scottish throne. We should again be careful not to impose modern conceptions of nationalism or cultural identity onto this decision. As we shall see imminently, the same Guardians proved willing to approve of an English groom for their young queen but under carefully negotiated circumstances. The Norwegian king's bid for the throne was rejected not because of fears for the integrity or sanctity of Scottish cultural identity but because those making the decision feared for their own prosperity and status.

With his own bid for the throne empathically rejected by the Guardians and their provisional royal government, Eric elected to adopt a new tactic, dispatching one of his most trusted councillors, Bjarne Erlingsson, to Scotland.[63] His mission was to secure the Scottish throne for Margaret. It must have been a tricky balancing act for all involved. The Guardians and the aristocracy would have to accept the vice-regal authority of this Norwegian proxy as a necessary condition of the still dim prospect of Eric feeling secure enough to release his infant heir to the Scottish. This is when the second of the obstacles to Margaret's accession to the Scottish throne made its presence felt. The Bruce family rose in rebellion, raiding and ravaging the lands of their neighbours and political rivals. This included attacks on several castles in Balliol-dominated Galloway.[64] Indeed, the two families, who together among the Scottish aristocracy possessed the best claims to the Scottish throne, had already been at the centre of some sort of disruption at the parliament held after Alexander III's death.[65] It seems likely that this initial flare-up in hostilities was triggered when either one or both of the rival claimant families took the opportunity to gauge their support among the gathered Scottish aristocracy.

The Bruce family were, like their Balliol relatives and rivals, originally of Anglo-Norman extraction. However, their roots within the Scottish political community ran considerably deeper. The exact parentage and family background of the first Robert de Brus, or Bruce, to come to prominence is unknown. It is probable though that the family name is derived from the village of Brix in Normandy's Cotentin Peninsula and that Robert was a member of the region's lower nobility.[66] King Henry I of England had a special association with the Cotentin, having purchased the lordship of the region from his cash-strapped elder brother, Duke Robert of Normandy, shortly after their father's death.[67] Duke Robert eventually reneged on the deal and attempted to drive Henry out of the region in concert with their other brother, King William Rufus of England. Yet the local aristocracy remained surprisingly loyal to the prince, who was able to repeatedly re-establish a base of operations within the Cotentin.[68] If Robert de Brus was indeed from the Cotentin, this royal connection would go a long way to explaining his sudden emergence in the aristocratic circles of northern England shortly after Henry claimed the throne and the high degree of royal favour in which he was held subsequently. Robert first appears within records around the 1100s as a retainer and vassal of Earl Ranulf of Chester but his presence within the witness lists of contemporary charters suggests he had a wide portfolio of landed interests across Northumbria.[69] By the late 1120s he had built up a considerable conglomeration of lands in Yorkshire, much of which had been awarded to him directly by King Henry.

When King Edgar of Scotland died in 1107, the kingdom passed to his younger brother Alexander I but considerable aristocratic pressure led to a large swathe of the south of Scotland and the then ill-defined borders region being earmarked as the domain of the late king's second surviving brother, David.[70] Considering David's still tender age and Alexander I's considerable opposition to this division, it is unsurprising that most of the evidence for David's trans-border pseudo principality only appears from the mid-1110s onwards. Prior to this, David had been living in the court of his brother-in-law, King Henry, who both supported him in establishing control over his inheritance and furnished David with estates throughout the north of England, including the Earldom of Huntingdon.[71] At some point during this period, David was granted lands in the north of the Cotentin, probably in recognition of his service in helping Henry secure control of Normandy. It is highly probable, given their shared connection to the Cotentin and the court of Henry I, that David and Robert's friendship and association was forged during this formative period in David's career. Certainly, as David's position within the borders gathered definition and his authority grew, it became clear that the Scottish Prince enjoyed the support of a formidable coalition of Norman lords and adventurers, who could count Robert de Brus among their foremost members.

In 1124, shortly after the death of Alexander I and David's own accession to the throne of Scotland, David bestowed upon Robert the Lordship of Annadale in the Scottish borders.[72] David's simultaneous reign as King of Scotland and the King of England's chief deputy within Northumbria demonstrates a great deal about the porous nature of medieval polities and the highly personal, caveated, nature of power within them. As, of course, did David's extensive efforts to increase his authority in Scotland through his sponsorship of Norman immigration, alongside the adaptation of Norman cultural trappings and administrative practices.[73] Robert continued to co-operate closely with David within the north of England but does not seem to have spent a great deal of time within Scotland.

The fault lines in David and Robert's tangled and overlapping loyalties were brought into sharp relief in 1138 with David's invasion of northern England.[74] Robert, like the majority of English magnates at this juncture, supported, to one extent or another, King Stephen of England. Stephen, a nephew of Henry I, had more or less usurped the throne from his cousin, Matilda, having persuaded the Church to free the nobility from their oaths to Matilda by promising to do away with Church taxation. On the other hand, Matilda was David's niece, and the Scottish king naturally favoured her claim to the English throne. Moreover, David saw the unfolding war as a chance to secure his extensive lands in northern England, probably hoping to incorporate them into the kingdom of Scotland outright.

Robert de Brus was a member of an embassy dispatched by King Stephen's army on the eve of battle in an attempt to dissuade David's invasion and reach some agreement with the Scottish king. Despite Robert's impassioned plea and his invocation of the many times in which David had benefited from the co-operation of the Anglo-Norman aristocracy, the Scottish king was determined to press the issue. As a result, Robert angrily renounced his pledge of homage and loyalty towards David.[75] The ensuing Battle of the Standard was a bitter disappointment for the Scottish king, who saw his forces routed with heavy casualties. The chronicler John of Worcester claims that of the two hundred knights that David fielded during the battle, only nineteen made it back to the Scottish base at Carlisle with their mail hauberks, the others having all been killed, captured or compelled to discard their heavy armour during their headlong flight. One of these knights was

Robert de Brus' second son, the inventively named, Robert de Brus.[76] While his father had renounced all loyalty to David, the young Robert had fought alongside the Scottish army, thereby protecting his personal claim to the Scottish estates he one day hoped to inherit.

This conspicuous display of loyalty turned out to be a wise strategy and the younger Robert inherited the Lordship of Annadale and the family's Scottish lands upon his father's death in 1141. Meanwhile, his elder brother, Adam, inherited the lion's share of the family's English lands, becoming the Lord of Skelton. While the exact parentage of Adam and the younger Robert's mother, Agnes, is unknown, there is substantive evidence that she was a member or close relative of the Yorkshire-based Sourdeval family.[77] Likewise, beyond her name, Euphemia, very little is known about the identity or background of the younger Robert's own wife.[78] The couple's eldest son, Robert, was married to Isabella, an illegitimate daughter of King William the Lion. This Robert predeceased his unusually long-lived father and with no children of his own, the Lordship of Annandale passed to his younger brother William on their father's death in 1194. William, the third Lord of Annadale, married Christina, a daughter of the unfortunate Uhtred of Galloway.[79] While previous generations of the family had prospered through a connection to the Scottish royal centre, William was not a member of the king's inner circle or often at court and can only be found in the witnesses of one royal charter. It is under William's tenure as lord that it becomes apparent, through the records, that this branch of the Bruce family had once again acquired large amounts of land in northern England, establishing their status as an Anglo-Scottish aristocratic family. William even possessed a licence from King John to hold weekly markets in Hartlepool.[80] The exact circumstances under which this new wealth of English territory was acquired are unclear but the very fact that the lords of Annadale were able to amass a considerable concentration of lands in northern England, through either inheritance, royal service or most likely a mixture of both, tells us a lot about the manner in which the Scottish and English aristocracy flowed seamlessly together in the early part of the thirteenth century.

William's eldest son, named Robert in keeping with family tradition, became the fourth lord of Annadale upon his father's death in 1212.[81] This Robert, while a relatively minor figure within Scottish politics, opened the way for his family's eventual rise to political prominence and kingship by marrying Isabel of Huntingdon, the daughter of Earl David of Huntingdon and thus the great-granddaughter of King David I. As previously discussed, the family's claim to the Scottish throne originates from this marriage and their descent from Isabel and David. In addition to placing the family closer to the Scottish crown, marriage to one of the Earl of Huntingdon's heirs brought the family further estates within England. Their son Robert, known as 'Robert the Competitor' because of his pursuit of the Scottish throne, was married to Isabella de Clare, the daughter of Earl Gilbert de Clare of Gloucester and Hereford and his wife Isabel Marshall.[82]

This was a highly advantageous marriage that intimately connected the Bruces with one of England's most powerful and influential aristocratic families. Robert's collection of English estates, concentrated in County Durham and Essex, compelled him to take an active interest in the unfolding Second Barons' Rebellion. A royalist supporter, Robert was an active member of the English king's army during both the disastrous defeat at the Battle of Lewes in 1264 and the dramatic reversal that brought the rebellion to a crashing halt at the Battle of Evesham in 1265.[83] He was, like most of the royalist faction, rewarded for his loyalty and service during the conflict by a gift of further lands confiscated from rebel barons. As materially rewarding as Robert's engagement in the English royalist cause was, it did drive a wedge between him and his second cousin, Alexander III, who tacitly supported the rebels as a way of curtailing Henry III's attempts to exert overlordship in Scotland. Robert was able to secure a reconciliation with the Scottish crown, which likely had some modest financial component, and was, prior to the birth of the king's three children, intermittently acknowledged as the king's heir and closest male relative.[84] It was a status that clearly informed his expectations during the crisis that followed the death of Alexander and his children. The family's status was further enhanced in 1272 when Robert's eldest son, the future king's father, married Majorie of Carrick, securing for the first time a committal rank for a member of the family.[85] Control of both Carrick and Annadale made the Bruces a formidable presence in the south-west of Scotland, effectively encircling Balliol-dominated Galloway. It appears that following this marriage, father and son worked closely together to maintain and advance their shared familial interests, with the elder Robert devolving much of his authority in the south of Scotland to his son.

Interestingly, all the members of the Bruce family we have just covered, up to and including Robert the Competitor, the Fifth Lord of Annadale, were buried in Gisborough Priory in Yorkshire. The priory had been founded by the first Robert de Brus and its continued use as a burial site by the hereditary junior 'Scottish' branch of the family, across four generations, suggests that they maintained a strong association with the region and their Yorkshire cousins.[86] Like the Balliols, whose family history we surveyed briefly in the previous chapter, the Bruces were a family of Anglo-Norman origin, whose income and possessions from England were as great or greater as those from Scotland and whose members had in recent memory engaged in service to the King of England. Perhaps it is worth asking at this stage, before the precipitous plunge into war, what then exactly made the families Scottish rather than English? Possibly the inherent difficulty in answering this question and the fact that both families were accepted within the realm of Scottish politics and were able to attract the dedicated support of Scottish aristocrat affinities suggests that the line between English and Scottish aristocrats was so blurred as to have little to no meaning for contemporaries.

We have discussed how authority and power in thirteenth-century Europe were flexible concepts that were open to, and indeed predicated on, negotiation. To the minds of the medieval aristocracy, rebellion, war and violence were not necessarily viewed as irrevocable breakdowns in this system of mingled associations and loyalties but the extreme end of a spectrum of legitimate negotiating tactics. Aristocratic families that felt they had been hard done by or had their rights impinged, may well resort to rebellion as a means of drawing attention to their grievances and forcing other concerned parties to the negotiating table. It was all very Clausewitzian, with violence functioning as a natural extension of diplomacy rather than marking its failure. By early 1287, the uprising staged by Robert the Competitor and his allies in protest against the Guardians and their recognition of Margaret as queen had petered out. It had failed to meaningfully damage the military resource or political capital of his rivals. Nor had the rebellion gained the Bruce family and their allies much in the way of political leverage. What the uprising did achieve was to spook Eric II of Norway, which to be fair to Robert the Competitor may very well have been its primary purpose from the start.

While the Bruces' rebellion achieved very little in military terms, they suffered no major defeats of their own. Rather they had gained temporary recognition as a distinctive other within the Scottish aristocracy, a group formed in opposition of the Guardians and their supporters. This meant that in 1287 they were still very much a viable force within Scottish politics that could feasibly emerge as a centre of opposition to Margaret's rule. Eric was understandably nervous about sending his infant daughter to a kingdom threatened by the shadow of civil war. Instead, he withdrew his representative, Bjarne Erlingsson, from Scotland before taking the momentous step of contacting King Edward I of England and asking him to act as his proxy in securing both Margaret's throne and safety.[87] Eric was appealing to Edward not because of his unrecognised and historically rebuffed claims to overlordship over Scotland, which Eric was almost certainly ambivalent towards, but because he was family.

Edward was young Margaret's great-uncle. Indeed, it is clear from a relatively rare example of surviving personal correspondence that he had been reasonably close with Margaret's mother, Queen Margaret of Norway, taking the time and effort to reaffirm their personal and familial connection. From Eric's point of view then, Edward could be broadly trusted to look after Margaret's best interests while his status as King of England and established connections with many of the members of the mingled Anglo-Scottish aristocracy meant that he was well positioned to guarantee Margaret's safety and bring the issue to a satisfactory conclusion.

Of course, the wolfishly ambitious Edward I had his own plan in mind for the future of Margaret and the Scottish throne. In his own way, Edward was almost as unlucky as Alexander III when it came to his heirs. Edward's eldest three sons, John, Henry and Alphonso had all predeceased him in a cruel succession of tragedies, leaving the three-year-old Edward of Caernarfon as his presumptive heir in 1287.[88] The king intended to marry Margaret to Prince Edward, who it was envisaged, would one day rule the Kingdom of England through hereditary rights and the Kingdom of Scotland on behalf of his wife.[89] Indeed, depending on the vagaries of dynastic fortune, it was entirely possible that the royal couple would have a son or daughter, but ideally a son, who could claim both kingdoms by inalienable hereditary right.

While it may seem strange that the Guardians of Scotland and their supporters were willing to entertain the grave risk Edward's bold proposal presented to the continued independence of the Scottish crown, the reality was that they had very little room to manoeuvre. The Guardians were, alongside the rest of the aristocracy, oathbound to support Margaret and see her safely on the Scottish throne. They had no direct access to the Queen on whose behalf they were nominally running the country, while Eric's deputisation of Edward and apparently favourable disposition to the match made meaningful resistance to the stipulations and conditions imposed by the English king very difficult. Moreover, the Guardians' own authority was predicated upon their status as Margaret's protectors and deputies. The longer they went without the Queen, the more their authority to handle these negotiations was eroded and the remarkable co-operation and solidarity of the Scottish aristocracy threatened.

It is also worth bearing in mind that Walter Comyn, the most senior and influential of the Guardians, alongside a significant portion of the Scottish aristocracy, had already lived through Henry III's efforts to take advantage of Alexander III's minority to advance his imperial ambitions. This experience, in which many of Henry's demands were deflected or diluted by skilful diplomacy, probably suggested that Edward's influence could be similarly managed and informed their expectations of the limits of the English king's ambitions in Scotland. After all, while successive generations of English kings had tried to cajole their Scottish counterparts into acquiescing to their suzerainty over the British Isles, they had tried to do so in a manner that kept the integrity and authority of the Scottish crown largely intact.[90] In the late 1280s then there were, from the point of view of the Scottish aristocracy, few if any hints of Edward's later imperial ambitions to subjugate Scotland and rule it directly.

Edward had, of course, undertaken a series of aggressive campaigns in Wales with the goal of bringing the last autonomous Welsh princes to heel but there were key differences in the English kings' relationships with Wales and Scotland. English kings tended to intermarry and co-operate with their Scottish equivalents, whose authority had been actively enhanced by

Anglo-Norman migration. However, in Wales, long-running Anglo-Norman colonial efforts were largely de-centralised and autonomous, only occasionally fortified by royal expeditions launched in response to specific rebellions or crisis. The Guardians and their followers could therefore be forgiven for missing the sea change in Edward I's policy towards his neighbours in the British Isles and in viewing his conquests in Wales as just another in a long line of royal interventions within the region.

The negotiations that followed were both intensive and lengthy, necessitating as they did a great deal of back and forth between Edward I, Eric II, the Guardians and the wider Scottish nobility. But by November of 1289, the first iteration of the treaty was signed in Salisbury. This first version of the treaty was concerned primarily with the bare bone practicalities of the arrangements surrounding Margaret's journey to Scotland and coronation.[91] The treaty reaffirmed that all involved parties intended to see Margaret placed upon the throne of Scotland. It also stipulated that Edward I would arrange transport for Margaret from Norway to Scotland and that Edward would take responsibility for her safety until her position within Scotland was secure.[92] Edward also undertook to smooth over a few diplomatic cracks and agreed to pay Eric the remainder of the dowry that Alexander III owed him from his marriage to Margaret's mother.[93]

The second treaty signed early the following year in Birgham, from which the entire agreement would take its name, concerned itself with the marriage between Prince Edward and Queen Margaret.[94] Much of the treaty was shaped by the Scottish aristocracy's fears that the marriage would reduce their kingdom to a mere English possession or vassal. It therefore specified that Scotland would remain distinct and separate from England. In contrast to prevailing marriage practices and legal thought, it was stipulated that even following her marriage, Margaret would retain control over all her own property, including the Kingdom of Scotland.[95] Likewise, the continued independence of the Scottish Church was guaranteed, while the merging of the kingdoms' respective parliaments was forbidden.[96] These were all sensible precautions on the part of the Scottish aristocracy, but Edward worked actively to sow ambiguity and dilute some of these safeguards by playing upon the somewhat nebulous nature of the groups in question.

Tragedy was to render many of the carefully negotiated conditions and safeguards of the Treaty of Birgham moot. With the treaty in place and her betrothal to Prince Edward ratified, Margaret, the uncrowned queen of Scotland, at last made the crossing from Norway to Scotland. Falling ill while still at sea, the seven-year-old Margaret died on Orkney in September of 1290.[97] When the news reached Scone, where the massed ranks of the Scottish nobility had gathered to witness the coronation of their young queen, the long-simmering tensions boiled over in a flash.[98] With the death of Alexander III's last descendant and in the absence of any close Dunkeld male relatives, such as a brother or nephew of the late king, the various factions and familial groups of the Scottish aristocracy fell rancorously to pressing the largely tenuous claims of their own candidates.

The Guardians stayed more or less in place, representing as they did the broad balance of power within the Scottish aristocracy, but without a queen to rule on behalf of, their position was tenuous, and they lacked the authority to curb the spiral towards civil war. In 1287, aristocratic factionalism was a centripetal force, the Scottish aristocracy rallying around the vacant Scottish throne to preserve its authority and protect their mutual self-interest. In the winter of 1290, however, this vision for the future and continuation of the collaborative model of government that had flourished under Alexander III seemed increasingly remote. The crown of Scotland was potentially up for grabs and power blocs formed as the Scottish aristocracy simultaneously vied for a share of the spoils to come, while also seeking to protect themselves from the predatory impulses of their neighbours. When the ever proactively ambitious Bruce family dispatched a contingent of armed men to take control of the coronation site at Scone, all involved would have recognised the implicit threat of their actions.[99] Meanwhile, John Balliol, Robert de Bruce's neighbour and most prominent rival to the throne, began to openly refer to himself as the 'heir of Scotland'.[100] The horror and desolation of civil war loomed on the horizon. As we shall see, Edward I's intervention and imperial ambitions would forestall and then shape the coming war but not prevent it.

With war seeming all but inevitable, some members of the Guardians, supported by others within the aristocracy, reached out to Edward I to ask if he would arbitrate the rapidly escalating succession dispute.[101] Setting aside the English king's pretensions to overlordship, there was a lot to recommend this course of action. Both the Bruces and the Balliols, who were emerging rapidly as the heads of the most prominent factions, held considerable English estates. This meant they already had an established relationship with Edward, who in turn could easily use those English lands as leverage to ensure their co-operation. In addition to this, in many ways the arbitration between royal claimants was a natural extension of the diplomatic work Edward had already undertaken in his role as Eric of Norway's proxy. Edward was already familiar with the intricacies of Scottish politics having taken part in an intensive series of negotiations with the Scottish Guardians and the principal factions within the Scottish aristocracy. Likewise, Edward's previous agreement to the Treaty of Birgham and the acknowledgement of the principles of Scottish independence contained within, may have helped to convince the Scottish ambassadors that Edward's ambitions could once again be defused by careful diplomacy.[102] Of course, setting aside the English pretensions to the overlordship of the British Isles was something Edward I was entirely unwilling to do.

Having initially accepted the Scottish nobilities' request to act as an arbiter in the succession crisis, Edward then stipulated that his help was contingent upon acknowledgement of his status as Scotland's overlord.[103] The Guardians, perhaps taken aback by Edward's rapid shift in policy, denied Edward's claim vociferously, pointing out how it contravened the agreement they had reached previously at Birgham. Rather than advance evidence supporting his claim, Edward then rather facetiously demanded that the Guardians prove that they were not his vassals.[104] In the face of Edward's attempts to muddy the diplomatic waters, the Guardians of Scotland adopted a new diplomatic line of their own. Once again reiterating their refusal to recognise Edward's overlordship, they advanced the eminently reasonable argument that only the King of Scotland was capable of making such an agreement. Since there was no king, Edward would have to wait to bring his suit to whoever emerged victorious from the arbitration process. This denial was a brave assertion of authority from the Guardians and the Comyn family, who had retained their position of prominence within the rapidly fraying royal administration. By presenting a strong and united front, the Guardians and their supporters clearly signalled to both Edward and the Scottish aristocracy that they would seek to maintain the independence of the Scottish throne and use the model presented within the Treaty of Birgham as their touchstone in all negotiations with the English king. Hoping that Edward's ambitions could be deflected in the same manner as his father's had been during Alexander III's minority, the Guardians agreed to temporarily cede a few key royal castles to Edward on the understanding that they and the kingdom would be handed over to the new King of Scotland, whoever that maybe, within two months of his selection.[105]

As bold as this display of solidarity by the Guardians and their supporters was, Edward outmanoeuvred them in short order. Upon accepting the Scottish aristocracy's collective terms and garrisoning the kingdom's most strategically vital royal castles, Edward convened a grand council that under the English king's supervision would evaluate the many competing claims for the Scottish throne and select a new king. Edward then informed these competitors that a prerequisite for consideration of their claim before the council would be acknowledgment of his overlordship of Scotland.[106] With a prize as great as the throne of Scotland at stake, all the royal candidates hastily accepted, naturally afraid that any resistance or push back to Edward's demands would see the kingship awarded to their rivals. Edward then advanced the agreement that since one of the candidates was the rightful King of Scotland, their collective recognition of him as overlord meant that the King of Scotland, whichever of them that turned out to be, was now sworn to abide by English overlordship.

While the Bruces and Balliols had by far the strongest and most compelling claims to the throne, eleven other nobles brought their hereditary claims before this council.[107] These included the minor English noble, John Hastings, who like the Bruces and Balliols, was descended from a daughter of David of Huntingdon; in this case, David's third eldest daughter, Ada.[108] However, while, as we shall examine in further detail shortly, the hereditary principle of primogeniture favoured the Balliols' claim and the principle of proximity favoured that of the Bruces, the Hastings' claim was immediately and obviously subordinate, whichever principle the council elected to abide by. Additionally, John Hastings lacked the Scottish roots and connections of either of the lead competitors.

Count Floris V of Holland also traced his claim to the throne from an Ada, the aunt of John Hastings' grandmother.[109] This Ada was the daughter of Prince Henry of Huntingdon and the sister of Malcolm IV, William the Lion and David of Huntingdon. While Floris was certainly in line for the throne, his claim to superiority over the other candidates came from the assertion that David of Huntingdon had given up his rights to the Scottish throne as part of an alleged agreement regarding the succession to his father's English estates. However, David was recognised within Scotland as his uncle William's heir apparent for close to two decades and it is extremely unlikely that he would have ever renounced his right to the throne he was immediately in line for.

Interestingly, one of the Guardians, John Comyn of Badenoch, often referred to in later sources as the Black Comyn to distinguish him from his son and the numerous other John Comyns, was also one of the competitors who appeared before the council.[110] Comyn's claim to the Scottish throne came from his descent from Bethoc, a daughter of Donald III. Donald had come to the throne of Scotland way back in 1097 after the death of his nephew Duncan II. Donald's elder brother, Malcolm III, had established that the throne of Scotland would pass from father to eldest son, a deviation from the historical practice of tanistry under which an heir was selected from among the deceased king's surviving male relatives.[111] Because of cultural and practical factors, this system tended to favour the succession of a king's surviving brother over his sons. While Malcolm's son, Duncan II, had succeeded in claiming the throne, Donald retained a large following, bolstered by those among the Scottish nobility that resented the imposition of foreign inheritance practices. Upon Duncan's assassination, these aggrieved elements rallied around Donald, allowing him to displace Duncan's younger brothers.[112] Of course, upon Donald's death without a male heir a year later, he was succeeded by his formerly displaced nephew Edgar I, who would in turn be succeeded by his younger brothers, Alexander I and David I.

Of the remaining competitors, the majority of them were descended in one form or another from one of many illegitimate children of William the Lion. Similarly, Robert de Pinkeney's claim came from his descent from an illegitimate daughter of Henry of Huntingdon, while Eric II made a tentative claim based upon his status as the closest relative of Queen Matilda.[113] While the claims of some of these competitors, such as John Comyn and Count Floris, lend themselves to interesting discussions about the development of Scottish inheritance law, almost all participants were aware that the council's real job was to decide whether John Balliol or Robert de Bruce would be King of Scotland. All the other claims were demonstrably inferior to theirs and were brought by nobles who wanted their relationships to the Scottish royal family ratified by the council and placed on the record.

For such remote family ties to remain extant and politically useful they had to be pressed as a means of eliciting and spreading acknowledgement of them throughout the wider political community. Additionally, many of the competitors, while probably realising their claims to the throne would be rejected in favour of stronger candidates, hoped to receive some sort of compensation from either Edward or the new King of Scotland. After all, everything in the medieval world was negotiable to some extent. In fact, John Hastings' lawyers made the incredible argument based on the unique nature of the Scottish coronation ceremony that Scotland was not a real kingdom and therefore could be dived between multiple heirs.[114] That Edward ultimately rejected this line of argument, which naturally outraged the massed Scottish nobility, suggests that he may have still hoped in 1292 that he could exercise authority in Scotland using the Scottish king as a proxy. He had, of course, already extracted an acknowledgement from the royal candidates that they would recognise his overlordship. Meanwhile, a step as drastic as dissolving the kingdom outright would have surely led to war with a united Scottish nobility.

The shape of Edward's ambitions was reflected within the structure of the Great Council he presided over. The council was to be composed of 104 members and chaired by Edward. Of these councillors, only a mere twenty-four were appointed directly by Edward.[115] Rather than attempt to represent the balance of power within Scotland through the selection of the remaining council members, Edward allowed the Balliols and Bruces to each appoint forty councillors. Edward I was not interested in dealing with the Guardians or the spectrum of opinions that ran through the Scottish nobility. Instead, the king wanted to create the appearance of a precipitous deadlock between the two most powerful candidates and their supporters that he would then magnanimously resolve. The council was therefore structured in such a way as to communicate Edward's authority and make it clear that whichever candidate went on to be crowned, they did so specifically at Edward's sufferance. A perhaps unforeseen side effect of this binary structure and the politicking necessitated by the selection of councillors meant that both sides actively courted allies and fostered support within the greater Scottish aristocracy. This deepened tensions within the Scottish aristocracy as the Balliols, Bruces and other powerful Scottish families consolidated their followers into clearly demarcated factions.

As touched upon previously, Robert the Competitor's claim to the throne was based upon the principle of proximity. Picture kingship as a stream of water that passes down the channels created by dynastic connections. Flowing down from David I to his grandson, Malcolm IV, to his brother, William the Lion, and then to his son Alexander II. By back tracing the path of succession to the closest path not taken, the channel through which the kingship would have flowed if William the Lion had no children, we come to Henry of Huntingdon, the younger brother of Kings Malcolm IV and William. The long-lived Fifth Lord of Annadale was the son of Isobel of Huntingdon, the maternal grandson of David of Huntingdon and the great grandson of Henry of Huntingdon. This meant that he was closer generationally to the flow of kingship through the family, with fewer links in the chain separating him from this revised route of kingship than his Balliol rival, who was a mere great-great-grandson of Heny of Huntingdon.

This is, however, a fundamentally flawed metaphor; kingship is an artificial construct, not a natural phenomenon. Kings were not created by natural forces or mechanics but by the recognition and acclamation of their peers and subjects. Both Edward I and the Scottish nobility argued the inalienable nature of kingship and its paramount place within the Scottish political community while negotiating over its form and parameters. Returning to our earlier metaphor with that caveat in mind, the advocates of the Balliol claim and the hereditary principle of primogeniture argued that the stuff of kingship was far more rarefied than mere water. Rather than flowing down the closest dynastic tie available, kingship unerringly, magnetically, adhered to the line of the king's eldest son. If a king had no sons, then the title passed to their eldest daughter and then hopefully through her to her nearest male descendant. John Balliol's maternal grandmother, Margaret of Huntingdon, was the elder sister of Robert the Competitor's mother, Isobel.

John was therefore the eldest-surviving grandson of David of Huntingdon's eldest daughter. David, the eldest son of Prince Henry of Huntington, had a son John but he died without issue in 1237. This meant that under the rules of primogeniture, John Balliol was the rightful heir of Henry of Huntingdon and the true King of Scotland. The difficulty faced by Edward I therefore was in deciding whether to favour proximity or primogeniture. Proximity had a long history of primacy within Scotland, being related to and often conflated with the Celtic tanistry system in which an heir was elected from the king's surviving agnatic relatives. Even with the decline of tanistry, the principle of proximity of blood remained rooted within Scottish legal culture and practice. However, during the thirteenth century, Primogeniture began to gain increased traction within Scotland. Moreover, it was the system most widely accepted and utilised by Europe's nobility and the one that Edward I would probably have considered the default method of inheritance. The Bruces and their advocates sowed a degree of confusion by arguing correctly that were the rules of primogeniture to be applied conventionally then the kingdom should be divided between the descendants of David of Huntingdon's daughters in the manner argued for by John Hastings. According to the Bruces then, favouring their claim and the principle of proximity was the best way to avoid an outcome that both Edward I and the Scottish nobility found deeply unappealing.

Unfortunately for the Bruces, Edward I, who you will recall suffered the loss of numerous children, had determined that should both he and his son, Edward, die without further issue, the crown should pass to his eldest surviving daughter.[116] The English king was therefore deeply disinclined to accept the Hastings' and Bruces' line of argument because it risked creating a precedent that might one day be used to challenge his daughter and the integrity of England. The Bruces later reversed their position, advocating a division of the Kingdom of Scotland, but this was likely because it was becoming increasingly obvious that Edward was going to support the Balliol claim.[117] It was after all probably better to inherit a third of a kingdom than none of it. Unmoved, however, by this last-minute attempt to finagle a compromise, in mid-November 1292, Edward and the council members declared John Balliol the winner and King of Scotland.[118] This decision reflected the interest and proclivities of Edward I, protecting a daughter's right to inherit an undivided kingdom while simultaneously upholding the primacy of primogeniture. Yet it was also a decision that suited most of the Scottish nobility, who welcomed both the imminent end to the interregnum and a Balliol victory. The Balliols were, after all, supported by the highly influential Comyn family and their allies; John Comyn having made a spectacle of setting aside his claim to the throne in favour of supporting that of his Balliol father-in-law.

Looking at it in purely hereditary or legal terms, the Bruce family's claim to the throne should have been fatally compromised by Robert the Competitor's death in 1295. His son, Robert, was removed from the kingship by the same number of generations as John Balliol, while the Competitor's eldest grandson, also Robert, was a further generation removed, meaning that John Balliol's claim was superior by both primogeniture and proximity. Of course, we know regardless of the legal and hereditary niceties that this grandson of the Competitor succeeded in becoming king, defeating both the English invasion and his Scottish rivals. The groundwork for this success was partially laid by the way Edward I chose to structure and conduct the council, which allowed the Bruces to rally further support for their cause and to an extent formalise and validate their position in opposition to the Scottish crown and its Comyn allies. This meant, following Robert the Competitor's death, many of the Bruce family's allies and supporters, while a minority within the Scottish aristocracy, were now heavily invested in their success and committed to the cause regardless of the legal situation. As we shall see, the Bruces made the most of this core of support by skilfully taking advantage of the chaos that was to come during John Balliol's reign and his son Edward's attempts to subjugate Scotland.

John Balliol was crowned on 30 November 1292 at the royal centre of Scone.[119] His then nine-year-old son Edward would, as the heir to the throne, surely to have been present. John had successfully claimed the throne, whose authority had been preserved largely intact by the vigilance of the Guardians appointed in the wake of Alexander III's death and the Scottish nobilities' remarkable recognition that their best interests lay within presenting a united front. Indeed, Scottish royal government had shown a remarkable resilience during the interregnum that was in large part due to the diplomatic efforts of the Comyn family who supported the Balliol kingship in the same manner as they had prospered by lending their support to Alexander II and Alexander III. However, John had been compromised by recognising the overlordship of Edward I of England, who now styled himself the Lord Paramount of Scotland. The Bruces also remained a very real threat, their ambitions undimmed. In the next chapter we will cover how the war unleashed by Edward I's attempts to exercise sovereignty over Scotland dashed Balliol's initially promising reign. The subsequent English invasion eventually shattered the solidarity of the Scottish aristocracy, leading to and blending with a civil war between the Comyns and Bruces for control of Scotland.

Chapter Three

Invasion and Civil War

John Balliol was crowned King of Scotland in November 1292, ending a six-year interregnum characterised by bad faith bargaining, pervasive uncertainty, and increasingly bitter rivalries. The Balliols' ascendancy to the throne represented a major triumph for their Comyn relatives and allies, who had despite considerable challenges maintained a white-knuckled grip upon the reins of power throughout the crisis. What the dawn of Balliol kingship did not bring was an end to the bad faith bargaining, pervasive uncertainty, or bitter rivalries.

Unfortunately for John Balliol and his family, the circumstances that facilitated his ascent to the throne would prove to have a profoundly deleterious effect upon both the integrity and independence of the Scottish crown. The compromises and qualifications John accepted in order to secure the kingship of Scotland, as unavoidable as they appeared at the time, conspired to create a void of authority and credibility. So gaping and obvious was this wound in Scottish royal authority, so compromising was it to the Balliols' attempts to exercise kingship in the traditional Scottish manner, that war was all but inevitable. The clash of arms would decide if the Scottish king's vulnerability was sealed or torn further asunder.

This chapter is not a blow-by-blow account of Edward I's invasion of Scotland and the winding, crooked path upon which his imperial ambitions and military fortunes led him and his vision for Scotland. Instead, it is a prologue for the curious civil war that raged parallel to this invasion, as Edward's effort to enforce his suzerainty over Scotland created the opportunity for the Scottish nobility to violently pursue their pre-existing grudges and rivalries. It is foremost an explanation for the great mystery that saw the Balliols and Comyns transform from the incumbent government and acknowledged leaders of the Scottish political community to English collaborators living in exile.

In a mirrored process, their Bruce rivals, the architects of the Balliols' and Comyns' eventual banishment, would begin the war shamelessly co-operating with the militarily superior English. Through the fortunes of war and an immense personal political savvy, Robert Bruce would reinvent himself, a collaborator and leader of a spurned faction on the fringes of Scottish politics, into the great hope of Scottish independence. As we shall see, such a radical reversal of positions was not the result of a simple or swift process, instead it occurred by a matter of degrees over more than a decade of war.

The flaring of factionalism during the lengthy interregnum and the extended period of arbitration that John and his rival claimants had been forced to negotiate turned the Scottish crown into something of a poisoned chalice. The extraordinary conditions under which John took the throne revealed, or outrightly created, glaring weaknesses in the Scottish crown's ability to project and exert authority. It would have taken an exceptionally bold, energetic and talented ruler to answer this challenge effectively. Unfortunately for the Balliols and their allies, John, who had led a rather sedentary career prior to his bid for the Scottish throne, was not up to rigours of this enormous challenge. The root of the problem, legitimacy, was one faced by many fresh royal dynasties in the medieval period but was drastically exacerbated by the circumstances of the interregnum.

Unlike his Dunkeld predecessors, John did not hold the throne or exercise authority in Scotland as a result of an unquestioned and inalienable right. Instead, his power and position on the throne was seen as conditional, the result of painstaking negotiations and a carefully wrought system of dynastic and political alliances. Of course, in practical terms the Dunkelds were almost equally dependent upon the support of aristocratic allies to rule effectively. Their historical symbiosis with notions of kingship and their monopoly on governance was little more than a carefully guarded illusion meant to confirm and reinforce their grip on power. The Scottish aristocracy of generations past had co-operated with the kings of Scotland largely because these royal governments had been so successful in presenting themselves as bastions of authority and power that were capable and willing to reward effective and loyal servants generously.[1]

The interregnum had laid bare these mechanisms and stripped away some of the veneer of royal authority. John's hereditary claim to the throne was undeniably strong to the extent that the ephemeral loss of a degree of royal prestige should have been eminently recoverable. However, it was greatly compounded by the extended, highly factionalised nature of the succession crisis and the orchestrating role the King of England had been allowed to have in its arbitration. Despite his demonstrable descent from the eldest daughter of David of Huntingdon, it seemed clear to all contemporaries that John Balliol was not King of Scotland because of inalienable hereditary right. He was King of Scotland because King Edward I of England had proclaimed him so. It was a decision that was just as obviously informed by the large Comyn-led aristocratic coalition that supported John.

Edward had outmanoeuvred the Guardians and the massed ranks of the Scottish nobility by demanding recognition of his overlordship of Scotland directly from the royal candidates as a precondition of their inclusion in the arbitration process. With the English king already firmly ensconced in the role of arbiter and with a crown at stake, none of the royal candidates, including John Balliol, felt confident enough in their suit to defy Edward directly. In this regard, the similarities and rough parity of the Balliols' and Bruces' respective claims worked to Edward's advantage. It was in effect a permutation of the famous Prisoner's Dilemma. In the absence of an unambiguous front runner, candidates were strongly disinclined to risk crossing the English king, particularly when their rivals had such a strong reason to cultivate favour by capitulating to Edward's wishes. When viewed from this perspective, it was far safer for the royal candidates to accede to Edward's claims to overlordship, a course of action that would have, at worst, maintained parity between the various royal candidates. As noted previously, Edward chose to structure the council in a way that created a deadlock between the two leading candidates, a stalemate that could only be broken by the intervention of Edward and his appointees to the council. This was done deliberately in an attempt to emphasise his importance to the process and further the perception that the Scottish throne was his to award.

Reminders of the English king's decisive role in the events surrounding John Balliol's accession to the throne were prominent even within the new king's coronation. Traditionally the Earls of Fife held a role of central importance in the coronation of Scottish kings, including the task of actually placing the crown upon the new king's head. Because Earl Donnchadh IV of Fife was just three years old in 1292 and far too young to perform these ancestral duties, his crucial position within the coronation was occupied by the English nobleman John St John.[2] As one of the senior knights of King Edward's household, John had served the English king faithfully and reliably as both a diplomat and military lieutenant.[3] It was for this reason that Edward had appointed him the deputy and proxy of the young Earl of Fife during his brief curatorship of Scotland as he worked to arbitrate the succession dispute. That John not only retained his guardianship and control of the earl following Edward's nominal abdication of authority within Scotland but was allowed to occupy a position of such unparalleled importance within the Scottish coronation ceremony was a testament to the persistence of the English king's influence.

Meanwhile, the not inconsiderable religious element of the coronation was presided over by a second English magnate, Bishop Anthony Bec of Durham.[4] Because of the extensive Balliol estates within and around Durham, the new king was a long-term associate and ally of Bec. Indeed, it seems that John had made extensive and effective use of this relationship during the succession crisis by persuading the bishop to lobby Edward I on his behalf. When seen in this context, it easy to see why John Balliol and his supporters accepted his long-time neighbour and advocate in a role held traditionally by one or more of Scotland's native bishops. It is important to remember, however, that Anthony was so valued an ally and effective an intermediary precisely because he was a valued member of King Edward's inner circle.

Bec had been a long-term member of Edward's household, even accompanying the then prince on Crusade in 1270. Upon Edward's assumption of the throne, Anthony began to reap the rewards of royal service, first being appointed as Keeper of the Royal Wardrobe in 1274 and then securing the Archdeaconship of Durham and the Constableship of the Tower of London in 1275.[5] He then served Edward as an envoy and diplomat in North Wales and Aragon before being elected, as the king's nominee, to the bishopric of Durham. Bishop Anthony's participation in Scottish politics predated his advocacy for John Balliol's claim to the throne as he served as the English king's main proxy in the extensive negotiations that surrounded the betrothal of Margaret of Norway, the uncrowned queen of Scotland, and Edward's eldest son and heir.[6]

The presence of two English magnates at the coronation of John Balliol would not have been regarded as particularly notable by contemporaries. After all, many of the most prominent members of the Scottish nobility, including the new king and his Bruce rivals, held estates in England. But Anthony Bec and John St John were more than simple guests or witnesses. They were prominent members of the King of England's inner circle, his favoured proxies, and they were presiding over the coronation of the Scottish king. The assembled ranks of the Scottish nobility and Churchmen would, upon seeing their new king crowned and blessed by Edward I's deputies, have been left in little doubt of Edward's continued influence and interest in Scottish politics. Despite the agreements intended to limit Edward's control of Scotland, he had in short order picked the new King of Scotland and had that candidate crowned in a ceremony overseen and carried out by his proxies in Scotland.

Any Scots who felt a degree of trepidation upon witnessing this most unusual state of affairs had their fears almost immediately confirmed when John headed directly from the site of his coronation at Scone to Newcastle, where Edward and the English royal court were spending Christmas.[7] That the new Scottish king, who had an incredible amount of work to do to secure his position, felt that it was necessary to delay the calling of a Scottish parliament to attend a foreign court suggests both the immediate directions of Edward I's ambitions and the enormous amount of pressure he brought to bear upon John. As part of the English court's Christmas celebrations, John formally paid homage to Edward I.[8] He did so not only for his English lands but also for the Kingdom of Scotland, a legal recognition of Edward's feudal overlordship of the British Isles.

While this may seem like the final nail in the coffin for John's kingship of an independent Scotland, it is important to remember that as momentous and damaging as this step was, he was not the first Scottish king to take it. Following King William the Lion's capture at the Battle of Alnwick in 1174, he had been forced to submit to English overlordship.[9] Subsequent Kings of Scotland, under acute pressure from their southern neighbours, had made concessions or statements that fell just short of this Rubicon. In every case, these acknowledgments of English claims to sovereignty over the entirety of the British Isles were walked back as soon as circumstances would allow, either through subsequent diplomatic agreements or because it became clear there was no practical way to enforce their purported supremacy.

William the Lion was forced to contend with endemic rebellions and uprisings in the years following his swearing of homage to an English king.[10] However, it is unclear to what degree this aristocratic discontent was fuelled by anger at the loss of sovereignty or by naked opportunism. The other terms of the Treaty of Falaise, such as the garrisoning of key Scottish royal castles by English troops and the levelling of a huge war indemnity, had greatly weakened the military position of the Scottish king and changed the calculus of power within the kingdom. With William's ability to reward and enrich his allies curtailed, the nobility sought to slough off royal authority and pursue alternate means of empowering themselves.

When viewed in this historical context, John's performance of homage was, while deeply alarming and a severe blow to the prestige and integrity of the Scottish throne, not necessarily irreversible or fatally compromising. Indeed, as we shall see, when Edward subsequently became entangled in wars and uprisings, John did his best to emulate his predecessors by attempting to ignore the authority of the now embattled English king. It was a reticence that suggests he hoped to be able to reclaim his kingdom's independence. Potentially far more damaging was John's decision, a week after his coronation, to publicly free Edward from all the promises and agreement he had made with the Guardians of Scotland.[11]

Edward had once again sidestepped the agreement he had reached with the Guardians regarding the sovereignty of the Kingdom of Scotland by placing pressure upon the new king. A king who had been stranded and isolated within the English royal court. Among the agreements circumvented in this manner was the Treaty of Birgham, which had been signed and formulated as part of the negotiations around the marriage between Edward's son, Prince Edward, and the uncrowned queen Margaret. In signing the treaty, Edward had promised to recognise and uphold the independence of the Kingdom of Scotland and the integrity of its borders. It also contained clauses designed to prevent English Churchmen from attempting to influence or interfere with the running of the Scottish bishoprics and ecclesiastical community.[12]

In allowing Edward to discard the Treaty of Birgham, John was not only depriving himself of a potential legal argument for limiting or refuting

Edward's overlordship, but he was also opening a potential cleavage between himself and the Scottish aristocracy. More than a simple treaty with a foreign power, the Treaty of Birgham was a manifesto in which the Scottish nobility expressed their collective conception of the Kingdom of Scotland.[13] It outlined and defined the guiding political aims and principles of the Scottish aristocracy and the terms upon which the kingdom functioned. By carelessly abandoning the treaty in the face of pressure from Edward, John risked the perception that he was disregarding or outrightly betraying the wishes of the Scottish aristocracy.

The merging of Balliol finances and household administration with those of the Scottish royal government was by no means a straightforward affair, complicated as it was by the confusion and misunderstandings created by the long interregnum. Edward I shamelessly attempted to use his position as the feudal overlord of the Balliols' English estates and his claims to suzerainty over the British Isles to gain financial and political leverage over the new King of Scotland.[14] Even prior to John's coronation as King of Scotland in 1192, Edward had instructed the English Exchequer to prepare an exhaustive audit of the Balliols' finances. Of particular interest to the English King were the dues and fees attached to the estates John had inherited from his mother, Dervorguilla of Galloway. Reporting in May of the following year, Edward's investigators had found that Balliol owed the English crown close to £3,300, a questionably large sum.[15] Edward then pardoned the vast majority of the debt, while holding the remainder over Balliol's head. It was a crude but effective demonstration of where the balance of power lay between the two monarchs. One that Edward undoubtedly hoped would help keep John firmly under his thumb going forward.

Edward clearly recognised the importance of the Comyn family to the Balliol royal government and their position of prominence within the wider Scottish aristocracy. Just as he had done with the Balliol finances, Edward ordered an investigation into the debts owed to the Crown by John Comyn II of Badenoch, who probably not coincidentally, also held a considerable portion of Galloway through inheritance. Like his newly crowned cousin, Edward's investigators found that John owed a surprising, possibly suspiciously large, amount of money to the English crown.[16] Again, much of this debt was publicly forgiven while a payment schedule was established for the remainer.

Again, the purpose for this financial song and dance was to leave the Comyns with the understanding that they were subordinate to the English king and reliant upon his goodwill and co-operation.

In a sense, Edward was converting manufactured fiscal debts into political cachet. Interestingly, Edward's attempts to use the many financial mechanism at his disposal to ensure Comyn obedience and support extended to the carrot as well as the stick. In 1292, during his custodianship of the Kingdom of Scotland, Edward had granted the management and incomes of several Scottish royal forests to Earl John Comyn of Buchan. He had also granted the Earl license to export lead from the Isle of Man. Following John Balliol's election and the audit of the Badenoch branch of the Comyn family, Edward continued to make a point of pardoning many of the various taxes and fees accumulated by the family's English estates.[17] A natural corollary to this solicitous financial strategy was the marriage between John Comyn II of Badenoch's son, John the Red and Joan de Valence, who was a cousin of King Edward.[18] These special considerations were almost certainly an attempt by Edward to show the powerful Comyn family the potential benefits of co-operation and to open a breach between them and their Balliol relatives.

In fact, John Balliol's accession to the throne was something of a triumph for the Comyn dynasty, reaffirming the place they had occupied at the centre of Scottish governance since the reign of Alexander II. One of the new king's sisters, Eleanor, was married to John Comyn II, Lord of Badenoch, known sometimes as John the Black to differentiate himself from his son and heir, John the Red. As a descendant of Donald III, John was one of the claimants to the Scottish throne. But having secured formal recognition of his royal heritage, he had instead chosen to throw his support behind the superior and more straightforward claims of his brother-in-law.

The king was also related to the Buchan branch of the Comyn family. John Comyn, the third Earl of Buchan, was the son of Alexander Comyn and the new king's cousin, Isabella (sometimes known as Elizabeth) de Quincy. Isabella was, like King John I, a grandchild of Alan of Galloway and had inherited extensive estates within Galloway.[19] Indeed, as we touched upon in the first chapter, while neither Alexander nor his son ever challenged Balliol claims to the Lordship of Galloway, they had leveraged their considerable royal favour to gain control of almost the entirety of the Quincy estates within the Lordship. The Buchan Comyns then were not only relatives of the Balliols but their neighbours and the most powerful and prominent members of their regional aristocratic affinity.

The six Guardians appointed to manage the Scottish government following the death of Alexander III in 1286 reflected the position and prestige of the Comyn faction. Its members included representatives of both emerging branches of the Comyn family, Earl Duncan of Fife, whose daughter was married to John Comyn III, and their ally and partisan, Bishop William Fraser of St Andrews. This left only the Bruce-affiliated James Stewart and the originally largely non-partisan Bishop Robert Wishart of Glasgow as dissenting voices. With the death of Margaret of Norway in 1290, the Comyns and their allies quickly rallied around John Balliol. A Comyn relative, with a history of close co-operation with the family and an excellent hereditary claim to the throne, Balliol's candidacy offered the Comyns a golden opportunity to preserve their hold on power.

However, while their presence at the heart of royal government was consistent across this period, their remit and exact role had changed considerably. During the interregnum, they proactively and effectively defended their position in royal government by soliciting the co-operation of the larger body of the Scottish aristocracy, preserving their power through an appeal to the nobility's mutual self-interest. Similarly, the dominant role the Comyns and their immediate relatives would come to occupy in the royal government of John Balliol differed considerably from the one they had occupied under Alexander II or Alexander III.

While John's candidacy was supported by the majority of the Scottish aristocracy, his Bruce rivals still commanded a considerable following of their own. The contentious and drawn-out process of arbitration, which preceded John's accession to the throne of Scotland, had exposed the political fault lines and factions within the Scottish aristocracy. Previous generations of Scottish kings had been able to moderate and harness such aristocratic rivalries by adjudicating such disputes and co-opting the participants into royal service where their ambitions and drive for advancement would enhance the prestige and power of the crown. They had in fact gone to considerable efforts, backed by the increasingly sophisticated means and mechanisms of the royal administration, to present themselves as above regional aristocratic rivalries. As we have seen, one of the primary strengths of the Scottish royal centre was its ability to promote and attract aristocratic co-operation.

In contrast, John was correctly and almost unavoidably seen as an active participant in an aristocratic faction. The strength of association created by his reliance on the Comyns and their allies for both political capital and military resources meant that he inherited many of their enemies and rivals who were swiftly absorbed into the Bruce faction. The intrusion of factionalism into the royal government and the lasting wounds the interregnum had inflicted upon Scotland's body politic became immediately apparent when John, returning from his visit to the English king's Christmas court in Newcastle, convened a parliament in early February 1293.[20]

Rather than acquiesce to his loss and pay homage to the new king, Robert 'the Competitor', already in his mid to late seventies, attempted to preserve the Bruce claim by transferring all the family's Scottish lands to his son, Robert de Bruce, who became the sixth Bruce Lord of Annadale.[21] This Robert, in turn transferred the Earldom of Carrick, which he held through his wife, to his own heir, the future King Robert de Bruce.[22] The elder Bruce then departed on a mission to Norway in the hopes of securing a marriage between his daughter, Isabel, and the long-widowed King Eric II.[23] Perhaps gambling upon the success of this overture, which would have consolidated the claims of two of Balliol's most prominent rival candidates and brought the Bruces an extremely powerful ally, the new Earl of Carrick initially refused to attend parliament or swear homage to the new king. While the majority of the Bruces' allies and supporters during the interregnum attended, ready to accept on a provisional basis the authority and legitimacy of the new king, Bruce diehards such as Angus of Islay, Lord William Douglas and Earl John Magnusson of Caithness also absented themselves.[24]

John and his allies were keenly aware of the potential weakness of their position and the need to foster stability in Scotland. While those Bruce party members who failed to attend parliament were proclaimed defaulters, their lands and titles now potentially subject to confiscation by the throne, no practical steps were actually undertaken to make good on this threat. In the short term at least, this proved to be a wise strategy; despite the Bruce family's initially belligerent stance, the Earl of Carrick eventually did homage to John I in August 1293. Meanwhile, the royal party pressed on with the vital business of consolidating their hold on Scotland. However, many of their reforms to strengthen the position of royal government, necessary as they no doubt were after a long and often contentious interregnum, were executed in a distinctly partisan manner.

One of the new royal household's most ambitious and telling reforms was the creation of three new shrievalties that granted their office holders near vice-regal supervisory powers over vast swathes of territory in the west of Scotland.[25] Royal authority in the west of the country, which maintained significant political and cultural links with Scandinavian and Norse-Gaels polities, was traditionally fragile and hampered by the lack of royal estates in the region. These new western sheriffs were intended to function as extensions of royal government in this difficult to control and historically autonomous segment of the kingdom. In practice, this could only be achieved by delegating royal authority to those allies of the king that were already active and powerful within the region.

The first of these shrievalties, which included Skye and much of the northern Hebrides, was awarded to Earl William of Ross, a cousin of the Comyn family and Balliol auditor during the Great Council.[26] His mother, Jean, was the daughter of the Comyn family's former patriarch, William, who in addition to the Lordship of Badenoch had come to hold the Earldom of Buchan through his second marriage to its hereditary countess.[27] Through this connection, Earl William of Ross was closely related to both the Badenoch and Buchan branches of the Comyn family and a natural supporter of the Balliol government.

The Shrievalty of Lorn, whose authority and remit stretched to encompass neighbouring Argyll and Mull, was bestowed by the king upon Alexander McDougall.[28] Alexander was a brother-in-law of John Comyn the Black of Badenoch and very much a member of the Comyn-Balliol affinity.[29] The McDougalls were engaged in a long-running and fiercely fought struggle for control of the region with the Domhnaills, the future Clan MacDonald.[30] Alexander's appointment as Sheriff gave him the increased means and remit necessary to prosecute this conflict more effectively. John was essentially licensing Alexander to assume control of the area, which allowed him to reframe his ongoing regional rivalry as a royal directive. Of course, with the Balliols and the Scottish crown throwing their weight behind the McDougalls as their proxies within the region, the Domhnaills, under the leadership of Angus Mór and his son Alasdair Óg, attempted to compensate. With little hope of recourse from the Scottish royal centre, they sought alternatives by aligning themselves ever more closely with the Bruces and signalling an amenability to English intervention in Scotland.

The last of the new sheriffs appointed by John I at this juncture was significantly different from the other two. While the Sheriffs of Lorn and Skye conspired through their combined efforts to expand royal authority in the rugged and wild north-west, their colleague's remit lay within the south-west, an area already largely integrated into the Kingdom of Scotland. While William of Ross and Alexander McDougall were both close Comyn relatives and committed Balliol loyalists, James Stewart came from a family that shared traditionally close ties with their Bruce neighbours. In fact, James, one of the Guardians of Scotland appointed in 1286 at the start of the interregnum, had been a committed member of the Bruce faction, serving as one of Robert the Competitor's auditors during Edward I's council.[31] Nevertheless, James had answered the new king's summons to parliament and publicly performed homage to him.

James' appointment to the new office was almost certainly an attempt by John I to detach the Stewarts from the still active Bruce party and signal to the Scottish nobility at large that he was willing to work with and even reward his former opponents. It was in many ways a sensible, even canny appointment. However, James' authority as sheriff only stretched to cover Kintyre and the Isles of Bute and Arran. While this was by almost any measure a substantial collection of territories, James' family already had effective control over them. In contrast, the Earl of Ross and Alexander McDougall were furnished with offices that invested them with at least nominal authority over expansive territories well beyond the peripheries of their traditional spheres of influence. James' appointment as sheriff was a mere confirmation of his regional primacy while King John's more committed allies and relatives were afforded the means and opportunity to expand their personal power and status. Indeed, there is substantive evidence, even in the immediate aftermath of James Stewart's appointment as sheriff, of tensions between local Balliol and Stewart officials as they vied for control in southern Ayrshire.[32]

The Comyn-Balliol faction was also extremely willing to use the powers and prerogatives of royal government to strengthen their position by empowering and enriching favoured members of the faction. Earl William of Ross and Earl John Comyn of Buchan, who already held the Constableship of Scotland by hereditary right, were both granted additional lordships from the royal demesne and granted extremely generous leases on lands that had been placed under royal guardianship.[33] Andrew Moray, yet another brother-in-law of Lord John the Black Comyn of Badenoch, was reappointed as the Justiciar of Scotia, a hugely important administrative position that oversaw the maintenance of royal government in the northern half of the kingdom.[34]

Earl Gilbert III of Angus, whose mother was a member of the extended Balliol family and who later married a sister of Earl John Comyn of Buchan, was also granted a senior position within the royal government.[35] He was joined in the royal inner circle by his first cousin, Ingram de Umfraville.[36] Ingram's father, Robert, was the brother of Gilbert's father, while his mother Eva was the daughter of Ingram Balliol, the king's great-uncle. Meanwhile, the Comyn-Balliol ally Bishop William Fraser of St Andrews was rewarded by John I by being granted the highly profitable guardianship of the young Earl of Fife and his lands.[37] This decision, which effectively allowed the bishop to absorb the earl's extensive incomes with the king's blessing, was met with resentful outrage by the earl's relatives. It was a situation that, as we shall see, would come back to haunt Balliol and his allies.

Having triumphed in the legal proceedings over his Bruce rival, John now had to reward those relatives and allies whose support had helped him secure the throne or risk their abandonment and ire. On the other hand, the monopolisation of office holding and the other rewards of royal service by a comparatively small group of the king's relatives and allies naturally stoked the resentment of other regional and familial affinities within the Scottish aristocracy who found themselves being excluded from those same rewards. This was the classic dilemma of medieval kingship. The king's ability to exercise authority was derived in a large part from the co-operation of local proxies. In order for this co-operation to remain effective and consistent it had to be rewarded through displays of royal largesse. However, the political community as a whole tended to react badly to the emergence of clear royal favourites and the uneven distribution of royal favours. To remain effective then, kings had to reward their close allies and relatives while still retaining the financial resources to incentivise the co-operation of the wider aristocracy. Kings who got this precarious balance wrong often found themselves devoid of effective allies or were faced with widespread uprisings.

The committed support of the Comyns and their relatives had played a role of paramount importance in the Balliol bid for the throne and their subsequent consolidation of power within Scotland. Those same allies, having resecured their prominence within Scottish royal government, were now eager to make the most of their hard-won position. However, left unmanaged and untampered, the same political factionalism that saw Balliol make good on his hereditary claim to the throne could become a corrosive force that undermined royal authority and invited dissent.

The Balliols and their allies attempted to consolidate their authority in Scotland and bolster their supporters through the deployment of royal prerogatives and a much-needed raft of reforms to the royal administration. Interestingly, in the years immediately following John I's assumption of the throne, rather than openly seek to contest the throne, the Bruces and their allies were content to continue to prosecute their rivalries on an essentially local, region by region basis. Their persistent but low-intensity resistance sought to erode the Balliols' control of particular localities while avoiding concerted reprisals from the royal centre. As we have seen, the McDougalls waged a localised war on the crown's behalf against the Domhnaills and their allies in the extreme north-west of the kingdom. Meanwhile, the Stewarts attempted to resist the imposition of royal officials within their south-western power base.

The Balliols were aware of the rather tenuous nature of their hold on the Lordship of Galloway. Indeed, King John I's generous granting of the thanages of Formartine and Dereily to Earl John Comyn of Buchan had been made on the understanding that John renounce his hereditary claim to Galloway. However, this awareness of Galloway's vulnerability was not enough in and of itself to shield Galloway from the influence of the Bruces, who controlled the encircling Earldom of Carrick and the Lordship of Annadale. In 1294, the Bruces, perhaps acting under the direction of the energetic new Earl of Carrick, somehow managed to contrive the election of their candidate, Thomas Dalton of Kirkcudbright, as the new Bishop of

Galloway.[38] This was a significant blow to Balliol prestige, destabilising their grip on the lordship and severely curtailing the king's ability to leverage the financial resources of the bishopric. The king, who appeared to have been caught unaware by the appointment, made several efforts to have it reversed, including appealing to the Archbishop of York, but to no avail.

John's acquiescence to Edward's claims to the overlordship of Scotland and the increased factionalism of the Scottish aristocracy were individually both severe threats to the authority and integrity of the Scottish throne. Compounded, they were a yet more insidious threat, with the potential to hollow out the institution of Scottish kingship entirely and permanently yoke it to English overlordship. In late thirteenth-century Europe, where the political and personal were largely synonymous, claims to authority, just like inheritance claims, had to be exercised routinely to have any meaning. Claims that were not exercised successfully soon became irrelevancies. The proliferation of lawsuits and related developments in legal procedure that had begun in the late twelfth century had no real impact upon this truism. The only thing that really changed was the preferred method through which such claims were pressed.

Having received homage from Scotland and John Balliol's acknowledgement of his overlordship, Edward I was eager to further secure his claim through the actual exercise of this authority. Edward would almost certainly have been keenly aware of the manner in which his own father's previously successful attempts to exercise practical authority within Scotland had quickly disintegrated when changing circumstances had necessitated that his focus and resources shifted elsewhere. Factionalism within the Scottish aristocracy and the resultant discontent among certain groups with Balliol rule provided Edward I with the opportunity to begin intervening in Scotland. Isolated from the traditional rewards of participation in royal governance and co-operation with the throne, the Scottish rivals of the Balliols and their allies proved to be more than happy to bring their grievances with John I to a nominal higher authority, his overlord Edward.

This often-self-reinforcing cycle of opposition was an extremely difficult situation for John I and his allies to deal with. Scottish dissidents such as the Bruces and their allies wanted a way to sidestep Balliol possession of royal authority and resources, while Edward was actively on the lookout for opportunities to prove the substance and mettle of his overlordship by overturning royal Scottish decrees. In this manner, the sovereignty of the Kingdom of Scotland was undermined by its lack of political unity.

The reason why we know that Stewart and Balliol officials clashed in Ayrshire during this period was that Edward I wrote to John reprimanding him for allowing the situation to get out of hand and ordering him to leave the administration of the area to the Stewarts.[39] Alasdair Óg of Islay, the leader of the Domhnaill family who were embroiled in an ongoing war with the Balliols' McDougall allies, made frequent appeals to Edward, both complaining about mistreatment by the Balliols and presenting their own suit for control over the disputed region.[40] In this case, the Lord of Islay's invocations of Edward's overlordship had only a limited practical effect, probably because of the remoteness of the conflict and the insulation provided to the Balliols by their use of the McDougalls as proxies. Edward's goal was to create a public and decisive triumph in which he proved the reality of his overlordship by unequivocally overruling the wishes of the Scottish king. Likewise, complaints made against the Comyn-Balliol functionary and ally Patrick Graham by his local rival, Simon of Restalrig, were similarly vexing for John Balliol but again failed to provide Edward with an excuse for clear-cut and decisive action.[41] In May 1293 Edward took the momentous step of summoning the Scottish king to appear in an English court in response to a lawsuit brought by a wine trader who had been owed money by Alexander III.[42] However, John never actually had to appear before the court since the wine trader died before proceedings could begin, leading to the case's abandonment.

Edward found a more substantive opportunity in the ongoing discord and controversy surrounding the guardianship of Earl of Fife. As you will recall, the Earl of Fife in 1292, Duncan IV, was a child and unable to perform his hereditary role in John's coronation as King of Scotland. Being similarly unable to manage his own household or estates, the earl was placed under the protection of a guardian. Upon taking the throne, John Balliol had dismissed John St John, the guardian appointed by Edward I, awarding his ally, Bishop William Fraser of St Andrews, custody over Duncan. Comparative to the wealth of an earldom, meeting the financial needs of a five-year-old was not a particularly burdensome task, allowing the guardian to take the remainder of the earl's income for themselves. Indeed, the guardianships of orphans and widows were highly sort after and lucrative resources for members of the aristocracy and royal control over their distribution was a significant contributor to the extension of royal authority.

The decision to award this guardianship and control over the earl's considerable resources to the bishop was met with immediate opposition from the earl's extended family, the Macduffs, who naturally felt that the role should have been entrusted to one of them. This situation was made worse by the ongoing attempts of the Comyn-aligned Abernethy family to expand their power in Fife at the Macduffs' expense.[43] Shorn of the authority and resources they had traditionally enjoined, the Macduffs' ability to resist this opportunistic encroachment were curtailed significantly. This state of affairs was particularly egregious since the earl's father had been assassinated by supporters of Hugh de Abernethy during an earlier phase of this struggle, even after he had taken steps to defuse the conflict by arranging for his daughter to marry Earl John of Buchan.[44]

When a younger brother of Earl Duncan III, referred to within contemporary sources simply by their family name Macduff, tried to claim a portion of his brother's inheritance, his pursuit of these claims was rebuffed vociferously by Bishop Fraser and Macduff was incarcerated temporarily.[45] Upon his release, he found little support or sympathy from the Balliol royal government. Undeterred, Macduff appealed to Edward I, who was more than happy to hear the case. King John attempted to sweep the matter under the carpet initially, dispatching legal representatives to resolve the matter in May of 1293.[46] However, English law required that John appear in person and Edward was able to pressure him into attendance of his September parliament in order to answer Macduff's suit.

Even more so than Edward's insistence that as overlord of Scotland he had the right to intervene in Scottish royal justice and hear appeals, the notion that he had the right to summon the King of Scotland to appear in court was extremely damaging to the prestige and independence of the Scottish throne. That, of course, was precisely why Edward insisted upon it. Appearing before the English king and the assembled parliament, King John I Balliol initially attempted to put a brave face upon things. Invoking the language of the Treaty of Birgham and drawing upon Scotland's traditions of political solidarity and aristocratic consensus, John argued that he could not address the claims of Macduff's suit without taking the advice of the Scottish nobility.[47] He was in a sense attempting to sidestep his earlier acknowledgement of Edward's authority as overlord, a personal arrangement regarding the comparative standing of two hegemons, by casting himself as a representative and facilitator of the political community of Scotland.

Edward was, perhaps predictably, unmoved by this argument and unimpressed by John's attempts to suggest his legitimacy as king derived from the support of the Scottish aristocracy rather than his relationship with Edward. He had after all gone to considerable trouble to put a king of Scotland in place precisely because he did not want the trouble of dealing with the Scottish nobility himself. Instead, he declared that John's refusal to engage with the particulars of the suit constituted contempt of court and threatened to confiscate the Balliols' English estates and three of the primary Scottish royal castles.[48] John relented quickly in the face of such severe measures. Abandoning his line of argument and resistance to Edward's jurisdiction over Scotland, he once again swore homage to Edward and submitted publicly to the strictures of English overlordship.[49]

In exchange for this humiliating and more or less total capitulation, he won a postponement in the ruling of the Macduff case. Fife and Earl Duncan IV were left, for the time being, in the custody of Bishop Fraser. John had also avoided, or at least delayed, Edward intervening directly in Scotland to deprive one of his allies of an important prize. While such a result would have been a catastrophic blow to Balliol royal authority, the actual outcome was preferable only by comparison. Judgement on the Macduff case had merely been delayed, not averted, and John had shown the ease with which Edward could corral and bully him. Needless to say, John's swift capitulation to Edward's authority did little to win the respect and loyalty of the Scottish aristocracy.

In the same manner that Edward and his ancestors pursued the suzerainty of Scotland and the rest of the British Isles, the kings of France claimed, with considerably more historical and legal justification, overlordship over Edward's extensive French lands. A legacy of the Norman Conquest, Edward's ancestors inhabited dual roles as both the independent kings of England and the Dukes of Normandy, the latter of which, nominally at least, lay under the authority of the French throne. Such tangles of loyalties and obligations were relatively common during the twelfth century in which the pursuit and integrity of familial connections and inheritance came to transcend cultural and political barriers.

Anglo-Norman kings of England went to great pains to avoid paying homage directly to the kings of France for their French territories. Fortunately for them, the relative weakness of the French throne, whose authority was curtailed functionally to the modest region surrounding Paris and the royal demesne, meant that negotiating around French suzerainty was not inordinately difficult.

In the century or so following the high watermark of the family's success under Edward's great-grandfather, Henry II, successive generations of French kings had greatly increased their own power and authority, extending their writ throughout the entirety of France and successfully confiscating the majority of the English kings' continental domains. By the time Edward I had taken the throne, all that was left of this once vast conglomeration of territories on the continent was Gascony, a wine-producing region of Aquitaine, with particularly strong economic ties to England. Edward, like his father Henry III, had made several unsuccessful attempts to recapture their lost French domains.[50] However, the balance of power had shifted firmly in favour of the French kings, who were able to successfully leverage their greater resources, renewed royal authority and the split focus of the English crown. As a result, Edward's position in France continued to deteriorate.

Somewhat ironically then, in France, Edward was in much the same position he was attempting to ensnare John Balliol in. He was, not to put too fine a point on it, the victim of ill-faith bargaining by an ambitious feudal overlord looking for any pretext to extend their authority. In the summer of 1294, the French King, Philip IV, seized upon Edward's reluctance to make further concessions and declared that Gascony was forfeit, trigging a war between the two kings.[51] John Balliol, like many Scottish magnates, already owed Edward considerable military service for his English estates. However, his earlier acknowledgment of Edward's status as overlord of the British Isles opened up the possibility that John and his kingdom owed military service to Edward in this capacity as well. This was evidently Edward's preferred interpretation and one that would allow him to harness a greater portion of Scotland's military resources. Even as Edward enacted a series of reforms in

England to bolster manpower and cash flow through the assessment of feudal obligations, the principle of military service remained a key theoretical and legal component of the relationship between monarch and subject.

John, perhaps in an attempt to gain clarity on the subject, wrote to Edward asking what Edward expected of him in regard to the coming continental expedition. In keeping with his conception of himself as the overlord of Scotland, Edward summoned John and the entirety of the Scottish nobility, including the earls and baronage, to participate in his war in France.[52] The Scottish nobility deeply resented being summoned by a foreign king to participate in a seemingly hopeless foreign war from which they had little to gain. In fact, their reluctance was shared by many of their relatives and contemporaries in England. Many of Edward's military reforms and cultural initiatives were direct attempts to answer the resultant manpower shortage.[53]

John appears to have initially agreed to heed Edward's summons but then changed his mind, most likely at the urging of his advisors in Scotland. Edward was forced to go to war without Scotland. While John's retraction and the general refusal of the Scottish nobility to mobilise for war on Edward's behalf no doubt infuriated the English king, he had little practical recourse. News of the war between Edward and Philip was met in the supposedly freshly conquered Princedoms of North Wales with an outbreak of a massive rebellion. Edward was now in the precarious position of having to both defend his Gascon holdings and quell the rebellion in Wales. Fighting simultaneously on these two fronts pushed Edward's military resources to the limit. This lack of troops stymied any chance of carrying out any meaningfully punitive actions in Scotland, affording the kingdom a temporary reprieve from English royal wrath.

Incensed by Edward's persistent and heavy-handed attempts to exert authority within Scotland and emboldened by the apparent success of their defiance in the matter of military obligations, the Scottish aristocracy began to organise for systematic resistance to Edward's position in Scotland. Just as they had done in the interregnum of 1286, the Scottish nobility selected from their own number a council of Guardians charged with the responsibility of protecting the freedom and integrity of the Kingdom of Scotland and with it the co-mingled interests of the Scottish aristocracy.[54] Indeed, it may have been the intervention of this group that first convinced Balliol to walk back on his promise to support Edward militarily in France.

There were two significant differences between this group of Guardians and their predecessors. Firstly, the size of the council had doubled from six to twelve members. This greater membership meant, nominally at least, that the council could better represent the collective will of the Scottish political community and the various family and regional affinities of which it was composed. Secondly, in 1286 the Scottish nobility formed a council of Guardians because they had no king, in 1295 they did so because so few of them trusted the resolve or competency of the king they had.

The formation of this council has, somewhat understandably, often been seen within the modern historiography as an anti-Balliol coup and the end of his effective authority within Scotland. However, both the Guardians and the Scottish resistance movements they later came to preside over were explicit in their support for a Balliol kingship. The primary diplomatic initiative they presided over, the establishment of a formal military alliance with France through the marriage of John's eldest son and heir, Edward Balliol, to a niece of King Philip of France, further entangled the fates of the Kingdom of Scotland and the Balliol dynasty. Both the marriage and alliance would have required the king's close co-operation and consent to be implemented. In short, the Guardians and their supporters clearly believed that their interests were best served through the preservation of the Balliol kingship. They were, however, unconvinced of John Balliol's ability to resist Edward I's impositions unsupervised.

The exact composition of this new batch of Guardians is unknown, although its likely they were organised and selected along the same lines as their predecessors and were formed of four bishops, four earls and four barons. Subsequent events would show that the Comyns, represented by Earl John Buchan and John the Red, assumed a clear position of military leadership at the outbreak of the war. John the Red had become increasingly prominent among the Balliol faction as his father, Lord John the Black of Badenoch, entered a state of semi-retirement.[55] The Comyns' prominence in leading the Scottish political community to war strongly suggests that they were members of this new council of Guardians and that their influence over the Scottish royal government remained undiminished.

Likewise, two of the four diplomats dispatched by the Guardians to the court of King Philip IV of France were noted Balliol intimates, Bishop William Fraser of St Andrews and Ingram de Umfraville.[56] Of the two remaining members of the diplomatic party, John de Soules was related through marriage to the Stewarts, who despite historic ties to the Bruce party had come to a broad accommodation with the Balliols, while Bishop Matthew Crambeth of Dunkeld remained staunchly pro-Birgham.[57] While it is, of course, possible the Guardians were content to simply use John I as a figurehead, the balance of the available evidence suggests a less radical reorganisation and redistribution of authority.

It seems that Balliol's allies and aristocratic sponsors retained their position at the heart of the royal government. The establishment of a more representative group of Guardians allowed the Comyn-led core faction to foster an increased sense of unity and capacity for collective action among the Scottish aristocracy, in preparation for hostiles with Edward. Regarding the nobility's relationship with King John I, the creation of this council represented more formalisation than innovation. Rather than an attempt to overthrow or replace the king, the council of Guardians was an expression of the aristocracy's determination to defend their collective interests by bolstering the integrity of the royal centre. John had from the start of his reign been dependent upon the support and approval of his Comyn allies. While the arrangement was to an extent motivated by a lack of faith in John's ability to resist Edward's imposition of authority over Scotland, the relationship between the king and his allies remained at its heart co-operative rather than competitive. Its overall result was a strengthening of the Balliol party's hold on power.

The failure of John Balliol and the rest of the Scottish nobility to heed his summons to military service would have left the enraged Edward with little doubt of their increasing resolve to devest themselves of his claims to overlordship. In addition to the, from Edward's point of view, deeply worrying prospect of a formal alliance between the French and Scottish thrones, the Guardians had in the summer of 1295 sent representatives to the Papal court in the hopes of unravelling the legal basis for Edward's claim to suzerainty over the British Isles.[58] While Edward was still at war with France at this time, the fighting around Gascony was slow and sporadic, with much of the French king's attention consumed by the struggle in the north against Edward's Lowland and German allies. Once the situation in Wales had been contained, Edward, eager to extract revenge against Balliol and his followers for their earlier defiance and as determined to secure his overlordship over Scotland as ever, had begun mustering a sizeable army in northern England. In the meantime, he continued to use the Macduff appeal as a pretext by once again restarting legal proceedings, summoning the Scottish king to appear before him to answer for his conduct in the case.

This time however, John, likely at the urging or even instance of the Guardians, refused to attend, instead sending the Abbot of Arbroath to act as his legal representative. In October 1295 Edward, keenly feeling the threat of the Scottish-French alliance, raised the stakes yet higher, writing to his Scottish counterpart to demand that the key border fortifications of Jedburgh, Roxburgh and Berwick all be surrendered to him until the conclusion of his hostilities with France.[59] At the same time, he declared all the English lands of John Balliol and those Scottish magnates who had refused his renewed calls for military service in the north of England forfeit and instructed his sheriffs to see to their immediate confiscation.

One Scottish noble who did answer Edward's summons was the future King of Scotland and Earl of Carrick, Robert de Bruce. He was joined by a small number of relatives and allies, including his father and namesake, Lord Robert de Bruce of Annadale. As a reward for his loyalty, Edward invested Robert with a position of considerable authority, placing him in charge of the defence of Carlisle.[60] Robert's defection to the English would hardly have come as much of a surprise to the Scottish political community. His family held extensive estates in England, while his grandfather, Robert the Competitor, had been John Balliol's foremost rival for the throne; a claim Earl Robert was clearly unwilling to renounce.

Indeed, the Guardians retaliated to the Bruce family's declaration for Edward with their own declaration of forfeiture and granted custody of the Bruces' Scottish lands to the Earl of Buchan.[61] Of course, the Bruces had heavily fortified their key holdings and there was little that could be done in the short term to enact these confiscations. Much the same could be said for Earl Patrick of Dunbar, sometimes styled as the Earl of March. Patrick was yet another claimant of the Scottish throne, his claim springing from his descent from an illegitimate branch of the Dunkeld family. Although married to a sister of Earl John of Buchan, Patrick had extensive English estates and connections, leading him to throwing his lot in with the English king.[62] On the other hand, the arrival of Earl Gilbert de Umfraville of Angus in Edward's army must have come as something of a shock to the Scottish political community.[63] A relative of both the Comyn and Balliol families, Gilbert had occupied a position of some importance in the Balliol government. His defection can only have meant that he had severe reservations about the Scottish nobility's ability to weather the storm of English invasion.

Seeing the writing on the wall, the Scottish political community rallied around the king and mustered for battle. It was in many respects an impressive showing, indicative of the Scottish aristocracy's commitment to the principles of the Treaty of Birgham and willingness to support the independence and integrity of the Scottish throne. The core of the army was composed of the forces of the seven loyalist earls, Buchan, Menteith, Strathearn, Lennox, Ross, Atholl and Mar. Unwilling to secede the initiative to Edward, in March 1296, this Scottish army under the collective command of the loyalist Scottish earls and with the king in tow, launched an ambitious raid into northern England, probably in an attempt to disrupt Edward's planned invasion of Scotland.[64] It was a bold plan that went some way to minimise the effects of their numerical inferiority, but it quickly began to unravel when a Comyn-led attack on Carlisle failed to capture the town or dislodge the Bruces' forces stationed there.

Unwilling to risk being engaged directly by Edward's now advancing army, Scottish forces withdrew across the border. Under continual pressure from Edward, the Scottish army was next forced to abandon the border town of Berwick and its considerable garrison, led by Lord William Douglas. Douglas had been a committed member of the Bruce faction and his refusal to join the Bruces in their defection to Edward once again demonstrates the complex and tangled nature of loyalty and identity during this period. Besieged and stormed by the English army, in short order, the town was put to the torch and a large portion of its population and garrison slaughtered.[65] A small ray of hope, however, lay on the Scottish army's horizon. Earl Patrick of Dunbar's wife, Marjorie Comyn, had elected to side with her Comyn and Balliol relatives over her husband and had, in his absence, surrendered Dunbar Castle to the retreating Scottish host.

Edward, probably understanding that the small Scottish army was composed of the kingdom's aristocratic elite and their immediate retinues, was determined to press home the advantage and prevent the Scots from mustering fresh reinforcements. To that end, while he marshalled his own forces in the aftermath of the sacking of Berwick, he dispatched a strong force of cavalry under the command of John Balliol's father-in-law, Earl John de Warenne of Surrey, to threaten Dunbar Castle. Fearing that the castle, whose freshly invested garrison contained many of the Scottish commanders and their most valuable troops, would fall, King John and his advisors dispatched their own knights to intercept.[66]

Hampered by a lack of effective leadership, the Scottish knights misinterpreted the manoeuvrings of their English counterparts and launched an intemperate and ill-timed charge without the support of the castle's garrison. The result was a disaster, and they were completely routed by the carefully positioned and well-ordered English cavalry. Casualties were light but as many as a hundred Scottish knights or men-at-arms were captured. With the relief force neutralised, Edward moved to place the castle under siege the following day, triggering the surrender of another hundred or so Scottish knights, including the earls of Buchan, Ross, Atholl and Menteith as well as John Comyn the Red.[67]

That Battle of Dunbar, a comparatively small-scale clash between the two armies' knightly elites, precipitated the rapid collapse of the Balliol war effort. When news of the Scottish defeat began to circulate, many Scottish nobles such as James Stewart rushed to reach separate, and comparatively generous, terms with Edward.[68] King John and his retinue withdrew further into Scotland, eventually reaching Perth in late June but by then the tide was truly against them. John's attempts to source fresh troops were hampered not only by his lacklustre reputation as a leader but by the capture of the majority of his diehard supporters among the Scottish aristocracy. The remaining relatives and followers of the many incarcerated nobles were unwilling to risk their safety through further resistance. Advancing into the interior of Scotland virtually unopposed, Edward took Stirling and Edinburgh castles in short order.

Devoid of support and fast running out of places to withdraw to, John I of Scotland surrendered himself to Edward in late June.[69] Once in Edward's custody, John was forced to plead guilty to the charge of treason for rebelling against his rightful feudal overlord and to repudiate his treaty with France. Edward then made a grandiose display of stripping John of both his English and Scottish lands and titles. Legend has it that the Balliols' former ally and advocate, Bishop Anthony Bek of Durham, made a great show of symbolically tearing the Scottish royal arms from the erstwhile king's surcoat, dubbing him with the persistent moniker of 'empty tabard' or 'empty coat'. It certainly seems like the sort of gesture that the English king enjoyed making. He certainly took great care to remove all the traditional trappings and paraphernalia of Scottish kingship, including the Stone of Destiny, implicitly aware of the ability of such items to become a rallying point for further dissent. On the other hand, it is entirely possible that John's nickname, unfortunate as it was, actually predated his removal from kingship and instead referred to his somewhat unusually minimalist family coat of arms. These arms, *Gules an escutcheon voided Argent*, a red field containing an empty white shield, could easily have given rise to such a nickname, regardless of the ignominious circumstances that effectively brought his reign to an end. Whatever the truth regarding this legend, John and his young heir Edward were stripped of their royal status and imprisoned in the Tower of London.

Of course, history rarely leaves such a clean break. Regardless of the success in dismantling the Balliol regime, there were still many in Scotland who refuted Edward's claims to overlordship and, consequently, his right to confiscate the Scottish throne. Despite abandoning his marriage pact with the Balliols, King Philip IV of France continued to indicate that he regarded John Balliol as the legitimate King of Scotland into the 1310s. It seems that John also retained some hope of reclaiming his kingdom. When in 1299, he was being transferred from the Tower into Papal custody in France, it was discovered that John had hidden his crown and the royal seal of Scotland among his personal effects and was intent upon smuggling them out of English custody.[70]

Edward had secured the grudging submission of his opponents by holding those nobles captured at Dunbar and its immediate aftermath as hostage for the good behaviour of their remaining relatives and subordinates. However, the manner in which the Comyn-Balliol-allied earls had managed and organised the war, particularly the heavy reliance placed upon their own military retinues and Scotland's knightly classes, meant that Scotland still had large reserves of untapped military resources.

Early 1297 saw the outbreak of popular uprisings throughout Scotland. Many of these rebellions were triggered simply by the imposition of English overlordship and the local disruption inherent in accommodating English garrisons or establishing new hierarchies and proxies as the administration of lands were divided among Edward's allies and English followers. However, support for the restoration of the Balliol throne was a consistent element of these uprisings, a supposedly natural and preferable state of affairs that contrasted to the unfolding disruption and discord that provoked the uprisings. The two most successful rebel leaders were Andrew de Moray, operating in the north of the kingdom, and William Wallace in the west.

Andrew de Moray was a member of a highly influential baronial family; his father had served as sheriff of Scotia, while his mother was a member of the Badenoch branch of the Comyn family.[71] Wallace's origins in contrast are somewhat more obscure and are the subject of vigorous historical debate, although it at least seems clear that the was a member of the lower nobility.[72] Both men and their followers began waging highly effective guerrilla wars against Edward's remaining forces, attacking castles and burning garrisons. Wallace, in particular, was highly vociferous and explicit in his support for the imprisoned King John I, demonstrating that in the minds of many of the Scottish rebels, notions of Scotland's independence from England remained indivisible from not just Scottish kingship but a specifically Balliol kingship.[73]

A crucial consideration in understanding Edward's motivations and strategy during this conflict was that for him overlordship of Scotland was not a simple bauble or ornament. While there is a strong argument to be made that his efforts to conquer the British Isles were motivated by a desire to reclaim the pseudo-imperial status of his Angevin ancestors, recognition of his claims to overlordship had more immediate and practical benefits. Edward was in desperate need of additional soldiers for his still ongoing war in France. Recognition of his rights as overlord by either the Scottish king or the Scottish nobility would have allowed Edward to begin mobilising the kingdom's military and financial resources on his behalf.

Edward's ultimate goal in the war was to coerce the Scottish nobility into accepting his overlordship and agreeing to fight on his behalf in France.[74] His invasion of Scotland, carried out in a lull created by the intervention of his continental allies in northern France, was a gamble undertaken after the Scottish nobilities' refusal to acquiesce to these demands for military service. In many ways, it had succeeded; the campaign was short, not particularly bloody and was decisive. However, the heavy-handed manner in which Edward's English followers attempted to establish his authority provoked widespread discontent and rebellion, greatly hampering his overall goal.

In order to help alleviate the increasingly desperate situation in Scotland, Edward released Earl John Comyn of Buchan and a handful of other Scottish captives in exchange for their promises to help put down the uprisings and eventually undertake military service in France.[75] Edward must have selected Earl John Comyn in particular because the vast influence he wielded in the north of Scotland where his earldom and the heartland of his estates lay. He was therefore perfectly placed to crush the rebel forces gathering around Andrew de Moray. With many of his relatives still in Edward's custody, John undertook to play a dangerous double game. While openly making a great show of his co-operation with Edward, John did virtually nothing to hinder the rebels' efforts. Indeed, it seems that he may have actively facilitated the rebellion he was sent to squash, providing them with provisions and intelligence before ultimately conspiring to allow their successful rendezvous and unification with William Wallace's forces.[76] At the same time, John Comyn the Red and a number of other captured Scottish nobles were released and sent to fight for Edward in Flanders against their former French allies.[77]

Another example of the nuanced, occasionally tangled, loyalties created by the strange confluence of factionalism and occupation can be seen in the relationship between William Wallace and Lord William Douglas. Wallace was explicit in his desire to see John Balliol restored to the Scottish throne, yet one of his greatest regional allies in the struggle to drive Edward's forces out of south-west and central Scotland was Lord William Douglas, an ally and relative of the Bruce-aligned Stewarts.[78] When the extent of Douglas' opposition became clear to Edward, he sent instructions to his local proxy and ally in the region, Earl Robert de Bruce of Carrick, to arrest him.

Robert had probably harboured some hopes that following Balliol's capture, he or his father would be allowed to press the claim to the throne that they had inherited from his grandfather. After all, the Bruces were the effective runners-up of Edward's Great Council. If the Balliols had been proven unfit for the throne, should it not default to the family with the next best claim? However, in the summer of 1297, Edward's thoughts on the future of the Scottish kingship remained largely opaque to the Scottish nobility. Rather than being groomed for a position of leadership in Scotland, Bruce found that many of the offices and lands originally awarded to him in the aftermath of the Battle of Dunbar were being reassigned to Edward's English followers.[79] Far from facilitating his rise to the throne, Edward's attempts to exert authority throughout Scotland were threatening to erode Bruce power. Now on top of this already unsatisfactory state of affairs, Bruce was being asked to attack his own supporters.

In the face of this dilemma, the Earl of Carrick made the momentous decision to break with the English king and throw his support behind the rebels. The initial effects of this defection were muted. A frustrated Edward fed more reinforcements and resources into Scotland, swiftly forcing the Bruce and his aristocratic coalition to surrender. However, Andrew de Moray and William Wallace continued to fight on, despite the capitulation of their south-western allies. Uniting their forces, they struck out for the strategically vital lynchpin of Scotland, Stirling. Baiting and then ensnaring a large English army led by the victor of Dunbar, Earl John de Warenne of Surrey, the rebels won a stunning victory at the Battle of Stirling Bridge on 11 September 1297.[80]

When word of the victory at Stirling reached Flanders, John Comyn the Red and the rest of the Scottish nobles fighting there swiftly defected to the French, who provided them with passage back to Scotland.[81] Andrew de Moray had been grievously wounded during the battle and would die shortly afterwards, but the remaining rebels under Wallace's command began to raid deep into northern England.[82] The success of these raids and their revitalising effect upon the morale of the Scottish political community led to the appointment of Wallace as the Guardian of Scotland.

Despite his loyalty and success in winning the support of an increasingly fractured Scottish political community, Wallace's time as Guardian would prove to be short-lived. Alarmed by the defeat at Stirling and the subsequent invasion of England, Edward struck a rather disadvantageous truce with Philip IV before racing his army up to Scotland. The result was the English victory at the Battle of Falkirk.[83] Having routed Wallace's army, Edward launched a series of punitive raids against the strongholds of the Scottish leadership before withdrawing to the safety of Carlisle. Of particular note, among the dead of Wallace's defeated army was the Macduff relative whose initial appeals to Edward as overlord of Scotland had triggered war between him and John Balliol.

Despite Edward's inability to follow up the victory and the relatively narrow nature of the loss, Wallace resigned, or was forced to resign, his Guardianship, although he continued to serve as a diplomat and military commander. In the apparent hope of fostering increased political unity, the Scottish nobility appointed John Comyn the Red and Robert de Bruce as joint Guardians. It was a bold experiment but a largely unsuccessful one.[84] In theory, this power-sharing arrangement pooled the resources of the two largest aristocratic factions in Scotland and heavily invested them in continuing the struggle against Edward. In practice, the two rivals deeply distrusted one another and in the absence of any immediate threat of renewed invasion from Edward spent much of their time trying to outmanoeuvre and undermine one another, instead of co-ordinating the reduction of English-held strongholds.

Efforts made in 1299 to install the new Bishop of St Andrews, William Lamberton, as a third guardian who could mediate between his aristocratic colleagues came to nothing because his appointment as bishop had in itself been a cause of friction between the two factions.[85] A former canon and chancellor of Glasgow Cathedral, Lamberton was something of a protégé of Bishop Wishart of Glasgow. He had been a trusted member of Wallace's inner circle but had attained that position as a result of the sponsorship of Wallace's Bruce-aligned Douglas followers. Following the death of Bishop William Fraser in 1297, Lamberton, with Wallace's support, was elected as the Bishop of St Andrews. The Comyns, who had been closely allied with Fraser and regarded the Bishopric as being within their sphere of influence, were deeply resentful of the installation of a Bruce-associated candidate under the fog of war, making Lamberton a poor mediator between the two Guardians.[86]

The resulting deadlock was only resolved by Robert de Bruce's resignation from the Guardianship. Once more shunted from the centre of Scottish provisional royal authority by the Comyns' grip on the remains of the royal administration, Robert elected to make peace with Edward. He was replaced as Guardian in 1301 by Sir Ingram de Umfraville, a Comyn relative and Balliol associate who had fought for the English at Falkirk. Later that year, John Balliol, who had been released into Papal custody as a result of tireless Scottish diplomatic efforts, wrote to the Scottish parliament appointing his former envoy, Sir John de Soules, as Guardian of Scotland and indicating that he intended to return to Scotland imminently.[87]

Whatever the exact niceties of this arrangement and the distribution of titles, the Comyn family retained a great deal of their power and authority within the wider Scottish political community. This position of de facto leadership was reinforced as it became increasingly clear that John Balliol would not be permitted to return from exile in France any time soon.

By early 1303 the overall military situation looked increasingly desperate for the Scottish royalists, despite a minor victory at the Battle of Roslin. Edward had finally concluded a more substantive peace with King Phillip of France, a twin dolorous blow, to those hoping for the restoration of an independent Balliol kingship since it precluded French intervention in Scotland on Balliol's behalf and finally freed Edward to bring the full weight of his attention and military resources to bear in Scotland.

Having entered Scotland virtually unopposed, Edward, understanding the central importance of the Comyns in resisting his rule in Scotland, struck north to threaten the Comyn heartlands of Buchan and Badenoch. Convinced of the hopelessness of facing such a sizable English army in the field, the Comyns quickly made peace with Edward, precipitating the collapse of organised resistance to the invasion by the Scottish nobility.[88] As befits the enduring nature of his legacy, the indefatigable William Wallace resumed his guerrilla resistance to the English occupation.

Despite initial threats regarding the confiscation of the Comyn estates and titles, Edward not only swiftly returned the Comyns' lost property, but also appointed the Earl of Buchan to a regency council composed of Scottish nobles and the most senior of Edward's mostly English proxies and officials in Scotland. In exchange, the Comyns helped to persuade the remainder of the Scottish nobility to surrender; the family then playing a leading role in the negotiation in 1304 of a general amnesty for all those who had previously opposed Edward and his claims to overlordship. These were generous terms, which although curtailing the breadth of Comyn influence over the Scottish nobility, kept their assets and power bases intact.[89] The relatively favourable nature of this arrangement was not a sign of Edward's trust of the Comyns, who had already made false submissions to him, or an expression of his gratitude for their swift capitulation but rather an acknowledgment of their continued power and influence.

Perhaps, the now sixty-four-year-old Edward was keen to end the cycle of withdrawal, rebellion and invasion that had hitherto characterised the conflict in Scotland. Despite leaving the matter of Scottish kingship largely up in the air, Edward sought to establish a more permanent and stable basis for his administration in Scotland by soliciting the co-operation and support of the Scottish aristocracy. In order to achieve these concessions, the Comyns and their allies had sacrificed Wallace, who Edward harboured an implacable hatred for. While there is no evidence that they co-operated in attempts to detain Wallace, they had agreed to his exclusion from the carefully negotiated general amnesty. This meant that when Wallace was finally captured in 1305, the Scottish nobility did nothing as he was subjected to a show trial and gruesome execution. The last gasps of John Balliol's kingship died alongside his great champion.

With the dream of a Balliol restoration thoroughly quashed, Robert de Bruce began to take advantage of this lull in hostilities to quietly canvass support for his claim to the throne. In February 1306, Robert, John Comyn the Red and their respective retinues met at Greyfriars Church in Dumfries. The church setting for this meeting was far from incidental. Robert and John were the effective leaders of the two largest factions of the Scottish aristocracy. Both had claims to the Scottish throne, John's claim stemming from his status as Balliol's maternal nephew, and they were keenly aware of the generational rivalry that shaped the relationship between their families. With the Balliol kingship thoroughly discredited, at least for this generation, it must have seemed to the two men that if Scotland where to ever regain an autonomous kingship, then it would be either a Comyn or a Bruce sitting upon the restored throne. Meeting in a church would have been viewed as a mutual guarantee of safety because of the extraordinary strong religious prohibitions and taboos regarding violence and the spilling of blood on holy ground.[90]

Of course, it did not work out that way. The original purpose of the meeting remains unclear, obscured by a mess of contradictory sources. What is clear, on the macro level at least, was its conclusion. Both Lord John Comyn the Red of Badenoch and his uncle Sir Robert Comyn lay dead, killed by Bruce and his retainers. Some later Scottish sources allude to the existence of a previous agreement struck between the two men in which they agreed to co-operate in a renewed war against English overlordship.[91] According to these sources, Comyn planned to betray Bruce to Edward in exchange for further considerations from the English king. As a result, Bruce killed him in an act of patriotic desperation. According to near contemporary English sources, he lured his most powerful and bitter rival to the church before stabbing the defenceless Comyn lord at the high altar in a blasphemous and blatant political assassination.[92]

What actually happened is difficult to discern. Both the Bruces and Comyns had danced astutely across faction lines as the fortunes of war ebbed and flowed. The Comyns were intricately connected to the Balliol government but repeatedly sued for peace with Edward and expressed a willingness to accept his overlordship of Scotland once the military situation had become untenable. Bruce, on the other hand, started the war on Edward's side only to repudiate this loyalty and manoeuvre for a position of leadership among the Scottish nobility after Edward's occupation and administration of Scotland began to threaten Bruce interests.

Both factions were fighting not for ideals or principles but to defend and expand their families' properties and political positions. Ideas of patriotism and nationalism have little place in the discussion of these events because they were foreign concepts to the participants. The Scottish aristocracy had rallied around the vacant royal centre during the interregnum and during Edward's attempts to impose overlordship over Scotland not because the throne was vital to their own identity but because a failure to do so would remove their ability to tap into its resources and network of patronage. In a sense, recognition of Edward's claims to overlordship simply meant having to negotiate with him and his imported English officials for access to this network rather than doing so with a Scottish king or their peers among the aristocracy. The Scottish nobility became no more or less Scottish without a king and were no more or less Scottish because of their varied views on the desirability or practically of a Balliol restoration. The *Flores Historiarum*, written in 1307, cuts to the quick of the matter and in its simplicity probably provides us with the most truthful or at least pertinent version of events.[93] Bruce and Comyn quarrelled and then Bruce stabbed Comyn. They had, after all, been quarrelling for quite some time.

Bruce moved quickly following the bloody affray at Greyfriars, making his play for leadership of the freshly unsettled Scottish political community. Having crossed this personal Rubicon, Bruce attacked and overwhelmed the English garrison of Dumfries castle, loudly proclaiming his renewed opposition to the English occupation and Edward's claims to overlordship. He then hurried back to Glasgow in order to secure absolution for the Comyn murders from Bishop Robert Wishart and began preparations for his coronation.

The trepidation and insecurity that Robert and his supporters felt in claiming the kingship of Scotland, without the full or unequivocal support of the Scottish political community, can be glimpsed in Robert's decision to be coronated twice within two days; a state of affairs that would be comical were the stakes not so high for all involved. Six weeks after the killing at Greyfriars, Robert had gathered his supporters at the traditional royal centre of Scone. They were by any measure a formidable group, representing a significant portion of the Scottish political community with three bishops and four earls in attendance. On 25 March 1306, Robert de Bruce was crowned King of Scotland.

In the absence of a senior member of the Macduff family, the coronation was performed by Robert's former fellow Guardian, Bishop William Lamberton of St Andrews.[94] The next day, a Macduff arrived, and the entire ceremony was repeated. The new arrival was Isabella, the sister of Earl Duncan IV of Fife, who once again was unable to perform his family's hereditary role in the Scottish coronation ceremony, this time because of his status as an English hostage. In another revealing display of the tangled loyalties and overlapping connections that characterised medieval politics during this period, Isabella was also the wife of Earl John Comyn of Buchan. Isabella's father had been assassinated by members of the Comyn-backed Abernethy family and it appeared that the formidable countess had not forgotten this debt. Isabella's decision to support Robert's claim to the throne was the cause of a major rift between husband and wife. Following Isabella's subsequent capture by the English, John would make no discernible efforts to recover custody of his wife or win her a reprieve from the terrible conditions she was being held under.

John of Buchan was not predisposed to forgive Robert for the murder of his family members in Greyfriars Church, their former rivalry mutating into an implacable opposition to all things Bruce. Since Bruce was now openly claiming the kingship of Scotland and promising to lead his new subjects in a definitive rebuttal of Edward's imperial pretensions, John and the remaining Comyn allies found themselves fighting on the English side after more than a decade of staggered opposition to their occupation.[95] As we have seen, the Bruces had already recruited extensive allies from among the traditional regional rivals of the Balliol and Comyn allies.

The conflation of this historic rivalry, the struggle between two Scottish aristocratic factions for the throne and the war to oust Edward's occupying English forces, was a major boon to King Robert and a hindrance to the Comyns. With the once chaotic and tangled loyalties of the Scottish aristocracy becoming increasing delineated, the Bruces were able to mobilise the now ingrained anti-English sentiment of otherwise unaffiliated or neutral members of the Scottish aristocracy to solicit their aid against the Comyns. They were abetted in this by the initial slow pace of this new phase of the war. Buchan was not nearly as talented a soldier or leader as his slain cousin, while Edward I was suffering from increasingly ill health. At the same time, internal rivalries and a lack of clear leadership among Edward's English deputies hampered any co-ordinated action against Robert.

Edward I died in February of 1307 while in the middle of raising troops for a fresh invasion of Scotland.[96] His son and successor, Edward II, continued the planned expedition into Scotland but did little more than accept the homage of those Scottish lords who already supported him before departing for England.[97] Robert de Bruce seized upon this lack of drive and focus and turned his attention upon his now unsupported Comyn enemies. Having swiftly reduced Comyn lands in Galloway, Robert turned his attention to their primary power base in the north of Scotland. The following campaign was slowed by a bout of ill health on the new Scottish king's part, but the Comyns under the Earl of Buchan's leadership were unable to or unwilling to press this advantage. A still ill and partially incapacitated Bruce led his forces to the victory over the Comyns at the Battle of Inverurie.[98]

Far more terrible than the battle, however, was what was to come after. Commonly referred to as the Harrying of Buchan, the Bruces were determined to break the Comyn hold over the region once and for all. Robert, alongside his younger brother, Edward, destroyed all of the Comyn castles in the area and allowed their army to pillage freely, carrying off all the region's mobile wealth and burning the rest.[99] John, now bereft of supporters and destitute, fled south to the court of Edward II, where he died shortly afterwards. The Comyns had held a position of almost unparalleled prominence within the Scottish aristocracy since the reign of Alexander II. They had played a vital leadership role in the interregnum, led the Balliol government in all but name and consistently formed the core of Scottish aristocratic opposition to English attempts to exert authority in Scotland. Following the murders at Greyfriars and Robert the Bruce's coronation, they had found themselves consistently outmanoeuvred and firmly associated with the overlords they had once so energetically opposed.

Robert would continue his bid to drive the English out of Scotland and secure his position on the throne, but this was a slow process. Many Scottish aristocrats continued to switch sides in reaction to the changing fortunes of war, just as Robert had once done. Robert's position as king was therefore not truly secure until his spectacular victory over Edward II at Bannockburn. In the aftermath of his decisive triumph, Bruce sought to further consolidate his power and suitably reward the inner circle of battle-tested wartime allies by confiscating the lands of those Scottish aristocrats who had opposed his claims to the throne, drastically altering the face of the Scottish nobility. In the following chapter we will examine the circumstances surrounding the exile of the disinherited, many of whom were Comyn relatives and associates, the formation of the Disinherited in England and the changing face of the Scottish political community under the Bruces.

Chapter Four

A New Scotland and the Fate of the Exiles

Following the collapse of the Balliol regime with the disastrous defeat at Dunbar in 1296 and the subsequent capture of King John I, the war in Scotland adopted a curiously tidal pattern. New developments such as John Balliol's release from English custody in 1302 or proposed changes in the administration of Edward's occupation of Scotland would trigger local uprisings. Such rebellions were largely unco-ordinated and piecemeal; targeted, at least initially, at local and regional manifestations of English power. With Edward I preoccupied by a range of far more pressing foreign and domestic issues, suppression of the rebels was initially entrusted to his lieutenants in Scotland, many of whom were either members of the Scottish aristocracy or relied heavily upon their co-operation. When, however, Scottish resistance reached a tipping point, Edward would march north with a large army to re-establish his proxy administration within the kingdom.[1] Having done so, he would return to England with the majority of his army.[2]

Each iteration of the cycle over the many uprisings that took place during the decade following John Balliol's imprisonment and forced abdication had its own nuances, unique events, and rotating cast of characters. Nevertheless, these allow for an examination of some of the systematic weaknesses of the Guardianship and Scottish resistance to Edward's attempt to assert overlordship during this period. Setting aside the actions undertaken by regional powerbrokers and actors, the Guardians' strategic aims were largely limited and conservative in nature.

While the Guardianship acted as an effective rallying point for aristocratic resistance, its authority was, almost by design, diffuse and dependent upon its various incumbents. They were fundamentally exemplars and representatives of the Scottish aristocracy rather than its commanders; leadership, when exercised at all, was heavily caveated and unevenly applied. The Guardians were largely composed of and selected by the members of the Scottish aristocracy, whose continued support they depended upon. However, this system was inherently fragile because these aristocratic factions had both the most to lose in a rebellion and were the most capable of pursuing independent action, including striking separate agreements with Edward. This meant that they were strategically skittish and prone to abandoning ship at the first significant setback.

It is notable that the most prominent exception to this tendency towards strategic passivity, William Wallace's raid into northern England, occurred at the zenith of Scottish military success and was planned and executed while Wallace was sole Guardian.[3] In contrast, as we have seen, most other iterations of the Guardianship were composed of anywhere between three and a dozen individual Guardians. While Wallace's exact origins and personal history are a source of much historical debate, the general consensus suggests that he came from a social stratum far below that of the Sottish earls, barons, and great aristocratic families from which the Guardians were traditionally drawn.[4] These nobles would eventually prove all too ready to hang Wallace out to dry, ultimately accepting Edward I's demand that he be excluded from a carefully negotiated general truce.[5]

In the form preferred by the majority of its members, to which they returned, albeit with tweaks in numbers and membership, time and time again the Guardianship and the political establishment it represented proved ill-suited to the demands of the war they found themselves embroiled in. Continued infighting over the crown, the Guardians' disinclination to test their authority and the aristocracy's overriding preoccupation with securing their individual interests, all meant that Scotland under the Guardianship was largely constrained to a limited defensive war. Much of the fighting took place on a regional level, directed and carried out by local factions.

In an odd sense, the upper echelons of the aristocracy never really progressed beyond the tactically scaled, cavalry-based vision of warfare that had led to the disaster at Dunbar. Even the much-celebrated victory at the Battle of Roslin in 1303, won by the then Guardian John Comyn the Red of Badenoch, was little more than a pyrrhic victory. The English army surprised and routed by Comyn and his supporters was an advanced force dispatched by Edward to reconnoitre the area and prepare for the imminent arrival of the royal English host. When this main force arrived shortly afterwards, the Comyns and their allies once again felt they had little choice but to sue for peace. They struck what was in the circumstances a reasonably generous bargain with Edward that would preserve their landed interests and enmesh them at the centre of the English king's developing Scottish administration. In doing so, the Comyns not only ended their resistance to Edward's rule but displaced the Bruces as Edward's primary Scottish allies.

The coronation of Robert the Bruce as King of Scotland in 1306 marked the first faltering steps towards breaking this pattern and imposing a new more assertive dynamic upon Scottish resistance to English overlordship. The coronation was attended by four of the Scottish earls, the Bishops of St Andrews and Glasgow, as well as representatives of aristocratic families deeply committed to the Bruce cause, such as the Douglas, Hays and the Campbells.[6] It was an impressive gathering of support but one that still represented a distinct minority of the overall Scottish aristocracy. Despite a number of early setbacks, including a stinging defeat at the Battle of Methven, Robert and his committed circle of allies conducted a focused and aggressive series of campaigns.

The objective of this new spree of martial activity and the developing propaganda campaign that accompanied it was twofold: to refute English claims to overlordship of Scotland and to secure Robert's place on the throne of Scotland.[7] One of Robert's great achievements, considerably reinforced in the minds of later generations by historians writing during the reigns of his Stewart successors, was the conflation of these two goals.[8] While they had done so largely ineffectively, the Guardians and the Scottish aristocracy had through their frequent rebellions and calls to arms, made their antipathy for English overlordship clear. More populist rebel leaders, such as Andrew de Moray and William Wallace, were effusive in their support for the banished Balliol monarchy.

Moreover, it was not as if prior to 1306, Bruce or his allies had been a model of competency or conviction when it came to opposing the English. As we examined in the previous chapter, Robert's main goal over the previous decade had been to manoeuvre into a position, any position, that would best support another bid for the Scottish throne. He had frequently aligned himself with Edward in opposition to Balliol loyalists.[9] For example, in 1302, with his position threatened by the possible return of John Balliol to Scotland, Bruce once again reached an accommodation with Edward, marrying Elizabeth de Burgh whose father, the Red Earl of Ulster, was a close friend and ally of the English king.[10] Of course, such rapprochements were always temporary and Robert's savvy jockeying for advantage would see him once again switch sides whenever the opportunity presented itself to insinuate himself among the leadership of the Scottish opposition or when further adherence to the English threatened to unravel his power base.

The majority of the Scottish political community had good reason to discount the legality and binding nature of John Balliol's forced abdication in 1296. Indeed, both the Papacy and the King of France continued to regard John as the rightful King of Scotland for more than a decade following his imprisonment by Edward. Yet his extended absence and apparent unwillingness to return to Scotland when the opportunity became available was a major boon for Robert and the Bruce cause. The Comyns and other Balliol relatives dominated the Guardianship, rallying the Scottish aristocracy around the principles of the treaty of Birgham. Yet the continued lack of an actual monarch and their failure to make any long-term gains against the English not only placed limitations upon their authority but had the potential to erode the legitimacy of their leadership and position at the heart of the Scottish political community. Another, at the time, largely unremarked upon consequence of Balliol's absence was that even his supporters and relatives had little practical incentive to uphold Balliol claims and were largely free to bargain away acknowledgment of Edward's overlordship to preserve their wider interests.

As noted in the previous chapter, Robert evidently felt it was worthwhile to re-stage his coronation because of the arrival of a member of the Macduff family, who traditionally coronated Scottish kings.[11] That he did so reveals a profound anxiety in regard to whether or not the larger Scottish political community would regard his coronation as legitimate. As farcical as it may have appeared to those attending the repeat coronation, they were already committed supporters of the Bruce cause, heavily invested in his success. It was far more important, given the relatively small number of aristocrats participating in his acclamation, that word be able to spread throughout Scotland that the Bruce was coronated in accordance with the distinctive traditions of the Scottish monarchy.

The Scottish political community was still broadly dominated by the Comyns and other Balliol adherents, while Robert's largely self-proclaimed kingship was of dubious constitutionality. Faced with these difficulties, Robert and his relatively small but dedicated cadre of followers attempted to secure recognition of his kingship, primarily through direct military action. From his coronation in 1306 to Bannockburn and beyond, Robert the Bruce and his allies waged an aggressive and ultimately highly effective war to secure control of Scotland. A facet often overlooked in popular reckonings of the Bruce faction's victory in the First War of Scottish Independence is that a great deal of the fighting carried out to secure the Bruce kingship was aimed at their fellow Scots. As we shall see, this was particularly the case during the period before the triumph at Bannockburn and the expansionary campaigns into Ireland and northern England that followed.

Edward I died in the summer of 1207.[12] His eldest son and successor, Edward II, was beset by a number of domestic issues and crises that diverted his attention from the war in Scotland.[13] Because of their great expense and the somewhat precarious state of English royal finances during this period, the English garrisons in Scotland were relatively small, scattered across key castles and settlements throughout the kingdom.[14] The limited capacity of Edward II's English commanders and proxies for co-ordinated military action meant that the English king's position in Scotland was heavily reliant upon the continued co-operation of those members of the Scottish nobility who had been persuaded to acknowledge his overlordship. Ultimately, the lack of resources and attention Edward II invested in the war in Scotland allowed Bruce and his allies to systemically target their Scottish rivals.

This was the fate of the Comyns. One of the great strengths of the Bruce campaign to secure Scotland was its ruthless and incisive pursuit of direct military action against its enemies. Time and time again, the Bruces and their allies decisively seized the initiative, forcing their rivals, who were on the whole largely satisfied with maintaining the status quo, to react to them. The Comyns had dominated the inner circle of the Balliol royal government and had as a result developed a fierce and keenly felt rivalry with the Bruce family. This rivalry was, of course, immeasurably deepened by the Greyfriars murder, which led to the Comyns soliciting English support to better combat the mutual threat posed by the Bruces. In an attempt to refute Robert's claim to the throne, the Comyns, almost by accident, found themselves stranded on the side of an English monarchy who they had spent the last decade intermittently, but sincerely, trying to eject from Scottish politics.

This allowed Robert to effectively conflate his bid for the Scottish kingship with opposition to English overlordship and occupation; a growing perception that allowed him to mobilise anti-English sentiment and recruit among otherwise neutral or uncommitted members of the Scottish aristocracy.[15] Following the routing of the Comyn army under the somewhat inept leadership of Earl John Comyn of Buchan, Bruce's forces ravaged the Comyn heartlands, reaving and killing in an attempt to break the family's power base.[16] As barbarous as this act was, it signalled to Robert's remaining enemies the stakes of the conflict and the high price of opposing his bid for the Scottish kingship. The remaining Comyn family members were forced to flee and seek shelter with their numerous relatives or newfound English allies.

Of course, the Comyns were far from the only Scottish aristocratic family to oppose Bruce ambitions for the throne. While the Bruce party's rhetoric and propaganda continued to develop throughout the conflict, their most effective recruitment tool among the Scottish aristocracy remained military action. Some of the time this even meant focused military action against a particular family or affinity in order to force their submission and acknowledgment of Bruce kingship. When it came to undertaking such military actions, the Bruces and their allies enjoyed a number of structural and strategic advantages.

The Bruces and their party had first come together as a result of their mutual opposition to Balliol rule. This meant that many of Robert's most dedicated supporters already had strong historical and regional rivalries with Balliol supporters and relatives, the segment of the aristocracy most consistent in their opposition to his rule. Robert therefore could call upon dedicated allies strategically placed to support military action against his most committed enemies. Robert's campaign against the Comyn- and Balliol-aligned MacDougall family in 1308, for instance, enjoyed the support of the Lords of Argyll and the Bruces' other Hebridean allies who, as noted previously, had long resented and resisted MacDougall primacy in the region.[17] Similarly, Earl William of Ross' attempts to oppose Robert and come to his relatives' aid in 1307 were consistently hampered by attacks from the Bruce-aligned MacRuairis family, who were based within the western reaches of the earldom.[18] This struggle left the earl in such a tenuous and isolated position that he swiftly capitulated to Robert when confronted by him the following year.[19] Like Edward I before him, Robert the Bruce's main method of recruitment among the Scottish aristocracy was the application of military pressure.

It was fortunate then that Robert proved to be highly successful in his efforts to win the long-term support and co-operation of many members of the Scottish aristocracy, even those members whose initial submission involved a degree of coercion. Several such converts came to play important roles within the nascent Bruce administration, such as Earl William of Ross, Thomas Randolph and James Stuart.[20] The core members of Robert's developing inner circle would stay with Robert as he made the transition from warlord and self-proclaimed king to the acknowledged head of the Scottish political community.

Even though he counted Bishop Robert Wishart of Glasgow and Bishop William de Lamberton of St Andrews among his closest supporters, one of the major stumbling blocks facing Robert in his struggle to exert royal authority was that he had been excommunicated for the murder of John Comyn the Red within Greyfriars Church. In 1309, the Papacy, while inconsistent in regard to its stance on English overlordship of Scotland, still maintained a degree of sympathy for the banished John Balliol.[21] It was certainly not inclined to throw its support behind an excommunicated murderer.

By 1309, John Balliol had long ceased to be an effective figurehead; indeed most of his relatives and former supporters were so deeply threatened by the incoming Bruce tide that they were now willing to side with his English tormentors. Yet he remained both very much alive and someone who had been legally crowned King of Scotland.

The Declaration of the Clergy, produced by Bruce propagandists for circulation during the 1309 parliament that he held in St Andrews, was a manifesto meant to further cultivate Bruce support by expounding upon the details and righteousness of his claim to the throne. It also signalled that Bruce had the support of important sections of the Scottish church.[22] The phantom of Balliol kingship presented the Bruce party with a rhetorical and legal challenge, which in turn imposed complications upon their bid to win further Scottish support.

In response to these concerns, the Declaration of the Clergy outlined Bruce's hereditary right to the throne and attempted to position him as the legitimate and natural successor to the Dunkeld kings.[23] John Balliol's reign was dismissed as a demonically sponsored aberration, not to be counted among the glorious annals of Scottish kingship.[24] The Declaration further attempted to sidestep these legal quibbles by placing an extremely strong emphasis upon Robert's role as a war leader and his forceful reconstruction of royal authority within the kingdom.[25] It was a feat that required both the taming of those members of the Scottish aristocracy opposed to his rule and the ejection of the English. While clearly meant to be circulated throughout Scotland, the contention that Robert had restored the Kingdom of Scotland and the monarchy's rightful and ancient place at its heart was in 1309 rather premature. In fact, the 1309 parliament was not well attended, composed only of long-term Bruce supporters and the modest number of nobles whose submission he had extracted over the past three years.[26] In practice, Bruce control over many of the areas represented within the parliament was minimal or hotly contested. Large segments of the Scottish nobility still rejected Robert's claim to the throne, finding themselves increasingly aligned with the English.

While many of the claims put forward during the 1309 parliament at St Andrews were rather grandiose in nature, they formed the rhetorical foundations upon which Robert would build his royal administration. In the years that followed, Bruce and his allies eagerly capitalised upon Edward II's lack of decisive intervention in Scotland by continuing to systemically isolate and reduce both English garrisons and the forces of their traditional Scottish rivals. As one by one the Bruce's internal opponents capitulated or felt compelled to throw their lot in with the English, Scottish politics came to be dominated by the clique of hardcore supporters and military companions that had gathered around Bruce. Following his successful occupation of Linlithgow late in the summer of 1313, Robert and his newly ascendant allies felt sufficiently confident in their position to dramatically ramp up the pressure placed on their remaining Scottish opponents.

Robert issued a proclamation that those Scots aligned with Edward II and the English had a year to acknowledge and submit to Bruce rule, otherwise their Scottish lands would be forfeited and confiscated by the crown.[27] With Robert's star now firmly in the ascendancy, this ultimatum provoked his remaining Scottish enemies to dispatch immediate pleas for aid to Edward II.[28] Perhaps sensing that this would be the last opportunity to salvage the rapidly deteriorating situation in Scotland, or even calculating that a victorious foreign war would shore up his shaky position within England, the hitherto disengaged Edward II prepared for battle. Meanwhile, the Bruce party, unwilling to rest on their laurels while they waited for their ultimatum to expire, continued to campaign vigorously within Scotland.

This strategic pugnaciousness had consequences, however, and the Bruce party's success had not been without cost. When Robert had first declared his kingship in 1306, he had done so in the knowledge that he could count on the full-hearted support of his four younger brothers. Their commitment to securing their family's position on the throne of Scotland was an important consideration given that the Bruce's immediate heir was his ten-year-old daughter, Majorie.[29] Neil, who had been entrusted with the safety of Robert's wife and daughter, had been captured and executed by the English in 1306. Thomas and Alexander died in similar circumstances the following year.[30] The brothers, alongside their ally, Reginald Crawford, had invaded the Balliol stronghold of Galloway with an army freshly raised from among the Bruce's Irish allies. They were soundly defeated and captured by Comyn ally Dungal MacDougall, who handed his captives over to the English, who promptly executed them.[31]

In 1314, Robert's remaining brother, Edward, who had come to occupy an increasingly important role within his brother's inner circle, began the siege of Stirling Castle.[32] Its capture would be a major coup for the Bruce party, who had issued a demand for its surrender at the same time as the ultimatum demanding the swift submission of their Scottish opponents. The castle controlled access to the easiest and most-travelled route between the lowlands and highlands of Scotland. Many contemporary maps actually portrayed Scotland as two separate islands connected by Stirling Bridge.[33] The strategic importance of this location was such that it had already seen a considerable amount of fighting, most notably the great Scottish victory won by Andrew de Moray and William Wallace at the Battle of Stirling Bridge in 1297.

Determined to prevent the castle falling into Bruce hands, however belatedly, Edward II set out for Stirling at the head of a formidable army.[34] In his haste to relieve the castle, Edward may have pushed his army, made up of around twenty to twenty-five thousand men, inadvisably hard. The Bruces countered by mustering their own, much smaller army, and moving to intercept the English force. The Scottish position was chosen astutely, blocking Edward's route to Stirling, it deployed on a swathe of marshy ground with their backs anchored by a patch of woodlands originally cultivated as a hunting reserve for use by the castle's inhabitants.[35] The ensuing Battle of Bannockburn would prove to be a decisive Scottish victory that secured Robert's place firmly on the throne of Scotland.

On the first day of the battle, 23 June 1314, with much of their exhausted army still struggling into position, the English knights launched two impetuous cavalry charges. Hampered by the ground and a lack of support, both attacks were beaten back by the well-led and resolute Scottish army. The first of these attacks was led by Edwards II's nephew, Gilbert de Clare, the Earl of Gloucester, and Humphrey de Bohun, the Earl of Hereford.[36] Neither were strangers to the war in Scotland. Gilbert was the son of Joan of Acre, the eldest daughter of Edward I, whose potential right to inherit the throne of England the king had moved so carefully to preserve during his arbitration of the Scottish succession crisis in 1292.[37] Upon securing his inheritance and earldom in 1308, the sixteen-year-old Gilbert threw himself into the conflict in Scotland and was appointed as warden of Scotland later that year.[38] In this capacity, he spearheaded attempts to break the Bruce siege of Rutherglen Castle.[39] Further commands and the captaincy of the Scottish marchers followed in 1309, despite his lack of experience or substantial land holdings within the region. However, much like Edward II himself, Gilbert's attention was increasingly drawn south and towards the bitter struggle for control erupting within the royal English court.

A seasoned campaigner, Humphrey de Bohun can be identified as a member of the English army with which Edward I besieged Caerlaverock Castle in 1300.[40] Despite an incident in which Humphrey and number of other knights, including future royal favourite Piers Gravestone, drew

Edward I's ire by abandoning the war in Scotland to attend a tournament in England, the earl served in the king's Scottish campaigns consistently and with distinction.[41] He was married to Edward's daughter, Elizabeth of Rhuddlan, in 1302.[42] In recognition of his military service and connection to the English royal family, Humphrey was granted a large portion of the Scottish lands confiscated in the wake of Robert's coronation.[43] This included control of the Lordship of Annandale, the Bruce family's original and longest-held Scottish estate. Annandale had finally been recaptured by Robert and his supporters in 1312 but Humphrey, who would still have regarded it as very much his own, was eager to reclaim his lost Scottish territories.

Some English sources suggest that a partial reason for the rash and disorganised nature of this initial charge was the two earls' inability to decide who would lead it, and Hereford's reluctance to accept the younger Gloucester's authority as Constable. After the failure of this charge, a second attack was organised under the leadership of Robert Clifford and Henry de Beaumont.[44] Robert Clifford, Lord of Clifford, Skipton and Appleby, was among the most experienced and talented members of the English host. He had taken part in Edward's initial campaign to overthrow John Balliol in 1296, during which he was granted his own command and charged with securing the submission of Irvine.[45] He participated in the English victory at the Battle of Falkirk in 1298, during which he sufficiently distinguished himself that the king made him castellan of Nottingham castle.[46] He earnt further acclaim during the siege of Caerlaverock and the surrounding campaign. In addition, he held the position of Warden of the Scottish Marches. Following Edward II's accession to the throne, Clifford was briefly made Marshal of England before being appointed as head of Edward II's administration within Scotland.[47]

Henry de Beaumont, a French-born nobleman and adventurer in English service, will, as we shall see, become a founding member of the Disinherited and one of the masterminds behind their audacious invasion of Scotland in 1332. The son of Louis of Brienne and his wife Viscountess Agnes of Beaumont, Henry took part in Edward I's Flanders campaign.[48] While Henry's decision to fight with the English against his king, Philip IV of France, may seem strange, his sister, Isabella, was married to the prominent English noble John de Vesci, who was a close friend of Edward I. Despite his native Maine's firm allegiance to Philip, Henry, who had two elder brothers, may simply have decided his chances of inheritance in Maine were so remote that he would need to seek his fortune further afield. The young Beaumont, no doubt enabled by his connection to Vesci, followed Edward from Flanders as part of the king's expanded military entourage, in which capacity he would eventually take part in the Battle of Falkirk.

During his time in English royal service, Henry managed to insinuate himself within the Prince of Wales' circle of friends. Beaumont's affinity with the younger Edward began to pay substantial dividends upon the latter's coronation. Henry was awarded a large collection of estates in Lincolnshire, which were greatly supplemented in 1310s when he was given the Lordship of the Isle of Man. The Lordship of Man appears to have been stripped from Henry, never to be returned, during his temporary exile from court, by the opponents of his friend Piers Gravestone. Despite this loss, Henry was soon welcomed back to court alongside his new bride, Alice Comyn, the Countess of Buchan.[49] Alice was the daughter of Alexander Comyn, Earl John Comyn of Buchan's younger brother, and Joana Latimer.[50] Upon his defeat and ejection from Buchan by Robert Bruce, Earl John had sort shelter among his English allies, living in exile on this family's English estates until his death in 1308.[51] He was notionally succeeded by his niece, Alice, despite the effective loss of the now ravaged earldom to Bruce and his allies.

As militarily ill-advised as his and Clifford's charge was, Beaumont had an earldom to win back, his wife's ancestral seat, and such a prize could never be secured though passivity or the avoidance of risk. Our brief overview of the careers of the quartet of nobleman that directed these attacks during the battle's opening day demonstrates the tangled nature of contemporary politics and the effects of nearly two decades of war. These men and their companions and subordinates were not fighting for some vague or abstract notion such as one kingdom or one culture's superiority over another. Modern conceptions of nationalism were utterly foreign to them.

Instead, they had come to fight in Scotland because they were self-identified members of a martial class who expected to reap immediate material benefits from participation in war. Humphrey de Bohun had enjoyed ownership of the captured Bruce estates in Annandale until the vagaries of military fortune had seen them recaptured by Robert's revanchist campaign.

The family of Henry de Beaumont's wife had lost their long-held position of political prominence within Scotland and the majority of their landed estates as a result of their opposition to the Bruce monarchy. Even Robert Clifford and Gilbert de Clare rode to war in the knowledge that victory not only meant loot but the likely restoration of the profitable offices they had previously held within the English king's administration of occupied Scotland.

Following the dismal failure of these cavalry charges on the opening day of the battle, Edward and his commanders spent much of the evening shifting his army across the titular Bannockburn so that they might more easily come to grips with the Scottish host. However, in doing so, they traded space for ease of access, finding themselves crowded and cramped on the small amount of solid ground available. On the morning of the second day, Robert the Bruce boldly seized upon this opportunity and the hesitancy the previous day's defeats had engendered within Edward's army by launching an immediate attack.[52]

Once again, the commanders of the English army bickered among themselves, provoking the Earl of Gloucester into launching yet another frontal cavalry charge. The smaller Scottish army pushed back the leading elements of the English host, before trapping the English army against the burn and surrounding boglands. Deprived of the space they needed to manoeuvre or fight effectively, the English soon became disordered and began to panic. Edward II had to be wrestled away from the battlefield by his household knights, who could plainly see that the day was lost. This withdrawal heralded the full-blown rout of his remaining troops who, hampered by the difficult terrain, were pursued ruthlessly by the victorious Scottish army. Edward would flee to the dubious safety afforded to him by his ally, Earl Patrick of Dunbar. From there, the king and his immediate entourage were whisked away on a fishing boat that delivered them safely back to England. The defeat at Bannockburn severely damaged Edward II's already badly tarnished prestige and authority. While he was able to keep the throne, the welter of recriminations that followed saw Edward decisively sidelined and effective royal authority was delegated to his cousin, Earl Thomas of Lancaster.[53]

Earl Gilbert de Clare of Gloucester and Robert Clifford were among the many dead of the defeated English army, as was the disputed Lord of

Badenoch, John Comyn IV.[54] John was the son of John Comyn the Red of Badenoch and his wife Joan de Valence, the sister of Earl Aymer of Pembroke. Joan and Aymer's father, Willam de Valence, was the maternal half-brother of King Henry III of England, making them first cousins of the now deceased Edward I and acknowledged members of the extended English royal family.[55] Indeed, Edward had brokered the marriage of his cousin to John the Red sometime during his lengthy arbitration of the Scottish succession crisis. John, the rising star of the Comyn family, was the maternal nephew of Edward's preferred royal candidate, John Balliol. This meant that John and Joan's marriage would have strengthened Edward's connection to the Balliol party, his chosen instrument for the exercise of overlordship within Scotland. When his father, John the Red, was murdered in 1306, John IV of Badenoch's mother sent him to shelter with his English relatives. Earl Aymer de Valence was also a member of the English army at Bannockburn, and it seems probable that the twenty-something-year-old John accompanied his uncle to war, eager for a chance to avenge himself against his father's murderer and reclaim his lost lordship.[56]

It seems that John died amidst the chaos of the Earl of Gloucester's initial cavalry charge. Of course, not all enemy combatants were simply killed out of hand. When describing the death of the Earl of Gloucester in the same action, one English chronicle suggests that in his haste to meet the advancing Bruce army, the earl neglected to don his identifying heraldry and was therefore not recognised by his killers.[57] Although strained by the excesses of a lengthy war and the English king's execution of several Scottish nobles who refused to recognise English overlordship, the conventions of aristocratic chivalric culture dictated that enemy nobles were to be taken alive whenever possible.[58] This convention was reinforced and underpinned by powerful financial incentives in the form of the often-exorbitant ransoms captured nobles or their families would pay for their release.

The death of anyone as high ranking as an earl in battle was relatively rare and evidently required some sort of explanation, no matter how tenuous. The most probable explanation, although one that would not have been very assuring to the members of the early fourteenth-century aristocracy, is that both Earl Gilbert and John were killed in a chaotic and hard-fought phase of the battle in which the pressed Scottish soldiery had neither the inclination nor luxury to identify individual enemies.

One of the reasons why the Battle of Bannockburn proved to be so decisive in securing Robert's position on the Scottish throne, beyond the obvious thwarting of Edward's attempts to relieve Stirling Castle, was the large number of prisoners taken by the Bruce's army. This included several of his remaining Scottish opponents who had fought alongside Edward's army, such as Balliol relative and former Guardian of Scotland Ingram de Umfraville, as well as Earl Robert de Umfraville of Angus. Others such as William de Soules and Earl Patrick of Dunbar hurried to make their submissions to the Bruce king in the immediate aftermath of the battle, the latter pausing only to ensure Edward II's escape.[59] The triumphant King Robert the Bruce was also able to use the large number of English nobles captured during the battle, such as Humphrey de Bohun, John Seagrave and Ralph de Monthermer, to negotiate the withdrawal of the remaining English garrisons in Scotland. Just as his propogandists had boasted five years earlier at the St Andrews parliament, Robert the Bruce had through force of arms and by dint of his military prowess reconstructed the authority of the Scottish monarchy and dismantled the English occupation of his kingdom.

Scant months after the battle, Robert made good on the threat that had initially provoked Edward's expedition. At a parliament convened at the site of the battle, he declared the lands of those Scottish aristocrats in English service who had died during the battle or who still refused to submit to his rule, forfeit.[60] This meant that Galloway, Badenoch, the earldoms of Buchan, Angus and Atholl, the great swathe of land formerly controlled by the MacDougalls in and around Argyll and a plethora of smaller lordships and conglomerations of estates now fell under Bruce control. As previously noted, Bruce propaganda sought to legitimise his claim to the kingship and sidestep the difficulties created by the practically defunct but theoretically still extant Balliol kingship. This strategy continued even as the Bruce party gained effective control of more and more of the kingdom, transitioning from a military alliance of aristocratic families to a royal government. More than fifty of the acts passed by Robert during his tenure as king made explicit reference to his status as the direct successor of Alexander III.[61]

Despite this rhetorical emphasis on continuity with the former Scottish political establishment, the ascendancy of the Bruce party and the mass confiscation of lands that followed its victory at Bannockburn radically reshaped the face of Scottish politics. Robert Bruce and his allies had in eight years of warfare decisively overthrown the dominant political faction within Scotland and driven them into exile. In the place of the Comyns and their network of relatives, the Bruce's war-hardened coterie of long-term allies shouldered their way into the forefront of the Scottish political establishment.

This transformation was cemented by the gradual distribution of these confiscated lands among the Bruce's supporters, most notably members of the Douglas, Stewart, MacDonald and Campbell families who had helped the Bruces take the war to their mutual Comyn- and Balliol-aligned rivals. Neil Campbell, a long-term Bruce adherent who was married to the king's sister, Mary, was granted a large chunk of land confiscated from the now exiled David Strathbogie.[62] In 1320, Neil and Mary's son, John Campbell, was formally granted the Earldom of Atholl. Two years prior to the victory at Bannockburn, another of the king's nephews, Thomas Randolph, had been granted the newly created Earldom of Moray, the heart of which was built around the former Comyn lordships of Badendoch and Lochaber.[63]

In 1328, the king granted the Earldom of Angus to Lord John Stewart of Bonkyll.[64] John's father, Alexander, had initially opposed the Bruce kingship but was forced to submit in 1308, after which he served his former enemy loyally. This transition in loyalty was no doubt aided by his many Stewart and Douglas relatives within the Bruce faction. Confiscated lands in Lothian, parts of which had fiercely resisted the imposition of Bruce authority, were divided among the Bruce's local supporters such as Robert Lauder, Alexander Seton, and Henry Sinclair.[65] The Earldom of Buchan was similarly divided among the Bruce's supporters, while the Lordship of Galloway was placed under the control of Robert's remaining brother, Edward. In addition to these large grants, many other Bruce allies across the kingdom found their holdings substantially enhanced by the spoils of war.[66]

Such gifts not only drew upon those resources taken from the Bruce's vanquished enemies but stretched to encompass lands and incomes derived from the royal demesne and even lands traditionally held by the Bruce family. Thomas Randolph's Earldom of Moray was enhanced with grants of royal land in Elgin and Nairn.[67] In addition, Thomas, who had rapidly emerged as one of the Bruce's most able and dedicated military commanders, was granted the lordship of the Bruce family's ancestral lands in Annandale as a way to further protect the border.[68] In a similar vein, James Douglas, another of Robert's inner circle of trusted lieutenants, was granted Selkirk and Jedburgh.[69] Edward Bruce was granted the Earldom of Carrick.[70] Robert had previously held the earldom himself and it had first entered the Bruce sphere with their mother, Marjorie of Carrick. The grant placed Edward in a position of primacy within the south-west of Scotland, allowing him to exercise royal authority within the region and effectively police neighbouring and ever-troublesome Galloway on his brother's behalf. In total, Robert made grants of lands from thirty of the royal thanages, lands that represented the crown's principal source of income.

Robert granted the hereditary shrievalties of Dumbarton and Cromarty to the earls of Lennox and Ross respectively. Both earls had oscillated in their loyalties to Robert.[71] Earl Malcolm of Lennox's father had been a Bruce supporter but he himself had sworn allegiance to Edward II in order to prevent the English king from creating a rival Earl of Lennox.[72] When threats to the security of his earldom dissipated with successive Bruce victories in the late 1300s and early 1310s, Malcolm defected to Robert's party willingly and eagerly. As we saw earlier, Earl William of Ross initially opposed Bruce before being forced to submit to the would-be king. However, even after this submission, the earl continued to equivocate and was among those Scottish nobles who wrote to Edward II encouraging him to intervene more forcefully in Scotland. Such men, always searching for their own advantage but too powerful and influential to remove easily, required incentive for their future loyalty.

This strategy was at the heart of the Bruce's redistribution of resources and restructuring of the aristocracy. Such grants were meant not only as a reward for services rendered but a way of securing the aristocracies' future co-operation. By granting the lion's share of these rewards to his most faithful and effective followers, the king was not only incentivising them to defend and support the exercise of Bruce royal authority but granting them the resources to do so more effectively. Naturally, those nobles who received the greatest and most immediate rewards were his inner circle of trusted and effective supporters. Prior to Bannockburn, Edward Bruce, Thomas Randolph and James Douglas, had established themselves as Robert's most trusted and able lieutenants by dint of their ferocity and success in the struggle against the English occupiers and their numerous Scottish allies.

As more and more of the kingdom fell under effective Bruce control and Robert's position on the throne of Scotland seemed increasingly secure, this group of trusted commanders transitioned easily into their new roles within royal government. Edward and Thomas were both provided with substantive ready-made power bases in the south-west and north of Scotland respectively. Both were granted a high degree of independence and latitude, trusted to secure their respective areas of influence for the Bruce monarchy. Alongside James Douglas, who held a similar position of pre-eminence in the borders, they were freed from oversight by the administrative organs of the royal centre. The continued prominence of the Bruce's battle commanders within the royal administration was of particular importance because, as spectacular and effective as it was, the Bruce's victory at Bannockburn did not bring an end to the war.[73]

Victory at Bannockburn had allowed Robert to remove or force the submission of his remaining opponents in Scotland, evict English garrisons from Scottish royal castles and secure the release of his wife and daughter, who had been imprisoned and kept in harsh conditions by the English since their capture in 1306. Rather than attempt to parlay his victory at Bannockburn into a peace treaty or a renunciation of overlordship by Edward II and the pack of English aristocrats that now controlled him, Robert preferred the continuation of hostilities. Perhaps Robert, who derived much of his authority and legitimacy as king from his successful prosecution of the war effort in Scotland, was concerned about the effect of a sudden peace upon his still fledgling government. Alternatively, maybe Bruce and his advisors doubted if Thomas of Lancaster had the authority to negotiate on such a heady topic on behalf of the English crown. It is also possible that Robert was attempting to head off any future invasions of Scotland by the resurgent English.

While it is probable that all these concerns and more occurred to Robert and his allies, the simplest and most crucial factor behind the decision to continue the war was that they were winning. Having, after much effort and tribulations, finally succeeded in driving their enemies from Scotland

and giving the English aristocracy a bloody nose, the victorious Bruces were unwilling to cede the initiative and began to probe deep into northern England. If properly executed, warfare could be highly profitable, presenting as it did numerous opportunities to gather loot, ransom noble captives and gain new estates and territories. In the aftermath of the Comyns' defeat in Buchan, the earldom was deliberately and purposefully ravaged by the victorious Bruce army in an attempt to break Comyn power permanently, siphoning off or destroying its wealth and resources. In Lothian, Bruce loyalists used the threat of violence to extort considerable sums of money from unaffiliated or English-aligned communities and noble families.[74] The north of England now found itself subject to these same policies and practices.[75]

Robert resurrected Scotland's historical claims within the region, capitalising upon the ambiguity surrounding which territories and titles the Scottish kings had previously held personally and which they held in their capacity as King of Scotland. With this narrative in place, Robert wasted no time in granting parcels of this now disputed land to his Scottish followers, incentivising them to secure their new estates by continuing the war in England and signalling his intention to permanently annex northern England.

Much of this fighting and periodic raiding was carried out by Bruce allies based on the Scottish borders, such as James Douglas, and by those families to whom Robert had granted northern English estates.[76] The king also made forays into this warzone at the head of a royal army, often launched with specific objectives in mind, such as in 1315 when he made a concerted effort to capture the English stronghold of Carlisle.[77] Bruce was, of course, intimately familiar with the town and its defences, which in 1306 he successfully held for the English against a Balliol-led Scottish army. With Thomas of Lancaster struggling to exert authority over the English aristocracy and the nobility of northern England largely left to their own defences, the initial limitation upon the success of the campaign in England was a lack of consistent royal Scottish oversight and fresh injections of manpower. The principal reason for these shortages was the parallel war being fought across the sea in Ireland.[78]

The Bruce brothers had a long, if somewhat obscure, familial association with Ireland. They were through their paternal grandmother, Isabel de Clare, descended from Richard de Clare and Aoife MacMurrough.[79] Richard, often known as 'Strongbow', was the Earl of Pembroke and a leading figure in the Anglo-Norman invasion of Ireland.[80] Aofie, his wife, was a daughter of Diarmait Mac Murchada, King of Leinster and Dublin.[81] This provided Edward Bruce with a circuitous claim to the High Kingship of Ireland.

In 1314, King Donnell O'Neill of Tyrone wrote to Robert the Bruce asking for his support against his increasingly aggressive English and English-aligned Anglo-Irish neighbours.[82] There were, of course, several contributing factors to the Bruce's decision to affirmatively answer the King of Tyrone's call for aid and expand his war against the English into Ireland. Firstly, taking the fight against the English to Ireland effectively prevented the bitterly divided and disorganised English leadership from using their considerable martial and financial resources in Ireland to support further hostilities in Scotland. This consideration became even more pressing in January of 1315 because the Isle of Man, which had changed hands several times already in the war, fell to the forces of the English-aligned John of Lorn and the MacDougalls, leaving western Scotland particularly vulnerable to invasion from Ireland.[83]

The second consideration is simply that the war was going very well. The previous decade of warfare had revealed and honed Robert's overriding pragmatism. Robert was perfectly willing to work with and accept the submission of former enemies among the Scottish aristocracy, he even came to welcome the support of Earl William of Ross, who had delivered his wife and daughter into English imprisonment.[84] However, such reconciliations were contingent upon submission to the Bruce's authority as King of Scotland and was therefore a pragmatic means of securing Bruce control of Scotland. When it came to the war with England, Bruce had little reason to abandon a conflict that he was winning and which continued to provide the Scottish political community with a shared endeavour and mutual enemy. Opening up a second front in Ireland was a potential way to capitalise upon his continuing success.

The most important factor in the decision by the Bruces and their partisans to intervene in Ireland was intimately connected to the condition they attached as the price of their support. Bruce forces would come to Donnell O'Neill's aid if he agreed to recognise Robert's brother, Edward Bruce, as High King of Ireland.[85] Donnell's father had previously held the title, yet he accepted Edward's highly dubious claim without any apparent equivocation or further negotiation. That he did so is probably a testament to the pressure the English-aligned Earl of Ulster, and his allies, had placed Donnell under. Of course, Donnell had made no serious attempts to claim the title for himself and was seemingly reconciled to the fact that he lacked sufficient support from the remaining Irish kings and aristocrats.[86]

The Bruce brothers' decision to try to secure the High Kingship of Ireland for Edward and a second kingdom for the family meant that their campaign in Ireland would inevitably be one of conquest and subjugation as well as liberation. The Bruces would have been all too aware that while their actions against the English would win them some measure of support among the Irish aristocracy, others would resist the imposition of another foreign ruler. While the Bruce legal and hereditary case for holding the kingship of Scotland was far more substantive than Edward's phantasmal claim to Ireland, the brothers had already secured one kingdom primarily through force of arms and evidently felt capable of repeating the feat.

During a parliament held in the early summer of 1315, Robert officially recognised Edward as his heir.[87] This articulated the brothers' commitment to one another and the unity of their dynastic course, both within Scotland and Ireland. Of course, it sidelined the claims of Robert's now teenage daughter, Marjorie, leading to her husband, Walter Stewart, developing something of a rivalry with Edward. The other major purpose of holding the parliament in Ayr, a royal burgh and port town located just north of Edward's earldom, was to organise and make provisions for the army that would shortly embark there for Ireland.

At first, the Scottish campaign in Ireland was wildly successful with the two brothers, and their Irish allies, winning a string of battles in 1315 and breaking the power of Richard Óg de Burgh decisively within Ulster.[88] These early successes and the stunning reversal of the English position within Ireland encouraged a small but significant portion of Ireland's kings and princes to acknowledge Edward's High Kingship. Unfortunately for the Bruces, their attempts to exercise royal authority within Ireland and win the support of the larger Irish political community was hampered by a number of issues. While Edward continued to recruit heavily from his own earldom and the Scottish isles, which already shared many cultural and political connections with Ireland, much of Scotland's manpower was needed elsewhere, principally the ongoing war for the control of the north of England.

Edward was a veteran campaigner and an effective leader in his own right, but the personal withdrawal of the Scottish king was inevitably accompanied by the reassignment of crucial resources. Finally, from late 1315 to 1317, Europe was caught in the grips of an extended and devastating famine caused by a spate of bad weather and the subsequent outbreak of disease among malnourished livestock.[89] The famine robbed the Scottish campaign in Ireland of much of its momentum and significantly complicated any further military activity. All of these factors conspiring together meant that by the beginning of 1318, Edward's authority within Ireland was largely limited to the north-east.

This extended period of relative inactivity also allowed many of Edward's Anglo-Irish enemies time to reorganise. In mid-October 1318, Edward's diminished forces were confronted by a small alliance of Anglo-Irish aristocrats led by John de Bermingham and Edmund Butler. Bermingham was the son-in-law of the Earl of Ulster, while Edmund Butler was Edward II's Justicar of Ireland.[90] Earlier that year, Butler had, despite his hitherto poor military record, been granted the Irish Earldom of Carrick by the king. Somewhat amusingly, this meant that there was an Earl of Carrick on both sides of the Battle of Faughart. While the scale of the battle is hard to ascertain from the remaining mutually contradictory sources, the death of Edward Bruce during the battle meant that it was a major strategic defeat for the Scottish. In addition to the no doubt acute personal loss, the death of King Robert's remaining brother heralded the immediate collapse of the Scottish position within Ireland and dashed Bruce hopes of controlling the High Kingship.[91]

The severity of this check to the Bruce party's ambitions and the potential danger of the situation can be seen during the parliament Robert called at Scone upon receiving confirmation of his brother's death. There, Robert announced a raft of statues designed to enable the effective recruitment and provisioning of a royal army.[92] With the personal military resources of the Bruces and their allies drained by the ongoing war in northern England and their defeat in Ireland, Robert now sort to reform the Scottish military and pass some of that burden on to his less-committed subjects. As we have seen, Robert's principal supporters such as the McDonalds and Campbells had fought for the Bruce cause because they had mutual enemies and had a great deal to gain materially from their success. In the process envisaged by these reforms, contributions to the Scottish royal army were to become mandatory and impersonal, simply another obligation owed by subjects to their king.

The terms on which he held Scotland, the ongoing attempts to annex the north of England and win Edward Bruce the High Kingship of Ireland, further emphasised that Robert's ambitions and political horizons were fundamentally dynastic and personal in nature. Intelligent, energetic, and judicious, Robert Bruce was an exemplar of everything an early fourteenth-century European aristocrat aspired to be. He ably negotiated the transition of his supporters from an alliance of warlords co-operating in a campaign against their regional and hereditary enemies to members of a royal government. He generously rewarded his followers, incentivising them to co-operate further with his nascent government but was also careful to allow other members of the Scottish political community, including a number of his former enemies, to benefit from reaching accommodations with the throne.

Robert's most trusted and effective allies were not only enriched by the granting of new titles and lands but given a huge amount of authority and autonomy, trusted to pursue their mutual interests. A large contributing factor to this success was Robert's ruthlessness in confiscating the lands of those Scots who still refused to submit to his kingship. In obliterating the power of the Balliol's former supporters, Robert gained access to the resources he needed to secure his position on the throne through the judicious exercise of kingly largesse.

Almost unavoidably, the Disinherited, those Scottish nobles who had chosen exile in England rather than submit to Bruce kingship, retained numerous familial and personal connections within Scotland. Many former Balliol supporters and relatives had sued for peace, accepting Bruce sovereignty, but they had done so largely in recognition of the Bruce's ongoing military success. Such families, many of which remained considerable regional powers, had every reason to resent the dictates of a king who had cut his way to the throne, sword in hand. Robert's eagerness to legislate upon the raising and maintenance of the royal army was in part motivated by a fear of these internal dissidents and the possibility that they would seek to take advantage of the loss of Edward Bruce, alongside a significant number of experienced warriors, by attempting to shuck off the Bruce kingship.

Another concern for Robert and his allies that had the potential to embolden the remnants of the old political establishment within Scotland was the return of Edward Balliol to England in late 1318.[93] Edward was the only son and immediate heir of the dethroned John Balliol, who had died still in exile in 1314. As the heir of a lawfully coronated King of Scotland, there were those, mainly Balliol relatives or former allies, who believed that Edward was the rightful King of Scotland. Edward was born sometime around the early 1280s, during a period of time in which his father was still attempting to court the favour of Edward I of England. Upon his father's capture in 1296, Edward had been held prisoner within in the Tower of London before being released in 1299 into the custody of his maternal grandfather, and Edward I's chief lieutenant in Scotland, Earl John de Warenne of Surrey.[94] Shortly after this, he was relocated to his family estates within France. His return to England, which may well have been inspired by the news of Edward Bruce's defeat and death in Ireland, provided Scottish nobles that were less than enamoured with Robert's rule with a plausible alternative. In 1319, Edward began to involve himself in Scottish affairs and the ongoing hostilities, serving with the English in their attempts to recapture Berwick, which had finally fallen to Bruce forces the previous year after a lengthy siege.[95]

In 1320, Robert's fears regarding a pro-Balliol insurrection were proven true when a conspiracy by a number of leading Scottish aristocrats to seat Edward on the throne of Scotland was uncovered.[96] The primary leaders of this attempted coup were Willam Soules, after whom the conspiracy is usually named, and his aunt, Countess Agnes Comyn of Strathearn. William, the Lord of Liddesdale and the hereditary Butler of Scotland, was the son of Nichoals Soules and Margaret Comyn, the daughter of Earl Alexander of Buchan. He was therefore the nephew of both Earl John Comyn of Buchan on his mother's side and of John de Soules, the former Guardian of Scotland, on that of his father's.[97]

In accordance with these familial connections and loyalties, William submitted to Edward I in 1304 in the aftermath of the English king's latest campaign in Scotland and the capitulation of the Comyns. William remained in English service and steadfastly opposed to Bruce kingship up until Bannockburn. Finally persuaded to reach an accommodation with Robert in the immediate aftermath of the battle, William was accepted back into the fold by a king eager to consolidate his support among the wider Scottish aristocracy. Despite his former opposition and the awarding of some of his lands to the indefatigable James Douglas, William co-operated closely with the new royal government and by 1318 had been allowed to occupy his hereditary office as Butler of Scotland.[98]

Agnes, William's maternal aunt, was a daughter of Earl Alexander Comyn and his wife Isabella de Quincy. Consequently, both Agnes and William's mother, Margaret, were partial heiresses to their maternal grandmother, Helen of Galloway.[99] In 1275, Agnes married Earl Malise of Strathearn. Malise, probably influenced by this connection to the Comyn and their Balliol relatives, supported John Balliol during the succession crisis and was one of the earls that commanded the Scottish army during the disastrous 1296 campaign.[100] Captured in the aftermath of the defeat at Dunbar, Malise was forced to swear loyalty to Edward I, acknowledging his overlordship of Scotland.

In contrast to the Bruces or his Comyn in-laws, Malise remained largely consistent in his newfound loyalty to Edward, participating consistently in the English campaign to subjugate Scotland and even forming something of a friendship with the king's heir, the future Edward II. In 1306, Malise was captured by Robert Bruce and Earl John Strathbogie of Atholl and forced to pledge allegiance to Robert as King of Scotland.[101] While the legality of an oath made as a result of coercion was questionable, the news nevertheless greatly vexed Edward I, who ordered Malise imprisoned. He was subsequently released when Agnes made a personal plea to Edward on her husband's behalf, and he remained active in English service until his death in 1312.

Also prominent in the conspiracy were David Brechin and Earl Patrick of Dunbar, whose mothers, Eleanor and Majorie, were also members of the Comyn family and the sisters of Agnes and Margaret.[102] Yet other members, such as Roger Mowbray, John Logie, Patrick Graham, Hamelin de Trope, Ingram Umfraville, Gilbert Malherbe, Richard Broun, Walter Barclay, Eustace Maxwell and Earl Murdoch of Menteith, had long-standing ties to the Comyn family.[103] Not coincidentally, they also held outstanding claims to lands in Galloway and Ayrshire that the Bruces' redistribution of land among their supporters had further isolated them from.

It is unclear exactly what role Edward Balliol himself had played in the conspiracy. But its leader, William de Soule, a member of the Scottish king's council, had made frequent diplomatic forays on Robert's behalf to the north of England, providing him with plenty of scope to secure the support and co-operation of both Edward II and Edward Balliol. Had the Comyns and their allies been able to take control of Galloway, where they and their relatives held a great deal of land and which had continually resisted Bruce rule, they would have been able to provide Edward II with a viable invasion corridor into the heartlands of the new Scottish king.

The nascent plot was ultimately unravelled and crushed by Robert when it was betrayed by Earl Patrick of Dunbar and Earl Murdoch of Menteith.[104] This foiling of the conspiracy by the defection of its two most powerful and highly ranked members is of considerable significance because both men's loyalty to Robert was relatively new and untested. That they had done so was a promising sign that Robert's efforts to solicit the support of the Scottish aristocracy and legitimise his rule were bearing fruit. With the existence of the plot revealed, Robert moved quickly and decisively to arrest all of the conspirators and try them publicly during a parliament convened at the royal centre of Scone.

Gilbert Malherbe, John Logie and Richard Broun were found guilty of treason and brutally hung drawn and quartered, while Roger Mowbray died in prison before the trial could begin.[105] David Brechin was found innocent of participation in the conspiracy but was nevertheless executed for failing to warn the king once he became aware of its existence.[106] William Soules and Agnes were likewise found guilty but sentenced to life imprisonment, possibly in deference to their rank and numerous familial connections.[107] Certainly, Agnes' gender and William's former service to the king and possession of a prestigious office of state may have helped move Robert to comparative leniency. In addition, Ingram Umfraville, the former Guardian of Scotland, who may have only been tangentially involved in the plot, fled Scotland, travelling first to England and then France.

The Soules Conspiracy demonstrated the continued threat of Comyn and Balliol partisans to the security of Bruce rule. Yet Robert's swift dismantling of the plot and the somewhat unexpected display of loyalty by the Earls of Dunbar and Menteith greatly strengthened his reign. William Soules, imprisoned in Dumbarton Castle, died in mysterious circumstances and without an immediate heir in 1321. The king then granted William's strategically important border Lordship of Liddesdale to his illegitimate son, Robert, further strengthening the Bruce family's position within the region.[108] Edward Balliol and the Disinherited still looked to the Bruce's new Scotland with envious and acquisitive eyes, eager to reclaim their lost or stolen Scottish holdings. However, for the remainder of Robert's reign, they lacked the strength or opportunity to make the attempt.

Over the next ten years Robert continued to consolidate his position within Scotland and complete the transformation of the Scottish political community. In 1323 both Robert and Edward II agreed to a thirteen-year long truce. Edward II was once again in a position to make such treaties, having regained a measure of authority in England and reconciled with his cousin, Thomas of Lancaster in 1318.[109] However, fresh political instability in England, provoked by Edward's lavish favouritism of the Despenser family, once more set the cousins at odds, leading to Thomas' arrest and execution. Edward, now deeply embroiled in the conflict with his own aristocracy, abided by the letter of the truce but either failed to rein in or even actively encouraged the predation of English pirates on Scottish trading vessels. In response, Robert entered into an alliance with France.

In 1327, Edward II, who had in the meantime also found himself fighting a largely unsuccessful war with France, was overthrown by his wife, the French princess Queen Isabella, and her political and romantic partner, Roger Mortimer.[110] Having successfully sidelined Edward, who conveniently died shortly after his imprisonment and abdication, the couple ruled England as regents of Edward and Isabella's son, Edward III. Despite Edward II's lack of popularity, the couple's regency remained divisive within England, with many disputing their leadership. Sensing an opportunity in this division, Robert resurrected his ambitions for the annexation of northern England, dispatching his two most trusted commanders and confidants, Thomas Randolph and James Douglas to oversee the invasion.[111]

Isabella and Roger realised that their continued rule was predicated upon their effective handling of this challenge and that success against the Scots would greatly improve their legitimacy and position in England. Consequently, with the young Edward III in tow, they marched their hastily raised army north to drive out the Scottish invaders. The campaign was badly bungled by the couple and hampered by poor logistics. They at first struggled to even locate the Scottish army, which, due to the slow pace of their own forces, had plenty of time to concentrate and occupy a strong defensive position. The Scottish army was then allowed to redeploy unchallenged, taking up another strong defensive position at Stanhope Park, while the disorganised English looked on. Attempts to pin and starve out the Scottish force by the larger English army resulted in a night raid launched by the Scots against the English camp that proved so devastating the Scottish army was able to slip away and return to Scotland unchallenged.[112]

Having exhausted both their army and the goodwill of the English nobility, Isabella and Roger were forced to cut their losses by entering into negotiations with the Scottish king. The end result of these talks was the Treaty of Edinburgh-Northampton, signed in 1328.[113] Designed to permanently end the now decades-long war between the two kingdoms, the English regents were more than willing to concede a now unenforceable claim to Scottish overlordship in exchange for protection against further invasion. In exchange for the compensatory fee of £20,000, Robert at last gained formal acknowledgement of Scottish independence from English overlordship and the legitimacy of his rule. In addition, there were a raft of further terms, the most important of which was the agreement that the border between the two kingdoms revert to the position it had been in the reign of Alexander III. The Stone of destiny and crown of Scotland, confiscated by Edward I in 1294, were also to be returned to Scotland.

While Bruce had to give up his ambition of annexing the portions of northern England held by previous Scottish kings, he had gained firm recognition of his rule and a seemingly long-term peace that greatly enhanced his legitimacy in Scotland and ability to portray himself as Alexander III's rightful and sole successor. Conversely, in relinquishing the English king's claims to overlordship in Scotland, the regents were also effectively abandoning the numerous claims to Scottish lands and titles that the English aristocracy had amassed over the past three and a half decades of fighting.[114] These forfeitures of long-nurtured claims, combined with the abruptness and ignominy of their defeat, meant that the peace treaty and the regents were deeply resented by many within the English nobility.

No one resented it more than Edward III. He had been dragged north by his regents on a poorly managed and inglorious campaign, during which time his life had been placed in serious danger when the Scottish night raid at Stanhope Park had destroyed the royal pavilion. Then he had been forced to enter into a humiliating peace, won through the abandonment of the title his grandfather and father had gone to such efforts to maintain. As we shall see, the sixteen-year-old Edward III would prove disinclined to forget his grudge against either group. He would in the near future unseat his regents, imprisoning his mother and executing Roger Mortimer. While it was ultimately the Disinherited who drew first blood in the Second War of Scottish Independence, Edward III's determination to resurrect his family's dream of imperial overlordship of the British Isles would see the conflict escalate into a decades-long conflagration that would once more consume Scotland.

Another important step taken by Robert and his allies during this time to further strengthen their hold on Scotland was the reconciliation with the Papacy. While now commonly interpreted as a political manifesto in which the Scottish political community asserted its independence, the original purpose of the Declaration of Arbroath was to demonstrate to the Papacy that both the Church and Political community of Scotland was overwhelmingly in favour of a Bruce kingship. The purpose of this carefully orchestrated demonstration of solidarity was to persuade the Papacy that it would have to accept Robert as king and revoke his excommunication in order to manage the Church's affairs effectively and fulfil its pastoral obligations in Scotland. While the Declaration did not persuade Pope John XXII to revoke Robert's excommunication, it did lead to a softening of attitudes within the Curia and a greater awareness that a compromise would eventually have to be reached in regard to Scotland.[115] Building upon this moderate success, in 1324 Robert dispatched his nephew and close ally, Earl Thomas Randolph of Moray, to meet the Pope at his court in Avignon. Upon his arrival, Thomas, who was one of Robert's most trusted and talented envoys, was finally able to persuade

John to lift Robert's excommunication and formally recognise him as King of Scotland.[116] This was a diplomatic triumph, greatly bolstering Robert's legitimacy both within and without Scotland.

The most crucial of all Robert's achievements during the latter half of his reign, in regard to his contributions to the potential perpetuation of the Bruce family as a royal dynasty, was his successful fathering of a male heir. This was a particularly important concern, since the Bruce line, having forcefully wrestled power away from their rivals, was looking perilously fragile. All four of Robert's brothers had died in the struggle to make good their family's royal claims without producing legitimate heirs. In March 1324, Robert's wife, Elizabeth de Burgh, now long removed from the effects of her harsh captivity, gave birth to the couple's first son.[117] Significantly, Robert chose to break with his family's long tradition of naming their eldest sons Robert.

Rather than drawing from traditional Bruce naming stock, the family's royal heritage and place on the throne of Scotland was to be emphasised by naming his son David, after the Scottish king whose reforms established adaptations of continental aristocratic culture and administrative structures into Scotland. In fact, it is probably not a coincidence that David was the king who first granted the Bruce family land in Scotland. Robert and Elizabeth's marriage had previously produced two daughters, Matilda and Margaret. Prior to David's birth, the king's heir had first been his brother Edward, who had died fighting an army partially commanded by Elizabeth's brother-in-law, and then Marjorie Bruce, the product of Robert's first marriage to Isabella of Mar. Marjorie, who was married to Walter Stewart, died in a hunting accident sometime around early 1317, leaving her infant son, Robert, second in line to the throne.[118]

King Robert, who was around fifty at the time of his son's birth and who had begun to suffer from bouts of ill health, sensibly made provisions for a potential minority. Should Robert die before David came of age, the Guardianship of king and kingdom would fall to his nephew, Thomas Randolph. If Thomas died, then this crucial role would pass on to Robert's other great friend and companion, James Douglas. In this manner, Robert entrusted the future of his dynasty to the close friends and allies whose co-operation and support had helped win him the throne. Another potentially important consideration for the future of the realm was the marriage proposed as part of the peace negotiations with England between the infant David and Edward III's sister Joan.

This marriage took place in Berwick shortly after the signing of the Treaty of Edinburgh-Northampton and saw the four-year-old prince and seven-year-old princess marry. Normally the Church did not look particularly favourably upon child marriages.[119] Consequently, betrothals and extended engagements were far more common within the aristocratic world because the Church's stance meant that the validity of such marriages could easily be challenged. This could have profound and troubling implications for the inheritance rights of the couple's potential children.

Of course, the high aristocracy had long found ways to bend the Chruch's numerous criteria for a licit union. For centuries, they acquired special, and often expensive, Papal dispensations to allow them to marry their relatives or hold proxy marriages, joining two people who had never met in matrimony. In 1328, Robert's health was increasingly failing, while the other principal party involved in the treaty, Isabella and Roger, were eager to secure the Scottish border so they could turn their efforts to pacifying an increasingly truculent English aristocracy. Evidently both parties felt that securing the newfound peace with a union between the two families was potentially worth having to deal with some minor legal quibbles sometime down the line.

Robert Bruce had attained the throne of Scotland by dint of his great success as a military commander, triumphing against both the English and his family's' traditional Scottish rivals. In doing so, he and his allies had radically reshaped the face of the Scottish political community, displacing many of the kingdom's most powerful and influential families. Robert, keenly aware of the potentially ephemeral and fragile nature of this achievement, had done everything he could to secure the kingship for the next generation. Yet despite his provisions for the Guardianship and the obvious competency of Thomas Randolph, a royal minority was an almost inherently dangerous arrangement. With Robert's death in 1329 and an accession of a child king, Edward Balliol and the Disinherited, a still potent spectre of Scotland's former political order, sensed at last an opportunity.

Chapter Five

The Great Gamble of the Disinherited

Robert the Bruce's military success against his fellow Scottish magnates and the forces of successive kings of England provided him with the power and opportunity necessary to exercise royal authority meaningfully within Scotland. The string of Bruce victories in the early 1310s that culminated in the spectacular crushing of an English army under Edward II's personal command at Bannockburn meant that the Bruce's claim to the Scottish throne could no longer be ignored. Indeed, with many of Robert's former enemies or sceptics now tripping over themselves to conclude separate peace agreements with him, the opposition was more rhetorical than substantive. There remained a small, somewhat disparate, circle of Comyn and Balliol relatives that opposed Robert's assumption of royal authority but with their English allies humbled and their strongholds within Scotland broken, they were something of a spent force within Scottish politics. As heartfelt and bitter as their opposition to Robert and his allies was, these remnants of the old political establishment lacked the power to challenge the blossoming authority of the Bruce's incipient royal government.

Robert created the Disinherited as a result of his efforts to further consolidate royal authority and secure his family's position on the previously hotly contested throne of Scotland. As we have seen, in the immediate aftermath of his triumph at Bannockburn, Robert declared the lands of those Scottish and Anglo-Scottish nobles that still refused to acknowledge his kingship forfeit, confiscating them. Rather than simply attempt to incorporate this massive influx of property into the royal demesne, Robert redistributed these confiscated lands among his own supporters. He then further enhanced these gifts with lands from the royal demesne or even those held traditionally by the Bruce family. In addition to the vital task of displaying the king's largesse and willingness to reward his allies generously, this mass reallocation of lands formalised and completed a process that had begun naturally during the course of the war. By elevating his allies and placing them at the forefront of the Scottish aristocracy, Bruce was irrevocably changing the political landscape of the kingdom. In doing so, he all but ensured that a substantial and powerful section of the Scottish aristocracy would oppose a Balliol restoration and the return of the Disinherited.

As we have heard, across the remainder of his reign, Robert built upon these foundations in an attempt to consolidate his family's hold on the Scottish throne and, after his birth in 1324, pave the way for the succession of his son, David. The Treaty of Edinburgh-Northampton signed in 1328 and the peace it brought was perhaps the most important step taken by Robert and his advisors in securing the successful accession of David II and the continuation of the Bruce dynasty.[1] The secret behind the treaty was that the leadership of both parties greatly desired peace yet had to take steps to mollify the feelings of their more bellicose subjects. While the Bruce's latest invasion of northern England had achieved very little of lasting strategic value, they had humiliated and then successfully evaded the English royal host, reaping a great deal of prestige. Robert was consequently able to use what was in actuality a relatively minor victory to bring the English to a negotiating table.

He was secretly eager to do so because he was increasingly suffering from the effects of ill health. While, as we have seen, he had taken precautions for the succession of a minor to the throne, Robert was well aware of the potential precariousness of such an arrangement and the danger that a renewal of hostilities would have on the royal government of a king unable to lead his kingdom to war. John Balliol's failure to lead the kingdom effectively at a time of war had seen him become an irrelevancy, his support steadily siphoning off to those willing to engage in the struggle one way or the other. Robert was determined that his son would not be similarly undermined.

The English leadership, Queen Isabella and her partner Roger Mortimer, had already experienced one costly failure as a result of their attempts to press the war. Peace with Scotland would allow them to concentrate the entirety of their political and military efforts on maintaining their now precarious position within England and quelling internal aristocratic discontent. As we have seen, the result of this toing and froing of mingled political concerns was a series of stipulations that made a fair foundation for the establishment of a lasting peace between the two kingdoms. The English monarchy gave up its claims to the overlordship of Scotland and the various estates and castles it had claimed for itself and its followers over decades of war. By the same token, by agreeing to restore the border to the state it had been in the reign of Alexander III, the Bruce supporters' gains in the north of England were likewise reversed. To further soothe the English nobility and allow its rulers to save face, Robert agreed to pay the English crown an indemnity of £20,000 in exchange for the renunciation of overlordship.[2] Finally, the marriage pact made between Robert's son and heir, David, and Edward III's younger sister Joan was seen as a means to consolidate the deal.[3]

The negotiations around this treaty, envisaged to bring about a generational peace between the two kingdoms, made specific mention of the Disinherited, the group that would eventually shatter the peace established by the treaty just four years later. Robert sought to make it clear in the treaty that the exile of the Disinherited was permanent and that those nobles who had lost land as a result of their opposition to his now universally acknowledged kingship would not be able to claim it back. After all, he had already given them away, with the majority of these lands now grasped tightly in the hands of Bruce supporters. This stance provoked a certain amount of pushback from the English side and a number of exceptions and caveats were carved out from this blanket refusal to negotiate.

It was eventually agreed that a small number of the Disinherited, such as Henry de Beaumont, Thomas Wake and Alan la Zouche, would be allowed to present their case for the rightful ownership of Scottish lands to a court.[4] However, the political reality behind this procedure was that for an applicant to be successful, they needed both the support of the English Regents, Isabella and Mortimer, as well as Robert and his deputies. Isabella and Mortimer were controversial figures, deeply engaged in a highly factionalised struggle for control over the English throne, while the Bruces were naturally opposed to the restoration of their traditional opponents. Despite these hurdles, a small amount of Scottish land was restored or promised to be restored to its previous owners. However, as it transpired even those men who nominally succeeded in this process struggled to gain any measure of real or practical control of the awarded estates. Most significantly for our purposes, the earldoms and great lordships that had once formed the power bases of

Robert's most significant Scottish opponents remained firmly in the hands of Bruce allies, their restoration never the subject of a serious negotiation.

Robert's insistence on clarifying the permanent nature of the relegation of the Disinherited from Scottish politics and the English demands for the establishment of a procedure to evaluate and establish exceptions to this relegation were both the result of the exiles' own activities. Rather than simply retreat south of the border to lick their wounds and ruminate upon their losses, the Disinherited had, ever since their exile, busied themselves in both the continuing war effort and English politics. This meant that certain members were able to exert a significant amount of pressure upon the direction of Anglo-Scottish relations. The core of the Disinherited was built around the surviving members and relatives of the Comyn family, who had for generations stood at the heart of the Scottish political establishment. They were joined in exile by a diverse collection of fellow exiles and Anglo-Scottish claimants.

Several of the Disinherited and their English allies had some degree of association with northern England's most powerful aristocrat, Earl Thomas of Lancaster, Leicester, Derby, Lincoln, and Sailsbury. A paternal grandson of Henry III, Thomas was Edward II's first cousin.[5] Due to his royal blood and status as the most powerful lord in England, Thomas quickly became a figurehead for baronial discontent with Edward II and his small circle of favourites. As we have heard, Thomas and his allies successfully leveraged Edward's defeat at Bannockburn to sideline the king and take control of the royal government.[6] Ultimately, Thomas proved no more able to defeat the Scots or tame the turbulent English aristocracy than his cousin and was eventually forced to reconcile with the king, who he agreed to share royal authority with. However, this peace proved to be relatively short-lived, and Thomas was outmanoeuvred and defeated by Edward's forces at the Battle of Boroughbridge when tensions with the English barons began to flair once again, leading to the earl's perfunctory trial and execution.[7] Despite his death and the limited success he saw during his tenure as England's de facto ruler, Thomas had a profound influence upon the shape of English politics and of Anglo-Scottish relations for much of the 1310s and very early 1320s; an influence that was to an extent shared and informed by the wishes of his Disinherited supporters.

The Disinherited, like their relatives and hosts within the English aristocracy, were placed in a somewhat difficult position by the overthrow of Edward II by his Queen Isabella and her new political and romantic partner, the infamous rebel lord, Roger Mortimer. Edward's lack of popularity among the aristocracy can be attested to by the repeated armed uprising against his government and the success that Isabella had found. Yet many were uncomfortable with the way the couple had outright removed Edward from the throne and the obliging promptness of his death following his imprisonment. Moreover, while the pair claimed only to be acting as regents for Isabella's freshly crowned son, Edward III, Isabella was a French princess who had overthrown her husband with the help of French troops. This spiced the usual jealousies and factionalism of royal courtly politics with a potent mix of xenophobia and sexism that further engendered the distrust of the English aristocracy.

As we have seen, the Disinherited and their allies were able to apply enough pressure to the regents that they expended some efforts during the negotiations surrounding the Treaty of Edinburgh-Northampton to establish a mechanism through which outstanding claims to land in Scotland could be arbitrated. Yet the most powerful and influential of the Disinherited, such as Henry de Beaumont and David de Strathbogie, failed to benefit from this process. In protest at this bargaining away of their rights and ancestral lands by the regents, the Disinherited joined Earl Henry of Lancaster, the brother of the now deceased Earl Thomas, and their northern English neighbours in an uprising against the regents. This rebellion proved to be short-lived and largely fruitless, with Henry and his Disinherited allies quickly coming to terms with Isabella and Mortimer.

Interestingly, Henry de Beaumont was specifically excluded from this peace settlement by the regents and remained an outlaw. It is possible that they took his participation in the rebellion personally since he was a former ally of theirs, having aided their initial takeover of England. While no doubt distressing in the short term, this antipathy eventually placed Henry and his fellow Disinherited in an advantageous position. When Edward III forcibly overthrew his regents, Beaumont's status as an exile strengthened the young king's perception that Henry was a natural ally, the enemy of those who had oppressed him and bargained away his rights to Scotland.

As previously touched upon, the true weakness of the Treaty of Edinburgh-Northampton was not the Bruce's refusal to meaningfully consider the restoration of the Disinherited but the simple fact that one of the treaty's primary signatories, Edward III, considered it a blight upon his honour and pride. By 1332, the political situation had advanced so significantly from the stalemate that had shaped the treaty four years earlier that the leadership of the Disinherited judged that the time was right for their return to Scotland and another attempt to regain their ancestral lands and titles. However, before we examine the shifting political factors behind these changes, we should explore the background and lives of some of the most prominent members of the Disinherited, in order to gain a better understanding of how the group coalesced and functioned.

We have already touched briefly upon the lives and careers of the coming expedition's joint leaders, Edward Balliol and Henry de Beaumont. As we shall see, of the two, Henry played the far larger and more proactive role in organising the Disinherited and paving the way for their invasion by securing the necessary funding, logistical resources and negotiating the tacit approval of the English royal court. Henry was a minor member of a prominent French aristocratic family. He was the third born son of Louis of Brienne and his wife Viscountess Agnes of Beaumont.[8] His paternal grandfather, John of Brienne, was perhaps one of the great chancers of the Middle Ages; a mixture of guile and good fortune seeing him reign at various times as both King of Jerusalem and Emperor of Constantinople.[9] Henry's paternal uncle, also called John of Brienne, held the title of the Grand Butler of France, one of the kingdom's great offices of state, and he had been the stepfather of Alexander III of Scotland.[10]

Despite his family's close ties to the French royal court, Henry, perhaps inspired by his grandfather's example, took service with Edward I during his campaign in Flanders.[11] As a result of his sister Isabella's marriage to one of Edward I's companions, he was afforded direct access to the king's inner circle. At the conclusion of the campaign, he was consequently able to accompany Edward I back to England as part of his military household, in which capacity he served in a number of the king's Scottish campaigns, eventually taking part in the victory at Falkirk. During this period, Henry and his sister had increasingly gravitated toward the inner circle of Prince

Edward. Upon his accession to the throne, Edward II, as he was wont to do, richly rewarded his friends and intimates, granting Henry a substantial portfolio of estates centred in Lincolnshire. While the most prestigious and valuable of his new titles, the Lordship of the Isle of Man, was stripped from Henry by the king's baronial enemies, Henry stood loyally by the king during the numerous trials and tribulations that characterised his relationship with the English aristocracy.[12]

As we saw in the previous chapter, in his zeal to break the Scottish Army and reclaim the lost earldom of his wife, Alice Comyn, Henry had jointly led one of the ill-fated cavalry charges on the first day of the Battle of Bannockburn.[13] Henry continued to serve Edward II steadfastly following this defeat, only for their association to end abruptly in the aftermath of the Battle of Boroughbridge and the removal of the king's cousin, Earl Thomas of Lancaster in the spring of 1322.[14] Freed from the burdensome need to share power with his cousin and temporarily ascendant over his enemies in the English aristocracy, Edward II sensed an opportunity to consolidate and recover his authority within England. To best capitalise upon this opportunity, Edward rather sensibly decided he would need to end the war with Scotland, which had become something of black hole that swallowed much-needed manpower, money and royal prestige. He therefore opened tentative peace negotiations with King Robert.

This abandonment of the war effort, and consequently the numerous territorial claims of his wife, greatly angered Henry de Beaumont, who protested the proposed peace in the most vehement terms possible. Tempers became so fraught that Henry lost his seat upon the privy council and was even briefly imprisoned by Edward. Retreating into the political wilderness, Henry eventually gravitated to the exiled lord of the Welsh Marches, Roger Mortimer, and would go on to be a key supporter of Queen Isabella's and Mortimer's coup in 1326.[15] However, as noted above, Henry soon fell out with the regents when it became clear that they too were willing to sacrifice the claims of the Disinherited in order to reach a workable peace agreement. Henry and a number of the Disinherited and their allies joined the new Earl of Lancaster in a military rising meant to protest and overturn the peace treaty.[16] Henry, perhaps because of his former association with the regents or his status as a ringleader, was excluded from the general pardon that ended this rebellion and was forced into exile in France.

In March 1330, Earl Edmund of Kent was tricked into entering into a conspiracy against the regents when he was falsely led to believe that his brother, Edward II, was still alive.[17] At the subsequent trial, Edmund indicated that he had been in touch with Henry de Beaumont, who had allegedly been willing to lobby his former ally, Earl Donald of Mar, to support the regent's overthrow. Clearly exile had done little to persuade Henry from his constant scheming and manoeuvring. Despite his quarrels with Edward II and his complicity in the king's removal and death, Henry's public and persistent opposition towards the self-appointed regents put him in good stead following their forcible removal by Edward III and the execution of Roger Mortimer in October 1330. Henry was subsequently allowed to return to England, where his shared opposition to Mortimer's government and the Treaty of Edinburgh-Northampton provided a surprisingly solid foundation for his later negotiations with Edward III.

Upon his return to England, Henry began to draw the Disinherited closer together, organising them and enlisting new allies in preparation for the commencement of a private war and the inevitable invasion of Scotland that this conflict would require. Henry had extensive military experience, fighting for decades alongside the military households of Edward I and Edward II with some distinction. Possibly inspired by the example of his late grandfather, Europe's most unlikely emperor, and with the once prestigious and wealthy earldom of Buchan as a potential prize, Henry was uncompromising and daring in his pursuit of the restoration of his wife's lands and titles. As a former companion of Edward II and early ally of Roger Mortimer and Isabella, Henry was, despite his lack of formal rank, the most influential of the Disinherited within English politics. Every iota of his influence was directed towards the recovery of the lost Scottish lands of the Disinherited, a stance he held with such belligerence that he was willing to spurn otherwise highly advantageous relationships in its pursuit. This combination of experience and influence, alongside his wife Alice's status as the Countess of Buchan and the head of the highest-ranking branch of the Comyn family, meant that Henry was able to emerge as the de facto leader of the Disinherited.

Unfortunately, very little is known about Henry's wife, Alice Comyn, or the extent to which she participated in the struggle to reclaim her family's lands, titles and position of pre-eminence within the Scottish aristocracy. Born in Scotland sometime around the late 1280s, Alice was the eldest daughter of Alexander Comyn and his wife Joan Latimer.[18] Alexander was the second son and namesake of Earl Alexander Comyn of Buchan. This meant that Alice, in addition to her familial relationship with the Badenoch branch of the Comyn family, was also closely related to fellow Disinherited Gilbert de Umfraville, the exiled earl of Angus. Another of Alice's cousins was Earl Patrick of Dunbar, who would soon play an important role in the attempt to repel her husband's invasion.

Alice's father, Alexander, served as the sheriff of Aberdeen, however, he wove an atypical path through the already complex web of alliances and betrayals that constituted the First War of Scottish Independence.[19] Rather than follow the lead of his elder brother, Earl John Comyn of Buchan, and their Badenoch cousins as they danced between opposition to English overlordship and grudging participation in Edward I's Scottish government, Alexander formed an alliance with Lachlann Mac Ruaidhrí. Together, the two fought against all comers to protect and expand their control over the Scottish Highlands with little regard for who sat on the throne of Scotland.[20] Alexander died in 1308, just as he and his partner's campaign against Earl William of Ross finally forced the embattled earl to make peace with the Bruces.

Alice's mother, Joan, was the daughter of Lord William Latimer, an English soldier and adventurer who had accompanied Edward I, then a mere prince, on Crusade in the 1270s.[21] He took part in the majority of Edward's military campaigns, fighting in Wales, Burgundy and Scotland, where he fought at both the Battles of Stirling Bridge and Falkirk.[22] Alice also had a younger sister, Margaret, who died without issue sometime in the late 1310s, leaving Alice to inherit a number of English estates she had held. With the death of her uncle, Earl John Comyn of Buchan, in December 1308, Alice inherited a claim to a war-ravaged earldom confiscated by Robert Bruce and his allies. Alice married Henry in 1310 and while the extent of her input and involvement in her husband's attempts to reclaim her family's earldom are unclear, the marriage was extremely fecund, producing at least eleven children. Which, if nothing else, indicates that the couple were willing and able to co-operate closely. It is entirely possible, even likely, that Alice played an important role in the formation of the Disinherited as a political movement, co-ordinating closely with her numerous relatives.

In contrast to the depth of military experience and political connections that Henry and Alice brought to the leadership of the Disinherited, Edward Balliol was a minor noble of no real achievement or discernible talents. For many contemporary observers it must have seemed very much a case of like father like son. Edward almost certainly had extensive contacts with the other members of the Disinherited when he arrived in the north of England in 1320. The circumstances around the Balliol family's return to the war, originally triggered by his father's refusal to bend further to the dictates of a king of England, highlight the complexities of the politics and culture of the era. The Disinherited, the descendants of those nobles that ruled Scotland alongside Edward's father, were now, thanks to the vagaries of war and the complexity of Scottish politics, firmly aligned with the son of the man who had deposed John Balliol. Consequently, in 1320, Edward Balliol believed that his best chance for reclaiming the throne of Scotland lay in supporting the English king's efforts to conquer the kingdom, hoping that he would prove himself reliable enough that Edward II would install him as a puppet ruler.

As it happened, Edward Balliol's foray into the war proved to be less than glorious. Edward took part in several skirmishes and yet another interminable siege of Berwick, yet he failed to assert his leadership over the Disinherited or leave a significant mark on the course of the conflict.[23] Indeed, by prematurely provoking the formation of the doomed Soules Conspiracy, Edward's campaigning in the north of England ended up damaging his cause and drastically weakening his support in Scotland. With his dreams of glory thwarted by the slow pace of the war and Edward II's inability to undertake a large-scale campaign within Scotland, Balliol drifted away from the conflict, returning to the safety of his family's French estates.

At some stage in late 1330, Edward become embroiled in legal troubles in France and was arrested by his feudal overlord, King Philip VI.[24] Edward was accused of the murder of a squire named Jean de Candas. It appears that Jean's family had a degree of regional influence and were able to pursue the case aggressively in court. Although the truth of the allegations is difficult to gauge, Edward certainly did nothing to help his case by refusing to appear to answer the allegations. Edward was freed from prison thanks to the intervention of Henry de Beaumont as part of his ongoing effort in organising the Disinherited for an invasion of Scotland.[25] Henry shouldered the considerable expense in political capital and money required by these negotiations because he realised that Edward Balliol's participation in the coming campaign was essential. Despite his lacklustre career prior to this point and the dubious legacy left by his father, Edward was a vital figurehead for the Disinherited cause.

Were the Disinherited simply to invade Scotland with the goal of compelling the Bruce party and the Guardians of young David II to return their land, they would even, if successful, be surrounded by their ancestral enemies and vulnerable to royal reprisals down the road. Moreover, while David II's minority represented a major opportunity for the Disinherited, it also came with a number of complications. Most pertinently for the Disinherited, the Bruce royal government was increasingly dependent on the support of a powerful clique of allies whose fortunes came from the redistribution of the confiscated estates of the Disinherited. The leading members of the Scottish aristocracy were therefore extremely unlikely to permit the king's Guardians to reach any sort of compromise or agreement with the invaders.

Instead, the Disinherited required a king of their own. By placing Edward, the legitimate son and heir of a crowned King of Scotland, on the throne, the Disinherited would be able to displace the Bruce regime and have their lost estates and titles lawfully returned to them in perpetuity. There was also a commonly held belief among the leadership of the Disinherited that there were still many in Scotland who would rise up against the Bruces in support of a Balliol restoration to the throne. The invasion would prove this belief to be overly optimistic; thirty-six odd years after the end of a functional Balliol royal government, and with the most powerful and determined member of their party in exile, there were not many Scots willing to flock to the Balliol banner out of loyalty or nostalgia.

However, it could still be possible to argue somewhat convincingly that Edward's heritage and claim to the throne meant that members of the

Scottish political community were more willing to negotiate with him and his followers than they might otherwise have been. While, as we shall explore later, no major Scottish aristocrats joined the Disinherited army prior to the Battle of Dupplin Moor, in the battle's aftermath, Edward's royal credentials surely made submission more palatable as many across Scotland were induced to acknowledge his right to the throne.

Born in Roxburghshire sometime around 1283, Edward was the son of royal claimant John Balliol and his wife, Isabella de Warenne.[26] Edward was only nine when he attended his father's coronation at Scone, meaning that he carried with him for some of his most formative years the expectation that he would one day succeed to the throne of Scotland. Edward would have been educated in a manner similar to any other European prince or member of the upper aristocracy until his father's forced abdication from the throne in 1296. Following his release from imprisonment in the Tower of London into the custody of his maternal grandfather, John de Warenne, in 1299, Edward would have almost certainly continued in his martial and chivalric education. Meanwhile, John Balliol made little to no effort to establish himself in Scotland following his own release from English custody, despite numerous requests by his then still numerous supporters within Scotland that he return at once.

Edward Balliol was therefore a man who had been raised to adulthood with the expectation that he would one day compete for and win the throne of Scotland. In 1320, when he had first attempted to involve himself in the war against the Bruces, Edward was twenty-seven and in the prime of his life. Yet in 1320, Robert Bruce was near the height of his own power and authority, while England, where Edward would have to recruit his army and allies from, was being wracked by political turmoil. Edward was forty-nine years old when the Disinherited finally launched their invasion of Scotland. He must have been aware that it would be his last serious chance to reclaim the throne.

Despite his lack of military experience and nominal inclusion as a mere figurehead, the invasion of Scotland by the Disinherited would see Edward come into his own. In the war to follow, Edward would establish himself in a position of direct leadership that belied his previous passivity and mediocrity. Edward Balliol would ultimately fall far short of the great men of his age – his talents and achievements were dwarfed by those of Robert Bruce – yet the Disinherited's invasion provided him with an opportunity he had been waiting half a lifetime for, and when that opportunity finally came he seized it with both hands.

Born in exile in 1309, David III Strathbogie, the titular Earl of Atholl, was the son of Earl David II of Atholl and his wife, Joan Comyn.[27] Joan was the eldest daughter of John the Red Comyn, the Lord of Badenoch, and his wife, Joan de Valance, providing David with a familial connection to the Comyns, Balliols and, more distantly, the Plantagenet kings of England. David II's father, Earl John of Atholl, had been an early supporter of Robert Bruce, being one of the few high-ranking members of the Scottish nobility to attend his coronation in 1306.[28] John had previously been captured in 1296 at the Battle of Dunbar and, like many of the Scottish nobility, had only been freed by Edward I on the proviso that he fought for Edward in Flanders and acknowledged the English king's overlordship of Scotland.[29] In response to John's profession of loyalty to Robert as King of Scotland and the breaking of his previous agreement with the English king, Edward I, confiscated the Strathbogies' English estates.

Unfortunately for John, he was captured once again shortly afterwards during the Battle of Methven. Edward I proved to be far less forgiving the second time around and John was transported to London and hanged in the manner of a common criminal.[30] Edward could argue, with some justification, that John had previously acknowledged his sovereignty and that his public repudiation of this agreement constituted treason. Yet the execution flew in the face of every protocol and expectation the aristocracy had of warfare. Indeed, he was the first earl to be executed in England in over two hundred years. King Edward's treatment of John was a signal to the Scottish aristocracy of the brutal new character of the unfolding war and the terror that Edward was willing to inflict upon his enemies in the pursuit of victory.

Almost undoubtedly influenced by his father's grim fate, David II abandoned his family's loyalty to the Bruces, instead turning to the familial connections his marriage brought him. With the help of his wife's Comyn and Valance relatives, David II was able to recover his ancestral lands and earldom, although he had to pay a considerable sum to Edward I's son-in-law, Earl Ralph de Monthermer of Gloucester and Hereford, who had been awarded ownership of Atholl following its initial confiscation. [31] In doing so, the Strathbogie family had just bartered their way onto a sinking ship. In 1307, Earl David II was driven out of Atholl by a concerted Bruce offensive and his lands and title declared forfeit.[32] David II took shelter with his English allies, who returned to him parts of his family's former English estates, such as Chilham in Kent and three new manors in Norfolk, by way of compensation.[33] Following the death of Joan's maternal uncle, Earl Aymer de Valance of Pembroke in 1324, the Strathbogie family inherited substantial estates in Northumberland and Yorkshire, as well as ownership of Mitford Castle.[34] Interestingly, despite, or perhaps because of the severity of his losses in Scotland, David II remained very much engaged in the war effort in Scotland and military service to the English kings throughout his exile. In 1322, he was placed in charge of the defence of Northumberland, while in 1325 he was awarded command of the English king's garrisons in the last of their continental domains, Gascony.

When David II died the following year, his lands and the now purely nominal title of Earl of Atholl fell to his eldest son, David III. The young earl, who had been born and raised on his family's English estates, was married to Kathrine de Beaumont, the eldest daughter of Henry de Beaumont and Alice Comyn. Connected as he was to both the Badendoch and Buchan branches of the Comyn family, and with an outstanding earldom of his own to claim, David III Strathbogie occupied a position at the heart of the Disinherited's leadership cadre. David III, who was only twenty-three when the Disinherited launched their invasion of Scotland, was also among the wealthiest of the Disinherited. This meant that, despite his personal inexperience or lack of familiarity with Scotland, his contribution and involvement with the Disinherited cause was vital to the successful organisation and staging of their invasion.

The third would-be earl to accompany the Disinherited alongside Beaumont and Strathbogie was Gilbert de Umfraville. He was the eldest son of Earl Robert de Umfraville of Angus and Lucy de Kyme, a wealthy heiress whose family had considerable estates scattered across Yorkshire and Lincolnshire.[35] The Umfraville family had acquired the Earldom of Angus when Gilbert's great-grandfather, Lord Gilbert de Umfraville of Prudhoe in

Northumberland, married Countess Matilda of Angus sometime in the early 1240s.[36] After this Gilbert's death in 1245, Matilda would leave their infant son, also named Gilbert, in wardship to the English magnate and future rebel Simon de Montfort. She would then marry an English magnate, Richard de Dover, with their daughter, Isabel, marrying Earl David I Strathbogie of Atholl, creating a distant line of kinship between the Disinherited's Gilbert and his fellow member and exile, David III Strathbogie.

Due to the circumstances of grandfather Gilbert's childhood in the 1240s and 1250s, the Umfraville family were, while Anglo-Scottish in terms of heritage and the distribution of their lands, largely English in their outlook. As a result, upon the outbreak of war in Scotland, both this elder Gilbert and his son Robert fought in support of the English king's claims of overlordship. In 1308, Edward II had appointed Robert as joint Guardian of Scotland and the head of the English king's proxy government.[37] Following the further deterioration of the English position in Scotland, Robert fought at the Battle of Bannockburn, where he was captured.[38] Robert was released soon afterwards but his Scottish estates, including the Earldom of Angus, were confiscated by Bruce and his allies. Robert's son, Gilbert, our Gilbert, was born sometime around 1310, just a few years prior to the loss of his Scottish inheritance.[39] Sometime around 1329, Gilbert married Joan Willoughby, whose father was lord of Willoughby de Eresby in Lincolnshire.[40]

Gilbert was something of an outlier among the leadership of the Disinherited. His ancestors had fought directly for the kings of England rather than for Balliol or the Comyn-dominated Guardians. In contrast, even the Strathbogies had originally fought for the council of Guardians governing on behalf of Balliol in 1296. Neither was he particularly closely related to any of the other Disinherited and his own marriage had been made with the goal of securing and expanding the family's English estates. However, Gilbert had a clear-cut claim to the Earldom of Angus, as well as the resources and youthful verve necessary to pursue it.

In addition to their uncrowned king and the three claimants to Scottish earldoms, the Disinherited were composed of an eclectic mix of relatives and English aristocrats who held, either through familial ties or the result of military service, territorial claims within Scotland that were rejected by the Bruce royal government. Richard Talbot was probably the most prominent example of the former group. The son of Gilbert Talbot and Anne Boteler, Richard's family were middling members of the Welsh Marches' regional aristocracy. He was through his paternal grandmother descended from the Welsh rulers of Deheubarth.[41] Richard was born around 1306 but, unlike his contemporaries in the Disinherited, Richard's father was still very much alive and in control of the family estates in 1332. Indeed, Gilbert was a man on the rise.

He had previously fallen foul of Edward II as a result of his participation in Thomas of Lancaster's efforts against the Despenser family, who were greatly favoured by the king. As a result of the failure of this uprising, Gilbert was stripped of his office as castellan of Gloucester Castle and left with a large fine levied against him.[42] However, this fine was scrapped upon the accession of Edward III, almost certainly because of Mortimer's own interest in and affinity for the Welsh Marches. In 1328, Gilbert was appointed High Chamberlain of England, while in 1330 he was made Justicar of Wales.[43] Signs of royal favour continued even after Edward forcibly removed his regents from power, and in 1331 Gilbert was raised to the Baronage.[44]

Gilbert's earlier opposition to the Despensers, which probably helped bring him to the attention of Edward III's regents upon their rise to power, was in part motivated by the same familial politics that drew his son to the Disinherited. Richard was married to Elizabeth Comyn, a daughter of John the Red Comyn of Badenoch and the sister of Joan, David III Strathbogie's mother.[45] Hugh Despenser had used his relationship with Edward II to greatly enrich himself through the confiscation of lands and levelling of arbitrary fees. Among the lands and estates plundered in this way was Goodrich Castle and its surrounding estates, rightfully the property of Richard's wife, Elizabeth Comyn.[46]

The young Richard participated alongside his father in Thomas of Lancaster's rebellion and was captured following the royalist victory at the Battle of Boroughbridge, the same victory that first triggered the quarrel between Edward II and founding member of the Disinherited, Henry de Beaumont.[47] Following Despenser's removal and death upon the overthrow of Edward II, Richard and Elizabeth were able to reclaim her family's lost estate. In 1332, with no immediate responsibilities in England, it seems that

Richard was eager to replicate this success on a greater scale by accompanying his wife's relatives in their attempts to reclaim a kingdom.

Another, but substantially more distant, relative of the Comyns and Balliols found among the Disinherited was Henry Ferrers. Born sometime around the early 1300s, Henry was the son of William Ferrers, the Baron of Ferrers of Groby and Ellen de Menteith, the daughter of Earl Alexander of Menteith.[48] William's father, also called William, was the son of yet another William Ferrers, Earl William de Ferrer of Derby, and his wife Margaret de Quincy. Margaret was, of course, the eldest daughter of Roger de Quincy and Hellen of Galloway, meaning that she was, like her sister who married Earl Alexander Comyn of Buchan or her aunt Dervorguilla Balliol, a partial heir to the lords of Galloway. While this relationship was somewhat distant, Henry's father William deliberately adopted the coat of arms of his Quincy great grandfather as his own.

William, the Lord of Ferrers of Groby, was a minor at the time of his own father's death and found himself burdened with serious financial difficulties. Upon attaining his majority, William began undertaking military service to Edward I. As a result, in 1296, in the aftermath of the overthrow of John Balliol's kingship, William was once again granted control of his family's lands in Scotland, which had briefly fallen under the English king's de facto control. William fought for the English king at both Falkirk and the famous Siege of Caerlaverock Castle.[49] William died in 1325, having avoided the worst of the infighting and civil disorder that characterised so much of Edward II's reign, although it was during this period that the Bruce party and its allies confiscated the family's Scottish estates.

Henry fell into the orbit of Earl Henry of Lancaster, joining many of his fellow Disinherited in the earl's unsuccessful attempts to remove Isabella and Mortimer from power. In punishment for this act of rebellion, Henry's lands were confiscated and a large fine was imposed upon him, although both punishments were soon waved.[50] Henry was subsequently involved in the trial and execution of Roger Mortimer for treason in 1330, an involvement that probably helped bring him to the king's attention.[51] Henry had been closely allied with and fought alongside the leaders of the Disinherited in their uprising against the Regents. Moreover, his family had previously held extensive lands in Galloway, inherited from their Quincy ancestors.

Another important consideration is that Henry's maternal uncle, Earl Muireadhach of Menteith, had also been responsible for the unravelling of the Soules Conspiracy.[52] Consequently, Henry may have hoped that a restored Balliol monarchy would award him the Earldom of Menteith, following his uncle's removal.

In contrast to these long-standing and tangled familial ties, Henry Percy joined the Disinherited in pursuit of lands awarded to his family by Edward II in his capacity as overlord of Scotland. Naturally these grants had been repudiated by the English crown during the Treaty of Edinburgh-Northampton, leading Percy and those adventurous and ambitious young nobles like him to throw their lot in with the Disinherited in a bid to reclaim these lost estates and share in the rewards of a potential victory. Henry Percy was born in 1301.[53] His father, also called Henry, had served extensively in the early portion of the war in Scotland under both his father-in-law, Earl John de Warenne, and Edward I directly, and was eventually placed in charge of governing a massive portion of south-west Scotland, including Galloway and Ayrshire. In doing so, he had earnt himself both a formidable reputation and a considerable fortune.

In 1309, the elder Henry purchased Alnwick Castle from the Bishop of Durham and established the family as one of the great powers of northern England and the Scottish border. In 1314, this elder Henry died, leaving the newly established baronage to his eldest son and future member of the Disinherited. In 1316, while the Bruce was continuing to divide the lands confiscated from the Disinherited among his followers, Edward II granted Henry control of Earl Patrick of Dunbar's lands in Northumberland following the earl's defection to the Bruces. Henry was married to Idonia de Clifford, the daughter of the English commander killed at Bannockburn. In addition to hoping to reclaim the Scottish lands formerly controlled by his own father, Henry was likely looking to advance some claim on the extensive Scottish lands awarded to his father-in-law.

Of the remainder of the Disinherited's English allies, the most notable two were probably Thomas Wake and Thomas Ughtred. Wake was the second son of Lord John Wake of Liddel and his wife, Joan de Fiennes.[54] John had engaged in extensive military service to Edward I, fighting in both Gascony and Scotland. He was present for the English victory at Falkirk and was in 1297 promoted to the status of marcher lord and charged, alongside his peers, with the defence of the Anglo-Scottish border. Thomas, who was born in 1297, was married to Blanche, the daughter of the future Earl Henry of Lancaster.[55] Like Henry de Beaumont, Thomas initially supported Queen Isabella and Roger Mortimer, only to fall out with them and flee into exile in France. Indeed, it is probable, given their shared association with the Lancaster brothers, that Thomas accompanied Henry de Beaumont during their time in exile. When Edward III rid himself of the regents and took power on his own, Thomas was greatly honoured by the king, probably as a result of his wife's familial connection to the English crown and his late father's reputation as a soldier. Thomas had a strong hereditary claim to the Lordship of Liddesdale, which under the Bruces had been awarded to Robert Bruce, the illegitimate son of Robert I.

Thomas Ughtred was yet another member of the aristocratic community of northern England, although one far less well connected than the Disinherited's other leaders.[56] Unlike many of his later allies, Ughtred remained loyal to Edward II, fighting on the king's behalf against Thomas of Lancaster. Atypically for the Disinherited, Ughtred had no confiscated or lost lands in Scotland to reclaim; instead he was an adventurer seeking to make his fortune through this high-risk military enterprise. However, while not necessarily a natural or intuitive member, once attached to the Disinherited, Thomas' martial abilities and developing relationship with Edward Balliol soon saw him gravitate towards the inner circle of Edward's quickly developing alternative royal court.

The majority of the Disinherited had lost their Scottish estates in the immediate aftermath of the Battle of Bannockburn in 1314, sixteen years prior to their eventual invasion of Scotland. After such a long time, it was a confluence of interrelated factors that finally convinced the diverse members of the Disinherited to start organising for the waging of their private war in the dawn of the 1330s. The first and most obvious of these factors was that England had been going through a period of prolonged political turmoil. Edward II's reign was blighted by aristocratic uprisings aimed at ending the monopolisation of power and its alleged abuses by consecutive royal favourites.

The circumstances in which Edward II's reign ended were no less troubling or disruptive, overthrown and murdered by his own queen, leading an alliance of French troops and English rebels. The regents' time in power was equally controversial, seeing the execution of members of the royal family and further aristocratic uprisings. A measure of peace and stability within English aristocratic politics was only reached at the tail end of 1330, when Edward III forcibly removed his regents and began ruling in his own right. Prior to this, the future members of the Disinherited, no matter what their disparate loyalties, were focused on negotiating this cascade of crises. They were, with the possible exception of Henry de Beaumont, too consumed by the need to safeguard their English estates to seriously contemplate the recovery of their lost Scottish lands.

Another major factor pushing the Disinherited towards action had to do with the changed circumstances of the Bruce monarchy. Robert Bruce died in 1329 after an extended period of poor health, leaving the throne to his five-year-old son, David II.[57] A minority reign carried with it certain inherent dangers for both monarch and kingdom. Robert I had taken sensible and effective steps to mitigate these difficulties by investing the entirety of royal power in a single trusted Guardian, his nephew Thomas Randolph.[58] Prior to Robert I's bid for the Scottish throne, the supporters of the exiled John Balliol had often attempted to consolidate their authority and protect the internal coherency of the kingdom by appointing multiple Guardians and courting the support of broad segments of the Scottish nobility. Robert I had eschewed such a policy, having experienced at first hand the fragile nature of the consensus binding the participants together and their all too often truncated capacity for decisive action. Instead, Robert poured all of the king's authority into a singular supremely talented and loyal Guardian who could manage the kingdom and the Scottish aristocracy on his son's behalf. This arrangement combined with Randolph's own reputation as a hero of the First War of Independence and the king's young age meant that Randolph was free to run the kingdom on David's behalf without having to contend with the attempts of other courtly factions to exert influence over the king.

Promisingly for the Disinherited, word had begun to percolate down through the Scottish borders that Thomas Randolph was ill. King Robert had made provisions for Thomas' death in his own will but his choice of replacement Guardian, James Douglas, was already dead. In fact, James died in 1330. Supposedly he was on a mission to fulfil his king's dying wishes by taking Robert's heart on a pilgrimage to the Holy Sepulchre in Jerusalem.[59] Rather unusually, Douglas and his party had decided to travel through Spain, where they somehow became involved in King Alfonso XI of Castiles's war against the Muslim polity of Granada.[60] Given the circuitous route and time this would have taken James' party and the potential difficulty of gaining access to Mamluk-controlled Jerusalem, it is possible that Bruce, still harbouring some doubts for the safety of his soul, merely requested his heart be taken on Crusade.

Whatever the case, while Alfonso's campaign proved successful, James Douglas was killed during the fighting, possibly as a result of his heedless pursuit of the retreating elements of the Muslim army. Douglas' death in Spain meant that Thomas Randolph was the last of the late king's inner circle of proven and trusted commanders. Should Randolph's illness kill or incapacitate him, then the Disinherited would be faced not by one determined enemy, but by a hastily constructed coalition composed of a new, as yet unproven, generation of the Bruce-aligned families, and fence-straddling aristocrats waiting to see in which direction the wind blew.

While the Disinherited's invasion of Scotland was a personal and private enterprise, an alliance of aristocrats determined to capture a kingdom, the practicalities and logistical concerns of assembling an army, even a small one, on English soil meant that the Disinherited required Edward III's tacit blessing. In fact, subsequent events suggests that Edward Balliol and Henry de Beaumont may have recognised that the conquest of Scotland would probably require English royal support further down the line. Edward III was formally bound by the Treaty of Edinburgh-Northampton, which his mother and Mortimer had cajoled him into signing. Knowingly abetting an army, composed mainly of English soldiers, invading Scotland from England was tantamount to breaking the treaty and with it his word. Such a course of action would be a major blemish on the young king's honour and have potentially severe repercussions on his domestic and international reputation. The same pride and insecurities that fuelled Edward III's resentment of the Treaty of Edinburgh-Northampton and the surrendering of his ancestors' claim to the overlordship of Scotland also prevented him from breaking the treaty unprovoked.

However, there were a number of promising signs and contextual factors that led the leaders of the Disinherited to believe that they may be able to negotiate some form of agreement with Edward. During the rather one-sided trial of Queen Isabella's partner and former regent, Roger Mortimer, one of the supposedly treasonous activities Roger was accused of was betraying the best interests of the realm by forcing the king to agree to an iniquitous treaty.[61] This was as highly encouraging to the Disinherited as it was alarming to the Scots, unambiguously signalling that the new king viewed the treaty as a hindrance.

Past kings of England had, in their attempts to exercise influence or overlordship within Scotland, been wary of the intermittent alliances reached between Scotland and France.[62] Such agreements meant that English kings had to be cognisant of overcommitting in the struggle against either of their neighbours for fear of becoming embroiled in a war on two fronts. Edward III's maternal grandfather was Philip IV of France. Philip had been succeeded to the throne of France by his three sons, Louis X, Philip V and Charles VI, each of whom ruled in turn before dying without issue. Upon the death of Charles VI in 1328, the French nobility selected a cousin of the Capet line, Philip of Valois, to rule as Philip VI.[63] As the eldest legitimate nephew of Charles VI, Edward III had an excellent claim to succeed his uncle as King of France. However, the French nobility, perhaps understandably, preferred that the throne go to one of their own rather than a young and unproven foreign king. While it seems likely that the French nobility of 1328 felt no need to explain the reasoning behind their declaration for Philip, an argument was retroactively proffered by his successors that Philip's claim was superior to that of Edward because it followed the male line exclusively. In England, Isabella and Mortimer were so consumed with the task of consolidating their own positions, they gave little thought to the pursuit of a hereditary claim that would have necessitated war with France.

Shortly after claiming the throne in 1329, Philip summoned Edward III to France to pay homage to him for his lands in Gascony and Aquitaine.[64] Edward or his regents initially left this call unheeded, busy as they were with pressing concerns within the British Isles. Philip, frustrated by this delay and eager to demonstrate the superiority of his position over his dynastic rival, repeated the summons with the addition of a threat that should Edward fail to appear, he would be in breach of his obligations as a vassal and that his French land would be confiscated. Philip's litigiousness had the desired effect, with Edward arriving in the French court in the summer of 1329, where he duly paid homage to Philip for his French lands.[65] Oddly enough, the two kings rather hit it off despite the age difference between them and the potentially humiliating nature of one monarch swearing homage to another. In addition to feasting and jousting, the two even made plans to go on Crusade together, tentatively setting 1332 as a preliminary date for the expedition.[66] While there were no ironclad agreements in place, Edward's friendly relationship with the French king meant that Philip was far less likely to intervene on behalf of David II's protectors in the event of a renewal of hostilities between England and Scotland.

Another complicating factor in winning Edward's endorsement of an invasion of Scotland was that David II was married to Edward's younger sister Joan, a marriage arranged alongside the Treaty of Edinburgh-Northampton with the goal of securing a generation-long peace between the two warring royal houses. However, this was not as much of an obstacle as it first appeared. In early 1332, the Scots paid the final instalment of the considerable sum they had agreed to pay for an English royal bride. This meant that Edward could now repudiate the agreement and break with his brother-in-law's Guardians, without fear of missing out financially. The saving grace of this arrangement from the Disinherited's point of view was the age of the royal couple. In 1332, David was seven years old while Joan was eleven. This meant that the validity of the marriage could, if deemed necessary, easily be challenged in court and dissolved.

Publicly Edward III went to some pains to obscure his co-operation with the Disinherited. Maintaining a shroud of official deniability, Edward sent orders to his northernmost sheriffs to disperse any men at arms gathering around the Scottish Marches.[67] Of course, Edward knew perfectly well that the Disinherited were not going to muster their army on the Scottish border. He knew this because he himself had forbidden them from invading Scotland directly from English soil. He had, however, after extensive negotiations with Henry de Beaumont, acquiesced to allowing the Disinherited to undertake a seaborne invasion and was in the summer of 1332, perfectly aware of the existence of the small army gathering across the ports of Yorkshire's north-eastern coast. Rather than risk breaking the Treaty of Edinburgh-Northampton and tarnishing the reputation of the young English king by marching out of their power base in northern England, the Disinherited would arrive unbidden as anonymous outlaws from the wild and trackless seas, over which no man or king could claim authority.

It was a neat political fiction that jarred somewhat with Edward's other actions in the lead-up to the Disinherited's departure. Accompanying the Disinherited was Walter Muny, one of the most trusted and distinguished of the king's household knights.[68] Muny had almost certainly attached himself to the Disinherited at the king's behest, probably to act as Edward's eyes and ears. Edward III, who was now well aware of the Disinherited's plans, had on 27 March granted Henry de Beaumont the princely summon of £500, nominally in order to compensate him for the losses in income he had suffered during his earlier exile under the regents.[69] The king also gave permission to Beaumont, David Strathbogie, Richard Talbot and Thomas Wakefield to lease their estates, effectively granting the commanders of the Disinherited an additional avenue to raise much-needed cash.[70] Money was, as ever, the essential sinew of war, the crucial resource that would determine if the Disinherited were able to raise a viable army. As discussed, many of the Disinherited's leaders had extensive estates in the north of England and elsewhere, giving them the means to raise the skeletons of military retinues.

The reign of Edward I had wrought considerable changes on the nature of military recruitment within England. This is quite a complicated topic, the intricacies and functionality of both old and new systems being the subject of ongoing historical debate, as indeed is the extent to which they differed from one another in practice. The gist of the topic is this: the traditional method of raising military forces in England, based on feudal obligation, had a number of limitations. For instance, it was generally understood that vassals owed their lords a certain number of days of military service.[71] Such agreements were, as always for the medieval period, personal rather than systematic but available evidence suggests that in England around forty days was generally considered the upper threshold of such service. Beyond this point, army commanders would find it increasingly difficult to maintain troops in the field, their armies suffering from desertion and sapped moral, meaning that generals would have to resort to extreme measures, like offering to pay for their soldiers' services.

This system, while not entirely devoid of flexibility, struggled to keep up with the demands for troops imposed by Edward I's frequent and long-running campaigns. In addition to a number of reforms to bolster the numbers and martial character of the knightly class, Edward increasingly showed a preference for the collection of scutage, a cash fee vassals paid to their lord in lieu of military service.[72] Edward could then use this money to pay the wages of professional or semi-professional soldiers who could be relied upon to stay in the field or perform garrison duty for an extended period of time without relief. This increased the performance of Edward's troops, relieved the king of many of the most pressing logistical issues inherent to the movement and supply of troops and allowed him to wage the sort of longer, more sustained campaigns required to facilitate true conquest.

The effects of these reforms continued to be felt into the reign of Edward II and would be further developed and refined later in the reign of Edward III. Fortunately for the Disinherited, years of fighting in both Scotland and the north of England had created a surplus of professional or semi-professional soldiers who had been rendered largely redundant by the signing of the peace treaty and who were consequently looking for employment.

All in all, the Disinherited were able to raise a small army of some one thousand and five hundred men. Of these, around a thousand were archers, lightly armoured missile troops recruited largely from the lower classes of English medieval society.[73] The English, probably as a result of the influence of their Welsh neighbours, exhibited a particular cultural attachment to the bow. While still somewhat ubiquitous across Europe, the bow had largely been replaced as a military tool by the crossbow, which were both more powerful and considerably easier to master. The English largely resisted this trend, continuing to value and promote the bow as a weapon of war. In 1252, Henry III emulated his grandfather, Henry II, by publishing an Assize of Arms, a decree outlining the terms of military service owed to the king by his English subjects.[74] In the Assize, the bow was identified as the base level of armament that every Englishman of military age was expected to bring with them for military service.[75]

Indeed, archers had historically made up an important part of the English armies during Edward I's and Edward II's war to secure overlordship of Scotland. Archers were potentially deadly in the right circumstances but upon the battlefield needed to be deployed and utilised with care. At Falkirk, under Edward I, they had proved decisive against the tightly packed but slow-moving formations of William Wallace's host. At Bannockburn under Edward II, they had been crammed into the small amount of solid ground available and were unable to hinder the enemy advance effectively.

The second component of the army was made up of five hundred men at arms. These were simultaneously the army's front-line fighters and its dedicated martial elite. While the exact origins and quality of their arms and armour were highly idiosyncratic, most would have been well equipped with some degree of plate armour, helms and a profusion of weapons meant to counter similarly armoured troops. The core of the Disinherited's men at arms were made up of the retainers and vassals of the army's leaders, supplemented by adventurers and mercenaries looking to enrich themselves through war. The majority of these men probably came from the north of England and had been involved in the long-running war of raid and counter-raid that had raged across the Anglo-Scottish border, while others had come from further afield such as Germany and the Lowlands.

Such men, the inheritors of the traditional knightly class and its mode of warfare, tended to prefer to fight from horseback. Contemporary English armies usually took a survey and evaluation of the horses involved prior to the commencement of a campaign, due to the understanding that the king would recompense men for the value of their lost horses.[76] Such records reveal that in addition to their prized warhorses, many knights and men at arms during this period were accompanied by three or four less-expensive mounts.[77] Such second-tier horses proved useful for the transport of goods, the undertaking of long marches and the launching of raids. While the Disinherited, as a private enterprise, kept no such records, it is possible that the seaborne nature of the invasion and its pressing financial limitations meant that the army contained a significantly smaller ratio of horses. This more than anything may have contributed to its members' later willingness to countenance fighting on foot.

It was by any contemporary standards an almost hopelessly small army with which to overthrow a dynasty and recapture a kingdom. Yet the members of the Disinherited had waited decades for an opportunity like the one presented to them in 1332 and were determined to press on while the political winds remained favourable to their cause. They were probably further emboldened by the likelihood of infighting among the Scottish leadership in the absence of the stricken Thomas Randolph. They also probably had good reason to believe that Edward III would imminently enter the war on their side. It is highly unlikely that Edward III would ever have permitted Edward Balliol to depart for Scotland with the intention of reclaiming his family's crown without securing some acknowledgment of his overlordship of Scotland, no matter how remote he believed Balliol's chances were. The young Edward III had raged when his mother and Mortimer had compelled him to surrender his ancestral claim to Scotland and it is unlikely he would not have seized upon the chance to reclaim it in his initial negotiations with the Disinherited.

Throughout late spring and summer, the Disinherited mustered their small army, procuring the necessary supplies and naval assets required to convey it safely to the battlefields of Scotland. Edward III's ruse had succeeded in maintaining only the thinnest veneer of official deniability. The Bruce royal government and the Scottish aristocracy were well aware that an invasion was imminent and were equally busy preparing for its repulse. The mastermind and driving force behind these mobilising efforts was, of course, the royal Guardian, Thomas Randolph. It is probable that the strain and pressure of directing these efforts and coercing elements of the somewhat reluctant Scottish aristocracy to contribute to the realm's defence exacerbated Randolph's existing illness, contributing to his death on 20 July 1332.[78] A mere eleven days later, on 31 July, the Disinherited took to sea in a cobbled together fleet of around eighty-eight vessels.[79] Their destination Scotland and the lost seats of their ancestors.

All too aware of this perilous development, the Scottish aristocracy, already in the early stages of mustering their collective military assets, convened a parliament at Perth on 2 August to decide upon Randolph's replacement as David II's Guardian and the de facto ruler of Scotland.[80] As we have seen, Robert I had transformed the political order of Scotland, enriching and upraising his allies at the expense of his enemies. His most trusted lieutenants had been given not just land and money but a large amount of autonomy and authority over the royal administration of Scotland, allowed to run their corner of the country and wage war in the pursuit of their shared interests. With Thomas Randolph's death, the last pillar of this system had fallen, the old guard finally removed. Yet these men had relatives that had risen with them and who were now eager to claim their place among the front ranks of Scotland's political community. It would now be for this new generation of Scottish nobility to see if they could co-operate with one another and rally around effectively and protect the throne of their child king. Meanwhile, after nearly two decades of being kept under the thumb of a powerful authoritarian king and his cabal of lieutenants, the remainder of the Scottish nobility suddenly found themselves with an opportunity to influence the course of Scottish politics once again.

After a day of rancorous debate, Earl Domhnall of Mar was chosen as the new Guardian.[81] Like his cousin and predecessor, Thomas, Domhnall was a maternal nephew of King Robert. He was in many ways an unusual choice, his election as Guardian and regent signalling the diminished influence of the Bruce family's traditional confederates. Born sometime in the early 1300s, Domhnall had been captured by the English in 1306 shortly after his uncle announced his bid for the throne. As a result, the young earl was raised in a relatively luxurious and gentle captivity in England. He was like so many other Scottish noble hostages freed following Edward II's defeat at Bannockburn. However, Domhnall chose to remain in England and subsequently fought against the forces of his Scottish royal relatives on Edward's behalf throughout the 1320s, even taking part in the Battle of Old Byland.

Domhnall's loyalties were, like most men of his time and class, overwhelmingly personal rather than cultural. Indeed, his eventual return to Scotland was prompted by the death and overthrow of his friend and patron, Edward II. He subsequently commanded a wing of the Scottish army during the Battle of Stanhope Park, facing off against an English army fighting under the command of Edward's usurpers, Queen Isabella and Roger Mortimer. Testimony during the trial of Thomas of Woodstock suggested that Domhnall may have been in contact with Henry de Beaumont and part of some scheme to solicit Scottish support for the forcible removal of the regents.[82]

In a sense, Domhnall was a compromise candidate for the silent majority of the Scottish nobility. He was backed by the significant portion of the aristocracy that was not particularly closely aligned with the Bruce dynasty and who wanted to avoid a drawn-out war with the Disinherited or their English backers.[83] He was also aided by his royal blood, a trait he shared, after a fashion, with his primary rival for the Guardianship, Lord Robert Bruce of Liddesdale, the illegitimate eldest son of the late King Robert.[84] Born sometime in the 1290s, Robert accused his younger cousin of plotting with the Disinherited to restore the Balliols, with much being made of Domhnall's former adherence to the English king. It seems, however, that Robert's bellicosity told against him at the Perth parliament. This political concern was probably compounded by his illegitimacy and the perceived danger of placing royal authority in the hands of someone with a compelling alternative claim to the throne.

With his authority and position as Guardian ratified by the Scottish parliament, Mar quickly set about building upon the work begun by Thoams Randolph to gather the supplies and weapons necessary for the coming campaign. All too aware, thanks to their numerous spies, that the Disinherited were proceeding up the east coast of Scotland but unsure exactly where they planned to make landfall, Mar organised the Bruce loyalists into two distinct armies.[85] One of these armies was placed north of the Firth of Forth, while the other, probably of roughly equal size, was placed to its south. The plan was simple but elegant. Wherever the Disinherited landed, they would soon find themselves opposed by a substantial Scottish army. The closest Scottish force would seek to hem in the Disinherited, attacking them if deemed practical, while the other army marched to reinforce them.

Mar placed himself in command of the northern army and appointed Earl Patrick of Dunbar to the command of the force guarding the coast south of the Firth. Patrick's father, also called Patrick, had been one of the candidates for the throne of Scotland who brought their claims before the council arbitrated by Edward I in 1291.[86] In 1296 he had fought for Edward I against John Balliol and the Scottish Guardians. It had been his wife, Majorie Comyn, who had surrendered Dunbar Castle to the swiftly retreating Scottish army, and in doing so unwittingly triggering the disastrous Battle of Dunbar.[87] Succeeding to the earldom upon his father's death in 1308, the younger Patrick had remained firm in his allegiance to the English king and the concept of English royal overlordship until Bannockburn. After this defeat, which he was not present for, Patrick smuggled Edward II and his immediate retinue onto a departing ship before hurrying to make peace with the Bruces.[88]

On 6 August 1332, with these Scottish armies still scrambling into place, Balliol and his army of the Disinherited made landfall at the port town of Kinghorn in Fife.[89] Shepherding a fleet of more than eighty ships of disparate sizes and packed with a small army of unhappy men and horses was no easy feat and it seems that the Disinherited leaders, having already crossed the Firth of Forth, were disinclined to push their luck further. Their landing in Kinghorn was opposed by a considerable force of local Scottish levies led by Earl Donnchadh of Fife and Alexander Sexton, whose father commanded the garrison at Berwick.[90] This force of Bruce-aligned Scots, which may well have outnumbered the entire Disinherited army, launched an immediate attack, hoping to catch the enemy as they attempted to disembark and pin them against the sea. It was a bold and daring attack that placed the Disinherited army in acute peril.

Recognising the danger, Henry de Beamont and his fellow Disinherited commanders countered with a large force of archers supported by a handful of men at arms and they bloodily repulsed the Fife levies. Sexton was cut down during the attack alongside a number of other important members of the regional nobility. Under the command of the Earl of Fife, the survivors of the Scottish army withdrew, looking to rendezvous with the Earl of Mar's host, leaving the port town and first blood to Balliol and the Disinherited. The Battle at Kinghorn, brief as it was, foreshadowed the decisive role archery would play in the two full pitched battles fought by the Disinherited, the Battles of Dupplin Moor and Halidon Hill. The lesson was simple; on an open field, the lightly armoured and poorly trained levy troops would struggle to stand before the withering hails of arrows loosed by massed archery.

Undoubtedly pleased by their victory over the Earl of Fife's forces and having completed the rest of their landing unopposed, the Disinherited next struck out for Dunfermline, some 15 miles to the west.[91] Meanwhile, the fleet was dispatched further north with the goal of supporting an eventual siege of Perth.[92] The march to Dunfermline was something of a detour, but one they hoped would yield them much-needed supplies and intelligence regarding their enemy's disposition. The Disinherited reached Dunfermline, the traditional burial place of Scottish kings, without opposition. However, they did discover that the town and monastery were full of supplies and weapons, including several hundred of the famed Scottish pikes, gathered to support the Bruce loyalist armies.[93] There is some evidence that, while his troops rested and enjoyed the bounty gathered on their enemy's behalf, Edward Balliol, eager to step into the role of Scottish king, began aggressively negotiating the terms of his future relationship with the leaders of local monastic communities.[94] After two days of recuperation and shaking down monks for money, the Disinherited, probably aware now of the broad disposition of their enemies, marched north towards Perth and the Earl of Mar's army.

On 10 August the Disinherited reached the southern bank of the River Earn, to find that the bridge had been destroyed and their way across was blocked by the Earl of Mar, whose host had rendezvoused with the Earl of Fife's levy.[95] The rest of the day was spent in a tense stand-off with neither side wanting to make the first move. The Disinherited must have been keenly aware that the Bruce loyalists' second army, led by the Earl of Dunbar, was already probing north and that to hesitate too long would see them crushed between the two. On the other hand, the Scottish army arrayed on the opposite side of the Earn was a massive mobilisation of men when compared to the Disinherited's tiny army. The exact size of the Earl of Mar's army is greatly exaggerated in both later English and Scottish chronicles. A more realistic estimate, proffered by historians, formed by considering the manpower available within the Kingdom of Scotland and the suggestion that the Earl of Dunbar's army was roughly the same size, puts the army at around fifteen thousand men. Enough to outnumber the small Disinherited army by a grotesque ten to one.

That the Scottish nobility had been able to raise two such forces while negotiating a leadership crisis speaks highly of the thoroughness of the late Guardian's preparations and the Scottish aristocracy's continued ability to co-ordinate. Unlike their outnumbered counterparts in the Disinherited, the members of the Scottish army were not paid or fed for their service;[96] a situation that had a profound impact upon the character and organisation of previous military campaigns. There were two principal forms of military recruitment operating within medieval Scotland at this time. The first method of raising troops was a variant derived from traditional feudal obligation, in which a sort of army of retinues was formed as members of the nobility mobilised both their own military households and called upon their vassals and allies to do the same.[97]

Like England, Scotland nominally operated a system of knight's fees that supposedly denoted the number of knights a landowner was expected to raise for military service. However, much like in England, the actual relationship between the value of land and the number of knight's fees attached to it was inconsistent and notional at best. Numerous records exist of landowners being assessed as owning fractions of a knight's fee. Did these landowners have to co-operate with neighbours or relatives to equip a single knight between them? Was there some sum of money that equated directly to a knight's fee that such individuals could pay a fraction of? Were all knight's fees intended to be paid in this way? Overall, it is probably best to regard knight's fees as a comparative financial instrument used in negotiations between the nobility and royal officials, rather than a strict quota for the raising of troops. The reality is that the number of soldiers raised by any noble was highly variable and depended almost entirely upon their commitment and closeness to the royal government or an immediate royal lieutenant at the time a campaign was called.

While this system would produce its fair share of levies, it also raised a significant portion of well-equipped and trained soldiers in the form of the combined military households and immediate retainers of the participating aristocrats. Armies raised in this way, temporary military coalitions of aristocrats gathered together for a single campaign or objective, had carried out the majority of the everyday fighting in the Bruce's war to claim the throne of Scotland.

The second route for the mustering of soldiers in Scotland was the tradition that in times of emergency, the king, or in this case his Guardian, could summon every able-bodied man in the kingdom to military service.[98] Such musters were usually called only on a regional level to support ongoing campaigns being fought by more traditionally raised troops. While capable of raising formidable amounts of troops, their usefulness was invariably curtailed by their lack of equipment and military training. Worse, while such troops were instructed to bring their own food, they could not realistically gather or carry more than enough to support themselves for a few days.

In 1318, Robert I passed legislation in an attempt to mitigate some of the weaknesses of these levies, imposing standards of equipment that such men were supposed to bring on campaign with them. Such standards were invariably based upon an individual's income; a rich man with a yearly income in excess of £10 was required to equip himself in a manner of a man at arms with some measure of plate armour, an aketon, steel gauntlets and a helmet.[99] Armour such as this could be manufactured in limited amounts in Scotland but was largely imported from continental Europe and even England. Upon the outbreak of war, a frustrated Edward III made repeated attempts to halt the trade of weapons and armour across the Scottish border.[100] In contrast, according to Robert's legislation, the poor, those who owned property equivalent to the cash value of a cow or less, only had to bring a spear or a bow and twenty arrows.[101] However, a lack of evidence makes it impossible to judge the extent to which these reforms were effective in increasing the quality and armaments of such levies.

At times of emergency such as the Disinherited's invasion, Scottish commanders could call upon both methods of recruitment to raise surprisingly large forces with a core of well-equipped and disciplined soldiers quickly. Demographic necessity and tactical lessons gleaned from the previous war had taught the Scots to fight primarily on foot, their armies organised into large formations or schiltrons of tightly packed, spear-armed infantry. When used cannily, this system had proven formidable.[102] At Bannockburn, the use of such formations had neutralised the enemy's superiority in heavy cavalry, which proved unable to break through the tightly packed wall of spears. Then on the second day of the battle, they were used to successfully hem in the crammed and panicking English army and grind it down.

Mar's superior numbers made him confident of victory, yet the Earn was no less an obstacle to his forces that it was to the Disinherited. Rather than risk forcing a crossing in the teeth of the enemy archers, he instead planned to dispatch flanking forces the following day and envelope the small pro-Balliol army, making effective use of his superior numbers. As night gathered, Mar was content to post a guard over the now shattered bridge before sending to nearby Perth for ale and wine, which was distributed liberally to the entire army.[103]

While Mar's host began a night of drinking and carousing, the Disinherited, well aware of the perilousness of their situation, embarked upon a daring night march. One of the Scottish members of the army, Andrew Murray, was familiar with the region and knew of a small nearby ford.[104] This proved to be unguarded, allowing the entire Disinherited army to cross over to the north bank of the Earn. There, in the darkness and confusion, they came across and scattered a small number of Scots who were either the guard left at the bridge or possibly even a group of camp followers trailing the main army. The Disinherited withdrew to a new position on the edge of Dupplin Moor but seem to have half believed that they had already dealt a grievous blow to the main Scottish army.

Dawn would soon relieve them of this misapprehension. Mar and his fellow Bruce adherents were, upon awaking, confused but not dismayed by the Disinherited's night-time redeployment. Indeed, realising they no longer had to negotiate the river or co-ordinate a complex series of separate attacks, the newly roused Scottish army boldly descended upon their enemy. Word of the approaching attack was brought back to the Disinherited by Thomas Vesci and Ralph Stafford who, returning from their scouting mission, informed Balliol and Beaumont that the large Scottish army was not only intact, but closing rapidly with them.[105] Wasting no time, the Disinherited effected a redeployment of their own, taking a strong defensive position at the bottom of a depression on the edge of the moor, the flanks of which were guarded by two small hills. The Disinherited strung their men at arms in a thin line across this depression while the archers arrayed themselves upon the slopes of the two overlooking hills. In order to avoid being outflanked and rolled up, the Disinherited's small army had to span the entirety of the space between these two hills. As a result, their only reserve was a small force of forty mounted German knights whose task it was to crash into and fill any gaps in the fragile battle line.[106]

Yet even as the leading elements of the Scottish army came within sight of the rapidly repositioning Disinherited, the bad blood and rivalry that had characterised negotiations during the parliament at Perth reared its ugly head. Having seen the small size of the Disinherited army and the banners of the English lords that accompanied it, Earl Domhnall Mar had informed his subordinates that he intended to give Balliol and Beaumont a chance to surrender. After all, only mad men would attempt to fight on when so badly outnumbered and the command echelon of the Disinherited were seeded with the well-connected nobility of northern England, men whose ransoms would bring their captors a fortune.[107] However, this suggestion greatly angered his second in command and rival for the Guardianship, Robert Bruce, who immediately seized upon the chance to accuse Mar of treason.

The result of the blazing row that followed was that both Scottish commanders became determined to prove their loyalty and worthiness to lead by being the first to crush the Disinherited. The army had been divided into two massive schiltrons, commanded by Mar and Bruce respectively.[108] With their commanders desperate to outdo one another, the two halves of the Scottish army began racing each other across the Moor, abandoning any hope of a co-ordinated attack. This haste, combined with the rough and uneven terrain of the Moor, saw both formations become increasingly disorganised and deformed. The race was won by Robert Bruce and his contingent, who made first contact with the thin line of the Disinherited's men at arms. Yet rather than delivering a concerted hammer blow to shatter the enemy line, the Bruce's now out of formation troops staggered or stumbled down towards their foes piecemeal. As more and more of Robert's men arrived, the effects of this added mass began to tell and the Disinherited men at arms were inch by inch pushed back. Crucially though, the battle line remained intact. Meanwhile, the English archers positioned on the two hills on either side of this melee began raining arrows down upon the Bruce's troops. As the Disinherited line was pushed further back, it began to expose the sides of the Bruce's schiltron to greater volumes of enfilade fire.[109]

The Scottish army was, due to the mechanisms through which it was raised, composed of both hastily raised levies and the battle-hardened retainers and warbands of the nobility. Naturally enough, both Robert Bruce and Earl Domhnall had packed their best-equipped and trained troops in the front of their formations. After all, it was these men who were most capable of going toe to toe with their similarly equipped and trained equivalents in the

Disinherited army. It would be this martial elite that would chew through the thin line of Disinherited soldiers, breaking the army and putting a final end to Edward Balliol's ambitions for the throne. Of course, this meant that the formations more numerous less well-armoured and disciplined troops, those least equipped to withstand arrow fire, were left as the English archers' only real target. While the Disinherited's men stubbornly held in the centre, the archers systemically whittled away at the schiltron's poorly protected flanks. As the men on the flanks began to panic, they tried to press inwards into the formation in their desperation to seek shelter from the arrows. This caused a dangerous crush that greatly impeded the combat effectiveness of the formation, the constant pressure and churn of men not only preventing fresh soldiers from reaching the front line but began to pin fighters against the enemy without the space necessarily to fight effectively.[110]

This unfolding crisis was then pushed into the realm of outright disaster by the arrival of the second half of the Scottish army and the Earl of Mar's schiltron. Surveying the unfolding battle, Mar could have divided his command and attacked the archers directly. The close-knit formation favoured by his troops was ill suited to the rapid pursuit of light troops or skirmishers and it is likely that had he made the attempt, the enemy archers would have simply withdrawn further up hill and poured arrows down upon his slowly pursing troops. As inglorious as this would have been, it may have given the Bruce's' troops the time necessary to recover and break through the Disinherited battleline. However, Mar was a political creature, and he had no intention of leaving the lion's share of the glory to his rival. Rather, he wanted to be able to tell his fellow Scottish aristocrats that his personal intervention in the battle led directly to a swift and decisive victory. Mar was almost certainly unaware of just how much danger the men of the Bruce's battle formation were in; to him it must have seemed like the impossibly thin line of enemy combatants could not help but break and scatter should he throw the full weight of his forces into the melee. So, he did just that. Hurrying downhill, Mar's men crashed into their comrades, exacerbating the existing crush to the point of deadliness. A situation that only got worse as the flanks of Mar's formation also came under attack by archers.[111]

Perhaps as many as a thousand of Mar's soldiers died in the crush, suffocated, or trod under heel by their fellows as they passed out or lost their footing. In the end, the army was routed, leaving behind heaps of the dead and broken. The exact number of Scottish casualties are as difficult to estimate as the size of the army, although they were surely high.

Among the most prominent casualties were the Guardian of Scotland, Earl Domhnall of Mar, his rival, Robert Bruce of Liddesdale, Earl Muireadhach Stewart of Menteith and Earl Thomas Randolph of Moray, the son of the previous Guardian.[112] Earl Donnchadh of Fife, now bested by the Disinherited for the second time within a week, surrendered and formally swore loyalty to Edward Balliol. In contrast, we are told only thirty-five of the Disinherited's men at arms were killed. Through canny positioning, the power of the longbow and a healthy dose of hubris on their enemy's part, the Disinherited had triumphed over almost impossible odds.

The Disinherited moved quickly to besiege Perth, whose commanders surrendered the city in short order. On 18 August, a full week after the Battle of Dupplin Moor, Earl Patrick of Dunbar's army finally arrived and attempted to place Perth under siege. Patrick was immediately confronted with a problem. The number of archers now positioned on the walls of Perth would make any attempt to storm the city unimaginably bloody, if not outrightly suicidal. On the other hand, Perth was full of provisions, while Dunbar's large army was filled with hungry mouths, useless to the operation of a prolonged siege. Should he attempt to besiege the city, it was likely that his forces would starve long before the Disinherited.

Patrick's final gambit was to attempt to blockade Perth from further resupply with an improvised Scottish fleet.[113] This failed decisively when the Disinherited's own fleet smashed the blockade, sinking or driving off Dunbar's ships. Feeling he had no other option, Patrick withdrew before dissolving his army, sending most of its troops home to Bruce-aligned territories. The earl remained in the area with a smaller force of hardened soldiers, skirmishing with the forces of the Disinherited. Yet he was unable to threaten their hold in Perth or prevent Edward Balliol's access to Scone, the sacred coronation site of Scottish kings.

Chapter Six

Once More Under the Yoke

The outcome of the Battle of Dupplin Moor, fought in August 1332, was as spectacular as it was unexpected. The Disinherited, a mere handful of exiles leading a skeletal army composed of mercenaries and northern English adventurers, had routed one army of Bruce loyalists in battle, convincingly seen off another and captured the de facto capital of Scotland. The Guardian of Scotland, Earl Domhnall of Mar, had been slain in battle only days after his election. His primary rival for the regency, Robert Bruce of Liddesdale, two Earls from Bruce-aligned families, a dozen or so other lords and several thousand soldiers were killed alongside him. The scale of this defeat and the significant losses inflicted upon the new leadership cadre of the Bruce royal government sent them into a state of temporary disarray. The Disinherited and their figurehead, Edward Balliol, were all too quick to seize upon this momentary weakness and lack of leadership.

To many contemporaries in Scotland and beyond, most of whom would have heard only the bare details of the battle and its result, the Disinherited's victory against such long odds spoke of providence and a degree of divine favour for the Balliol cause. When viewed through modern secularly influenced eyes, it is easy to dismiss this consideration as tangential at best, just another layer to the blended cultural and political shock of the battle's aftermath. However, divine arbitration of worthy causes through feats of arms was a well-established, if rarely invoked, principle of both medieval theology and law, and it is worth noting that, following the battle, the majority of the formally staunch pro-Bruce Scottish religious establishment rushed to make terms with Balliol.[1] This sudden influx of clerical support included all but one of Scotland's bishops, as well as the abbots of Dunfermline, Coupar, Inchaffray, Scone and Arbroath.[2]

In addition to the hastily given support of the Scottish Church, the Disinherited's victory at Dupplin Moor and their subsequent occupation of Perth persuaded many of the surrounding region's aristocrats and power brokers to begin presenting themselves at Balliol's ad hoc court. The most important of these defectors was the hapless Earl Donnchadh, or Duncan, of Fife, who had been captured during the battle and had eagerly declared for Balliol as a means of securing his freedom. As the Earl of Fife and head of the Macduff family, Donnchadh's defection represented more than a simple model for coercing the support of the senior Scottish aristocracy. At Scone, on 24 September, before his fellow Disinherited, the assembled Scottish prelates and a smattering of local defectors, Edward Balliol was crowned King of Scotland.[3] Earl Donnchadh performed his family's traditional role in the coronation by placing the crown upon Edward's head, while the ceremony itself was presided over by Bishop William Sinclair of Dunkeld.[4] The Disinherited now had a lawful King of Scotland with which to legitimise and secure their numerous outstanding territorial claims, crowned in the correct place by the correct people.

Within modern historiography, the lasting legacy of the Battle of Dupplin Moor and the Disinherited's great adventure is its role in foreshadowing both the coming military ascendancy of the English archer and its status as the inciting incident of the, itself often overlooked and heavily abridged, Second War for Scottish Independence. Neither of these legacies would have been readily apparent to contemporaries in the autumn of 1332. While contemporaries would have been aware of the decisive role archery played in the battle, it is important to remember that the English, as well as many of their enemies, already made extensive use of the bow in a system of combined arms and tactics. Yes, archery had played a big part in securing victory at Dupplin Moor but the same could be said of the Battle of Falkirk thirty-five years before. Neither battle was hailed by those who fought in it as the beginning of a military revolution. The archers' legendary victories over the flower of French chivalry still lay off in the unglimpsed and unwritten future.

Likewise, the Disinherited's invasion of Scotland was a private enterprise by a clique of nobles that sort to reclaim the lands and titles confiscated from their immediate forebearers by installing their own alternative candidate on the throne of Scotland. While it was obvious to most that Edward III had abetted the Disinherited, it was still not clear, probably even to him, whether he would break the Treaty of Edinburgh-Northampton and intervene militarily on Balliol's behalf. He had, after all, gone to some pains to create a layer, albeit a tissue thin one of official deniability about his earlier support for the Disinherited.

The result of the battle that would have seemed the most momentous and world shaking to its contemporaries within Scotland, the crowning of Balliol, is often overlooked or treated in a cursory manner within many later examinations and retellings of Scottish history. This is partly because of their foreknowledge of the ultimate failure of the Disinherited and partly because they did not want to muddy the narrative of an Anglo-Scottish conflict with unwanted nuance. The Bruce's Stewart relatives and successors, in their attempts to effectively govern a very different and divided Scotland, found that it was advantageous to conflate Robert I's reconstruction of the Scottish monarchy with the establishment of a Scottish national identity.[5]

Yet the supporters of David II spent decades fighting both the King of England and a rival King of Scotland. Edward Balliol and his Disinherited supporters did not simply fade into history, dwarfed by the immensity of the Anglo-Scottish conflict they had unwittingly unleashed, they actively had to be reckoned with by their Bruce enemies. At times, backed by their English allies, the Disinherited came perilously close to turning the clock back and restoring the Balliol monarchy in earnest. Indeed, as we shall see, Dupplin Moor was far from the high-water mark of the Disinherited's success in Scotland.

This discussion about the immediate impact of the Battle of Dupplin Moor and its contrast with the long-term legacy of the Disinherited, of course, raises the question of just how strong the Disinherited position was at the time of Balliol's coronation in September 1332? As previously stated, the losses sustained at Dupplin Moor were a serious and shocking blow to the leadership of the Bruce faction. Yet the Bruce family had in its bid for the throne cultivated the support of some of the Scottish nobilities most-established and influential families, such as the Stewarts and Campbells; families that had only grown and thrived as a result of the new estates and titles heaped upon them in reward for their loyalty.

Barely a month after their defeat at Dupplin Moor, new leaders of the pro-Bruce faction were already beginning to emerge and, now cognisant of the danger of facing the Disinherited in pitched battle, were busy preparing a more surreptitious resistance. While it seems that few thanked him for his efforts at the time, Earl Patrick of Dunbar's decision to dissolve his army when it became clear that any attempt to besiege Perth would end in disaster preserved the lives of thousands of soldiers. The majority of such troops were raised from pro-Bruce regions and their safe return, alongside their commanders, greatly enhanced those areas' ability to resist the Disinherited.

The primary problem that Edward Balliol and the other Disinherited faced was that their army, while disproportionately formidable, was too small to meaningfully hold onto any significant territory. They could comfortably hold Perth and its immediate environs but attempting to stretch their authority further required dividing the already modest army, rendering its constituent parts excessively vulnerable to raids by Bruce partisans. In order to make good their claims within Scotland, the Disinherited required either reinforcements from England or a greater degree of support from the Scottish aristocracy. While Balliol had received pledges of support from segments of the Scottish nobility, most of these were relatively minor lords from the area now threatened directly by his army or who had been captured during battle and forced to submit at the point of a sword. Such defections were motivated by survival instinct and opportunism rather than genuine enthusiasm for the idea of a Balliol restoration. As such, these fresh adherents to the Disinherited's cause could not be relied upon to provide their whole-hearted support or even retain their newfound loyalties once the Disinherited's army moved on.

The Disinherited were probably hampered in this regard by the amount of time that had passed since the Bruce family's political ascendancy. The Disinherited were the sons, sons-in-law and even grandsons of those men that had been deprived of their Scottish lands and titles for refusing to submit to Robert I. An entire generation had passed in the eighteen years since Bannockburn and the communities once ruled over by the Disinherited's forebearers had been given ample time to form attachments to their new, Bruce-appointed, masters. It had been twelve years since the unravelling of the Soules Conspiracy that saw the arrest and execution of many of the Balliols' most adherent supporters in Scotland.[6] It had been a staggering thirty-six years since Edward's father, John Balliol, was forced to abdicate the throne of Scotland and ceased to exercise any measure of royal authority.[7] Perhaps time, just as much as the proactive policies of the Bruce royal government, had seen Balliol support within Scotland thin.

Balliol and his Disinherited allies had good reason to linger in Perth after the Battle of Dupplin Moor. Their army had to be rested after the colossal efforts it made during the battle, preparation for Edward's crucial coronation had to be made and time allowed for news of their victory to spread and Scottish defectors to make their way to Perth. However, the new leaders of the Bruce faction were organising rapidly and the Disinherited were keenly aware that to tarry in Perth further would risk them becoming isolated and encircled. Edward's solution to this threat was an aggressive one that sought to make the most of the lingering advantages won at Dupplin Moor.

Gathering what local reinforcements they could, the Disinherited struck out for the one area of Scotland that had seen large-scale pro-Balliol uprisings in response to their arrival; Edward's ancestral lordship, Galloway.[8] The plan had several points to recommend it. Firstly, if successful, it would allow them to establish a proper power base within Scotland, whose military and financial resources could be tapped to support further campaigns. Secondly the journey itself, an armed sojourn across the length and breadth of Scotland, at a time in which the Bruce government controlled no major armies, would provide plenty of opportunity to rally further supporters or at the very least to intimidate them into submission. Finally, establishing themselves in Galloway, located in the south-west of Scotland, would place the Disinherited in a position where they could communicate and negotiate reliably with Edward III of England.

Before departing, Edward left the Earl of Fife in command of Perth and a small garrison.[9] The earl was by far the highest-ranking defector to join the Disinherited and therefore needed to be treated with a measure of respect. By granting him the prestigious custodianship of the kingdom's capital, Edward may have hoped to further secure the earl's loyalty and signal to other potential defectors from the Bruce party that he was willing to treat them generously. Of course, by entrusting Perth to the Earl of Fife, who had his own troops and military resources, Edward was also preserving his valuable archers and veteran men-at-arms for the main expedition.

Over the course of the following two weeks, Edward crossed Scotland. The Disinherited army headed for Irvine on the west coast before cutting inland through Coylton in South Ayrshire and pushing on into Galloway.[10] At no point in this lengthy journey did they encounter any armed or organised resistance. Everywhere the army marched, David II's supporters would melt away, leaving the locals to make hasty, if perhaps largely insincere, submissions to Edward Balliol. By far the most notable of these submissions was that of Alexander Bruce, the perhaps illegitimate son of Edward Bruce and yet another nephew of the late Robert I.[11] Alexander, whose mother, Isabella, was an aunt of the Disinherited commander David Strathbogie, had eventually succeeded his father to the Earldom of Carrick.[12] His surrender and subsequent profession of loyalty to Balliol delivered them effective control of the south-west of Scotland. That Alexander Bruce, a first cousin of David II and senior member of the Bruce party, was willing to capitulate to a Balliol claimant is a highly instructive example of the perpetually caveated nature of loyalty and politics during this period. Alexander was, in the short term at least, willing to renounce his normally advantageous familial connections in order to maintain immediate control of his earldom and a position of primacy within its interconnected web of aristocratic affinities.

Emboldened by this utter lack of resistance and the warm welcome he received in Galloway, Balliol decided to press his advantage as far as he could and marched his forces back eastward into the heavily fortified border region. It was here that they at last ran into a semblance of opposition. As the Disinherited army was sweeping the countryside around the crucial border town of Jedburgh and its accompanying fortifications, they were ambushed by a force of Bruce loyalists led by Archibald Douglas.[13] Archibald was a younger brother of the Bruce's famed commander and companion James 'The Black' Douglas and had served in the Scottish invasion of England in 1327.[14] James' eldest son and heir, William, was a young man, likely in his early to mid-teens in 1332, and had left the management and defence of the family's numerous interests in the region to his uncle. Archibald was also the father-in-law of the defector Earl Alexander Bruce of Carrick. This attack, probably conducted in the hopes of catching the Disinherited army while it was still dispersed for travel, was discovered and repelled without difficulty. During the brief skirmish, one of Douglas' subordinates, Robert Lauder, whose father and namesake was the Bruce Justicar of Lothian, was taken prison.[15]

Flushed by this minor victory, the Disinherited pushed on to Roxburgh, occupying the castle on 3 October.[16] Roxburgh Castle had been built by David I of Scotland sometime around the early 1130s. In accordance with its status as a crucial border fort, its defences had been greatly strengthened by successive kings of Scotland until Robert I had partially demolished it as part of his policy of denying fortifications to the enemy. Despite this, its occupation was, even in its ruined state, of considerable strategic value, although it is notable that Edward himself was lodged in the nearby, but much more comfortable, Kelso Abbey.[17]

The Disinherited enthusiasm for this success and the continued lack of serious opposition was probably dampened somewhat when word reached them that Perth had fallen on 7 October to a Bruce army under the leadership of Robert Keith, the Bruce's hereditary Marshall of Scotland and a veteran of Bannockburn. Earl Donnchadh was captured alongside the city but soon talked his way out of captivity, once again inveigling his way into the upper echelons of Bruce loyalists. The Disinherited would also have been aware that as they progressed through Roxburghshire and the surrounding countryside, they were being shadowed by an army under the leadership of Andrew de Moray. Andrew's father, for whom he was named, had been an ally and co-commander of William Wallace before he died of wounds sustained during their celebrated victory at the Battle of Stirling Bridge.[18] The younger Andrew had been captured by Edward I as a child in 1303 and raised in captivity until he was finally freed in the grand prisoner exchange that followed the Battle of Bannockburn.[19]

Following the death of the Earl of Mar at Dupplin Moor, Moray had been hastily elected as the new Guardian of Scotland by a small conclave of Bruce supporters.[20] Aware of the potentially disastrous consequences of engaging the Disinherited in open battle, he began to stalk them through the borders. He attempted through frequent harassing actions and the threat of his army's continued presence in their rear to contain the Disinherited and arrest their advance. Moray and his subordinates spotted a potentially decisive opportunity in Balliol's insistence in quartering away from the main Disinherited army based in Roxburgh Castle.

However, rather than simply fall upon Balliol and overwhelm his bodyguard while sending a blocking force to the nearby Kelso Bridge, the Bruce commanders instead elected to attempt to demolish the bridge.[21] The arduous and conspicuous nature of this work alerted the Roxburgh garrison, who were able to ford the river and come to Edward's assistance.[22] Worse still for the Bruce loyalist, with the alarm raised they were soon driven off from the bridge, leading to Andrew Moray's capture, alongside the notorious Flemish mercenary, John Crabbe.[23] This was a serious blow to the coherency and continuity of Bruce leadership, who had now lost two Guardians in the space of a few months.

Interestingly, both men's captors were allowed to sell on their ransoms to King Edward III of England.[24] Cashing out of a ransom by trading custody of prisoners to a superior with the resources necessary to hold them in suitable comfort and security while engaged in the lengthy and complex process of negotiating and collecting the full sum was a relatively common practice.[25] It was also a way for lesser knights or men-at-arms to come to the notice and earn the gratitude of their commanders.

English interest in supervising the incarceration of John Crabbe was easily explained by his previous piratical predations on English shipping.[26] Andrew de Moray, on the other hand, was the Guardian of Scotland and the lawfully appointed regent of David II, the English king's brother-in-law. Moray may have exercised some influence on this decision by arguing that as the Guardian of Scotland he could not be ransomed by someone of lesser rank and that he therefore had to be handed over to Edward III of England.[27] However, this was clearly a politically motivated snub, meant to underline his continued rejection of Balliol's claim to the Scottish throne. As such Balliol and his fellow Disinherited were under no real legal obligation to acquiesce to Moray's demands. That they did so, and that Edward III actually accepted this offer, shows both the influence the English king wielded over the rank and file of the Disinherited and the keen interest he was now taking in their progress.

The transfer of such valuable prisoners to England shows either the ardency with which Edward Balliol was trying to court his English counterpart's support or that he, the king of Scotland, lacked the necessary influence over his largely English army to resist. Edward III was young, hot headed and excessively proud, traits that to contemporary eyes all had a distinctly romantic and kingly air about them. Edward Balliol must have been aware of the precariousness of his own position and the multitude of options available to the younger Edward, should he wish to embark on a great northern military adventure. Balliol and his allies were in a sense gambling that Edward III would see the value in supporting their claim to the throne of Scotland, in exchange for recognition of the English king's suzerainty over the British Isles. Yet Edward III could also choose to emulate his grandfather's strategy, sidelining the Balliols and attempting to rule an occupied Scotland through a council composed of English garrison commanders and Scottish aristocratic collaborators. Then there was the possibility that the young David II, who was after all Edward III's brother-in-law, would, once separated from the families of his father's supporters, make for a more expedient and pliant junior partner or puppet king. Such an arrangement would avoid the troublesome task of removing large swathes of the Scottish aristocracy from their treasured offices and estates to make room for Balliol's Disinherited allies.

In late November, Edward Balliol attempted to tip the younger king's hand and galvanise him into action by publishing the details of an agreement he alleged the two had reached prior to the Disinherited invasion of Scotland.[28] According to this agreement, Edward and his heirs agreed to pay homage to the Kings of England as the rightful feudal overlords of Scotland.[29] In addition to this, they committed to undertaking military service on behalf of the English king when summoned, alongside 200 Scottish men-at-arms.[30] In exchange for help in securing the Scottish throne for his family, Balliol further agreed to cede £20,000 worth of territory and fortifications which was to be permanently annexed by the English king.[31] A further clause stated that Edward Balliol promised to treat a dethroned David II equitably and proposed a potential marriage between the almost fifty-year-old Balliol and Edward III's then eleven-year-old sister, Joan, in the event that she chose to repudiate her marriage to David.[32]

It is probable that this agreement was genuine rather than a strangely belligerent offer meant to tempt Edward III into granting his support. It is difficult to imagine that Edward III would have allowed the Disinherited to invade Scotland and tacitly provided them with the necessary financial backing without establishing some method of benefiting from their success. The specificity of the terms in regard to the amount of territory to be seceded to England and the conditions surrounding the military service owed by the Scottish king suggest that they were the product of extended negotiations. Balliol must have been keenly aware that the surrendering of Scottish territory to England would be hugely unpopular among the Scottish nobility, whose support he eventually hoped to win. That he would risk further isolating them by publishing a hitherto secret agreement with Edward III is compelling evidence that he had become convinced that he required English aid to properly establish himself as King of Scotland, despite the current lack of significant opposition. This may well have reflected the cash-strapped would-be king's difficulties in continuing to pay the Disinherited army without resorting to the sort of plundering and extortion that would only have further alienated his potential subjects.

While Edward III pondered the issue and attempted to solicit the support of a rather unco-operative English parliament, Edward Balliol agreed to a winter truce with David II's caretakers. He did so on the understanding that the truce would last until early February when a parliament could be convened that would have the authority to discuss a more permanent agreement.[33] Content that matters would rest where they lay until February, Edward withdrew from Roxburghshire and prepared to celebrate Christmas in Annan in the south of Galloway. From there, most of the Disinherited's carefully scraped together army returned to their respective homes, scattered across the north of England. The keystone of the Disinherited's unprecedented success up until this point had been their audacity. In settling down for the winter, Edward had bartered away the strategic initiative. Worse still, he had badly underestimated the resolve of his enemies and the extraordinary lengths they would go to thwart the return of the Disinherited.

On 16 December, Archibald Douglas, who had succeeded the captured Andrew de Moray as Guardian of Scotland, fell upon Annan with a considerable contingent of troops.[34] In contrast to his earlier failure at Jedburgh, this attack was a spectacular success. The Disinherited, confident in the sanctity of the truce, were literally caught abed and several hundred of them were remorselessly slain. Among the losses were such senior members as Walter Comyn, Roger de Mowbray and Edward's brother and immediate heir, Henry Balliol.[35] Edward only escaped by breaking down a partitioning wall in his accommodation and fleeing half-dressed into the winter-shrouded Galwegian countryside.[36] Earl Edward Bruce of Carrick was captured and after narrowly escaping summary execution was allowed to make peace with his relatives and rather sheepishly return to the Bruce fold.

For all the ease with which they had been achieved, the Disinherited's territorial gains in Scotland were brittle. They were ultimately predicated on the half-hearted or outrightly coerced co-operation of those regions that had fallen directly in the path of the Disinherited's army. With the threat from that army now lifted by the massacre at Annan, Balliol's authority in Scotland, such as it was, simply dissolved overnight. All the hard-won gains made by the Disinherited over the past months had come to nothing, all as a result of the new Guardian's decisive, if treacherous, raid.

Balliol emerged, deeply bedraggled a few days after the disaster in Carlisle, where he was afforded a warm welcome.[37] It then appears that he dispatched envoys to York, where Edward III was holding a session of the English parliament. Indeed, many of the now scattered Disinherited would have been summoned to attend the parliament as land-owning members of the English nobility. The convening of this parliament in York was far from a coincidence, and it was dominated by the question of how to react to the unfolding events in Scotland. Edward III made a great show of soliciting the advice of parliament but when they remained stubbornly non-committal or outrightly leery of renewed war, he began preparing for the invasion of Scotland anyway.[38] Edward III would support Balliol in securing the throne of Scotland, but he was determined to negotiate as high a price as possible, eagerly taking advantage of his ally's now greatly reduced circumstances. Rather than £20,000 worth of land scattered across the borders, the English king would now aim to annex the majority of southern Scotland, including Edinburgh, Selkirk, Roxburghshire, Dumfries and Peebles.[39] The desperate Edward Balliol had little recourse but to accept, in the hope that his hawkish English allies could place him on the throne of a now greatly reduced kingdom.

The wheels of English royal administration began to roll slowly into action in January and February 1333, beginning the arduous task of assembling an English royal army.[40] Edward III sought to expedite the situation by allowing the Disinherited to reassemble their own forces. This mustering of troops was financed directly by the king, who made large cash gifts to the Disinherited's leadership, including Henry de Beamont, David Strathbogie,

Gilbert de Umfraville and Henry de Ferrers.[41] The Disinherited found their ranks swollen by the addition of yet more English marcher lords, such as their old ally, Earl Henry of Lancaster, Earl Richard FitzAlan of Arundel and Ralph Neville.[42] They were further reinforced by a small contingent of Balliol's Scottish supporters who had, either through a profound sense of loyalty or desperation, followed Edward to England after his defeat.[43]

This army, largely paid for by Edward III but still nominally under the command of Edward Balliol and his Disinherited supporters, would proceed into Scotland, preparing the way for the main English host. The Disinherited crossed the border via Carlisle in early March with a force of several thousand men, meeting no real opposition from Bruce supporters who, under Archibald, were concentrated on fortifying Berwick. With no serious opposition in sight, the Disinherited army began to spread out as they burnt and pillaged a path towards Berwick, a marked contrast to their far more measured and convivial advance towards Galloway the previous autumn. These rapacious tactics, sometimes formally known as a Chevauchée, would in the next decade or so emerge as a favoured tactic of English armies fighting in France.[44] The usually modestly sized army would array itself in a great line and then advance through enemy-held territory, burning and looting anything they came across.[45] Theoretically, exemptions were made for Church property but in the heat of the moment few raiders ever enquired too closely into such legal niceties.[46]

The tactical rationale for such wholesale destruction was twofold. Firstly, the population, seeing that their current masters were wholly incapable of protecting them, would, so the line of argument went, be more likely to transfer their allegiance to their tormentors, motivated by the simple desire to avoid further destruction. Secondly, by damaging the enemy ruler's income and prestige through the destruction of their territory, the aggressors hoped to tempt the opposing army into challenging them to open battle. Of course, it is also worth noting that such tactics greatly enriched the raiding army and its commanders and were therefore exceedingly popular. While the Chevauchée, the grandest and most euphemistic incarnation of this practice, is heavily associated with English armies fighting in France during the Hundred Years' War, similar tactics had been used throughout the struggle for mastery of Scotland. As we have seen, Robert I himself had deliberately ravaged the Earldom of Buchan, robbing and slaughtering its population, as a way of breaking the Comyn family's hold over the region.[47] Likewise, after Bannockburn, Bruce-aligned armies had spent the better part of a decade raiding and pillaging across the north of England.[48]

Upon reaching the now strongly fortified and well-provisioned Berwick, the Disinherited army moved quickly to place it under siege while their newfound English allies continued to ravage the surrounding countryside. The efficacy of these siege operations was greatly enhanced by the arrival of an English fleet dispatched by Edward III, which prevented the town from being resupplied and reinforced by sea, while simultaneously ensuring that the besiegers themselves remained well supplied, despite the devastation wrought upon the surrounding area.[49] Berwick was not only vital to the defence of southern Scotland, guarding the coastal road that led to Edinburgh, Stirling and Perth, it was also an important economic centre and source of royal income. Breaking the siege and relieving the town was therefore a high priority for Archibald Douglas and the remainder of the Bruce leadership. However, Archibald remained leery of the prospect of confronting the Disinherited in battle. After all, a significantly smaller iteration of the Disinherited's army had already defeated a previous Bruce Regent and his much larger army. The Bruce government could ill afford another such defeat. Archibald was a veteran of the First War of Independence and well versed in the type of skirmish-based attritional warfare that had allowed the Bruce party to weather the periodic large-scale offensives launched by English kings. Indeed, the new Guardian's greatest success against the Disinherited, the raid on Annan, had been a result of emulating such tactics.

Rather than risk facing the Disinherited in battle before the walls of Berwick, Archibald and his commanders instead decided to bypass the enemy army and launch a large raid of their own across the border. In doing so they hoped to force the Disinherited to break off the siege and divide their forces in an attempt to hunt down and engage the raiders.[50] If all went well, this strategy would save Berwick and open up the possibility of defeating the Disinherited in detail. This strategy, however, failed to appreciate the resources that Edward III was willing to commit to the war. This time around, the Disinherited were not in Scotland as an independent army whose goals incidentally benefited the English king. They were now the vanguard of a larger invasion. While the Disinherited maintained their siege of Berwick, Edward dispatched a force of eight hundred or so horsemen, probably drawn from the army he was gathering around York, to interdict the raiders.[51] Archibald had crossed the English border with a significant force of several thousand men, but the very nature of their objective required them to disperse widely in order to be effective. This allowed the English to intercept and defeat the raiders in a series of skirmishes. Unwilling to allow the remaining Bruce troops to simply slip back over the border laden down with loot, the English then began a series of counter-raids in Dumfries, during which William Douglas of Liddesdale, a cousin of the Guardian was captured.[52]

In addition to its questionable tactical success, Archibald's grand raid counterproductively reconciled the English parliament, which had previously attempted to steer their king away from military adventurism in Scotland, to the idea of resuming the war. This upswelling of support from the aristocracy greatly aided Edward's efforts to raise and finance a substantive army. The arrival of the English king and his newly raised host at Berwick on 9 May precipitated a marked increase in the intensity of the siege.[53] The young king, who had rather publicly and rashly sworn not to leave the town until it fell into his hands, oversaw repeated escalade attempts and the destruction of the town's primary supplies of fresh water.[54] With supplies growing low and his garrison increasingly hard-pressed, the Bruce commander of Berwick, Alexander Sexton, whose son had been killed during the skirmish at Kinghorn, agreed to surrender the town if they were not relieved in fifteen days.[55] Such negotiated deadlines were a common aspect of medieval siege warfare, allowing both sides to preserve their own honour and avoid the worst of the slaughter. It was such an agreement by the English commander of Stirling Castle and the besieging Bruces that had drawn Edward II and his army to open battle at Bannockburn.

News of this fresh deadline for surrender spurred Archibald Douglas, who had been busy raising and organising fresh troops, into action. Marching on Berwick with a substantial army, Douglas arrived at Berwick on 11 July, the last day before the town was to surrender.[56] This delay arose because the Scottish Guardian had taken his army on a wide looping route, hoping to intimidate the enemy into withdrawing with the sudden appearance of so many men from an unexpected direction.[57] Edward III stubbornly refused to leave, calling Douglas' bluff, and the Scottish army withdrew. However, in the confusion sown by their arrival from this surprise quarter, a small force of Bruce soldiers laden with supplies were able to make their way across a broken bridge near the town.[58] Much of this force was overrun and killed when they were spotted and intercepted by English cavalry but a small number of men and supplies managed to make it into Berwick, marginally improving material conditions and greatly boosting morale within the town.

Having failed to intimidate the now combined English and Disinherited armies into abandoning the siege of Berwick, Archibald once more defaulted to a strategy of punitive raids. Leading his army into Northumbria, Archibald's followers burnt and reaved huge swathes of land deep into English territory with the goal of forcing Edward III to break off the siege and give chase. However, while the loss of property and life in Northumbria was significant, Bruce forces failed to capture any significant English fortifications, despite attempts by Douglas to take Bamburgh Castle, in which Edward III's queen, Philippa was sheltering.[59] Heedless of this danger, the bloody-minded young English king maintained the siege while the northern border of his kingdom burnt.

Meanwhile, the commanders of Berwick argued that the supplies and reinforcements they received during Archibald's brief appearance before the town met the criteria for relief and that they were no longer obliged to surrender.[60] Edward III disagreed with this interpretation of their agreement, a position that he punctuated by executing Thomas Sexton, the garrison commander's son, who had been offered as a hostage during the earlier negotiations.[61] He then announced his intention to similarly hang one of the remaining hostages every two days that went by without the garrison's surrender. Perhaps thankfully for Edward III's later reputation as a paragon of chivalry, the garrison hastily reopened negotiations, agreeing to surrender by 20 July if they were not relieved, a term that was now strictly defined.[62] Edward also agreed that in the event of the city's surrender, he would maintain and protect the sanctity of the population's property. William Keith, one of the commanders who had entered Berwick during the foray on the 11th, was dispatched to send the ultimatum to Archibald Douglas, who was busily engaged with the raiding of Northumbria. When word reached

Archibald of Berwick's imminent surrender, he was able in the space of the few days left to him to regather his widely dispersed army and make the 40-mile march back to Berwick. A feat that required considerable military and organisational acumen.[63]

Forewarned of their enemy's approach from the south, the English and Disinherited armies left a small blocking force at Berwick, to prevents its garrison from sallying out, before taking up a strong defensive position on Halidon Hill.[64] Located just a handful of miles away from Berwick and overlooking both major routes into the town, it was the perfect place to lie in wait for the approaching army of Bruce loyalists. Combined, the English and Disinherited army probably numbered somewhere in the region of eight thousand men.

Edward had begun the siege of Berwick with a far larger army, possibly thirteen or fifteen thousand men strong, but his repeated attempts to storm the town and pressure its defenders into coming to terms had a very real cost in blood. The relatively protracted nature of the siege was an even greater factor in the diminishment of the English army. Edward III had yet to embark upon the great swathe of gold-thirsty military reforms that would later allow him to maintain garrisons and armies in France for protracted periods of time. Such reforms to military recruitment were still years in the future, the product of hard-won experience and a renewed strategic vision for the war. Therefore, large numbers of his army's most valuable troops had, upon serving the customary forty or so days of military service, considered their duty to their king fulfilled and returned home. Others simply deserted, fed up with the constant boredom and privations inherent to siege warfare. A deeply chagrined Edward III had, when ordering further reinforcements from his officials in York, noted that he had been all but abandoned in Berwick.[65] Unsurprisingly, given their far greater personal stake they had in the success of the campaign, the Disinherited seem to have been less affected by desertion, making them an integral component of the army arrayed on Halidon Hill.

The Scottish army, hastily called together from all quarters for the relief of Berwick by the Guardian, was comfortably larger than the opposing army.[66] Its composition and the way it had been assembled was demonstrative of both the extraordinary strengths and glaring weaknesses of the Bruce military system. Douglas had in a handful of days reconsolidated his highly mobile troops from across Northumbria and rendezvoused with reinforcements from Scotland to create an army of around fifteen thousand men. This was a force of considerable size, displaying both the efficacy of the army's command structure and the system of recruitment that allowed such an army to be raised in the first place. However, only a thousand or two of these soldiers were armed and armoured to a standard that qualified them as men-at-arms.[67] The majority of the army was composed of the kind of light infantry that had proven such a liability at Dupplin Moor. Such configurations of troops were highly mobile and effective in a war of hit and run guerrilla strikes. In addition, under the right circumstances and when well led, large formations of them had proven themselves capable of defeating mounted knights and men-at-arms. Yet the victories they achieved at Stirling Bridge and Bannockburn were predicated upon a masterful use of advantageous terrain and the actions of foolhardy and overconfident enemies. If used incautiously on the battlefield, formations of such troops had proven to be all too vulnerable to arrow fire.

Archibald Douglas, the Guardian and Bruce army commander, manoeuvred cleverly on his approach to Berwick, refusing to be rushed into a bad position by the urgent need to relieve the town. Arriving on the 19th from the north-west, the Bruce army carefully kept the English and Disinherited between them and the River Tweed; a manoeuvre that denied the two Edwards the obvious and least risky line of retreat from the larger army.[68] If their joint army was defeated, its routing troops would be pinned against the river with nowhere to run to, all but ensuring a slaughter. The Bruce army initially arrayed itself on a parallel hill but upon seeing that the Edwards had no intention of quitting Halidon, advanced cautiously. Archibald may still have been reluctant to engage the enemy directly, after all, he had declined to bring them to battle during his previous attempt to relieve the siege. However, his army was significantly larger than that of the two kings and his preferred tactic of drawing off the enemy through raiding had been thwarted by Edward III's stubbornness and brutal willingness to kill hostages. Scotland and Scottish honour demanded that Berwick be saved and, having now arrived on the battlefield, Archibald, whose army contained a large chunk of the Scottish nobility and a majority of its remaining earls, could not retreat without seriously endangering his position as Guardian.

On the slopes of Halidon Hill, the awaiting Disinherited and English armies' deployment and the command structure indicated just how central the Disinherited were to the battle and wider campaign in Scotland. The combined army was arrayed in three groups, sometimes referred to as battles, as a means of engendering tactical flexibility and ensuring effective command and control across the army. The first two of these segments were each commanded by one of the two King Edwards available to the army.[69] Balliol's status and royal dignity more or less demanded he be afforded such a command. However, rather than simply consolidate all the Disinherited forces under Balliol's direct supervision, command of the third of these battles was shared by the Disinherited co-founder, Henry de Beaumont, accompanied by Strathbogie and Umfraville, and the Marshall of England, Edward Bohun, who was accompanied by Edward III's younger brother, Earl John of Cornwall.[70] It was an arrangement that seemed to stress the Disinherited's role as partners, rather than mere subjects, of the English crown. Probably on the advice of Beaumont and the other veterans of Dupplin Moor, the men-at-arms that formed the core of each of these battalions elected to fight on foot, committing to a defensive battle. The army's large contingent of archers were dived between the three battles, deploying on their flanks.

The Bruce army was likewise organised into three schiltrons. The first two were commanded by Earl John Randolph of Moray and Archibald Dougals, while the third fell under the shared command of Earl Kenneth de Moravia of Sutherland and Earl Hugh of Ross.[71] John Randolph was the eldest son of Thomas Randolph, a nephew of Robert I's and David II's first regent. The Earl of Sutherland was married to a daughter of the late Earl of Mar, while Earl Hugh of Ross was married to a sister of Robert I. Hindsight would show that their decision to deploy in these tightly packed schiltrons was foolhardy, but the commanders of the Bruce army probably had very little choice. With so much of their army made up of untrained levies, the dense cohesive nature of the schiltron probably represented their best method of guiding such men across the battlefield and into contact with the enemy, while preserving the momentum and concentration necessary to overbear the enemy men-at-arms. Archibald and his fellow commanders must also have been aware of the possibility that the enemy men-at-arms may remount and attempt to sweep them off the hill with a downward charge, an eventuality for which the schiltrons could provide a robust answer.

The battle was not a drawn-out affair. In order to get to grips with the enemy, the Bruce army, already tired from a punishing days' long forced march to reach Berwick, had to advance downhill, cross a section of boggy ground that joined the base of the two hills and then ascend the deceptively steep slopes of Halidon Hill. They did so in the face of a hail of downward slashing arrows. Slowed by the need to maintain their formation and sheer exhaustion from the climb, the advancing army took severe casualties as it attempted to crest the hill. The first two schiltrons made contact with the mingled English and Disinherited battles commanded by the two Edwards but, already blooded and exhausted by the ascent, were quickly routed.[72] The third schiltron, commanded by the Earls of Ross and Sutherland and loaded with some of Scotland's most formidable troops, put up more of a fight against Beaumont's and Bohun's troops but it too eventually broke.[73]

One of the primary reasons that the third Bruce schiltron remained in the fight for so long was that rather than falling upon it with their full force, Edward III and Edward Balliol, having triumphed in their own engagements, hurriedly ordered their men-at-arms to remount and chase after the fleeing remnants of the defeated schiltrons.[74] The result was a massacre, with hundreds of Bruce-aligned Scottish soldiers being overtaken and rode down as the English and Disinherited men-at-arms vented all the frustrations born of a long and difficult siege. Of the seven Scottish earls present at the battle, five – Moray, Ross, Sutherland, Lennox, Atholl and Carrick – were killed.[75] Also, among the dead was the army's commander and Guardian of Scotland, Archibald Douglas, his nephew William Douglas and three prominent members of the Stewart family.[76]

The loss of manpower and the utter devastation of the Scottish nobility and knight classes all but shattered the power and authority of the Bruce royal government. Realising their opportunity to wrest away control of Scotland, the Disinherited and English armies raced across Scotland, taking advantage of the confusion and demoralisation of the remaining Bruce supporters as they seized and occupied the kingdom's most strategically vital fortresses.[77] Earl Patrick of Dunbar, once again unwilling to face the Disinherited in the aftermath of a stunning victory, rushed to swear loyalty to Edward Balliol;[78] a course of action emulated by a large portion of the Scottish aristocracy. King David II and his queen were evacuated to the safety of the French royal court by their household after it became clear that remaining in Scotland would almost inevitably lead to his capture and imprisonment.[79] Only a handful of castles on the fringes of the kingdom, such as Dumbarton and Urquhart, remained in the hands of the now isolated Bruce loyalists.[80]

In the aftermath of the Battle of Halidon Hill, Edward Balliol and his supporters were able at long last to take some measure of control of the Scottish royal government and administrative apparatus. With the forces of the remaining Bruce loyalists reeling on the back foot, the Disinherited now exercised either direct or de facto authority over the vast majority of the kingdom.[81] Edward used his royal authority and newfound military pre-eminence to distribute offices and wealth to his followers, finally restoring the Disinherited's lost lands and titles. The victory at Halidon Hill marked the apex of the Disinherited cause, but it also carried with it the seeds of their destruction.

With their enemy seemingly all but vanquished and the war for all intents and purposes won, Edward III sought to make good on the promises he had extracted from Edward Balliol in exchange for his help in securing the Scottish throne. Almost a full year after the Battle of Halidon Hill, on 12 June 1334, Edward Balliol formally signed over ownership of the south of Scotland to Edward III.[82] Roxburgh, Edinburgh, Dumfries, Peebles, Berwick and their environs were all handed over to the English king and legally sundered from the Kingdom of Scotland.[83] Edward Balliol had little choice but to acquiesce to this alienation of territory since refusing would mean abandonment by a large portion of his followers among the Disinherited and an almost certainly doomed war with England.

One dire problem created for Balliol by this arrangement was that the annexed regions were among the kingdom's wealthiest and most populous. The delicate web of reciprocal obligations and the calculus of power that held the kingdom together meant that their loss not only diminished the kingdom but severely and disproportionately curtailed Edward's royal incomes. This loss of income threatened his ability to exercise authority within the now truncated kingdom through the customary distribution of largesse. This loss of status and resources was particularly damaging to his authority over the remaining Scottish earls and the other leaders of the Disinherited, narrowing the distance between them. It is easy to see in hindsight why the transition from rebel band to the ruling faction of Scotland was almost inevitably going to place strain on the relationship between Balliol and the other Disinherited leaders.

The Disinherited were a group of related Anglo-Scottish exiles, united and motivated by the desire to recover their lost ancestral lands in Scotland. While several of the Disinherited were related to the Balliols and descended from supporters of the Balliol royal government, the ancestors of other members had been supporters of Edward I and taken part in the dismantling of the Balliol kingship.

Despite being the son of a king of Scotland, Edward Balliol had spent most of his life deliberately isolated from Scottish politics. His appearance on the border in 1320 had achieved very little, other than inspiring the premature unmasking of the Soules Conspiracy, and he soon withdrew in ignominy. Indeed, Edward was not involved in the initial formation of the Disinherited or their efforts to keep the cause alive during the rocky reigns of Edward II and Isabella. Henry de Beaumont had had to drag him out of a French prison.[84] He brought no real military experience and limited resources to the campaign. Edward's primary value to the Disinherited was his exceptionally strong claim to the throne, which provided them with a means of formally recovering their lost estates as well as a legal basis to act against common Bruce enemies. He led the Disinherited because they required a king to legitimise their territorial acquisitions. However, this meant that they were used to regarding him as a convenient ally rather than a superior.

Having waited so long and fought so hard to reclaim their families' lost Scottish estates, the leaders of the Disinherited were somewhat disinclined to recognise, let alone support, the imposition of any outside authority over these newly recovered territories. A potential weakness in the tangled nature of the familial ties that bound so many of the Disinherited together was that many possessed overlapping or competing claims to lands in Scotland, derived from shared family members. This led to a degree of bickering and the formation of grudges as the Disinherited attempted to take effective control over their former estates. A particularly bitter and self-destructive feud erupted between the king and Henry de Beaumont, when Henry attempted to claim the lion's share of the deceased John Mowbray's estates.[85] John's remaining family, including his brothers, resisted this attempt vociferously, appealing to the newly installed king for assistance. Edward, either because he was naturally sympathetic to their cause or hoped to use the incident to demonstrate his authority over Beaumont, sided with the Mowbrays and attempted to pressure Henry into relinquishing his claim on the lands in question. Incensed that Edward, who owed his throne and place within the Disinherited to Beaumont's sponsorship, would side against him, the earl reacted by effectively seceding from the kingdom. Withdrawing to his own estates, Beaumont refused to co-operate with his former allies in the intensifying struggle against David II's resurgent supporters.[86] Worse still, several other prominent members of the Disinherited followed suit, turning their attention to the administration and defence of their own lands to the exclusion of their commitments to one another or the king they had created.

While the Bruce's supporters had failed to prevent Edward Balliol and Edward III from subjugating the majority of Scotland in the aftermath of Halidon Hill, this inaction was indicative of confusion and a lack of co-ordinated leadership rather than of resolve or numbers. Indeed, in some ways their relative passivity following the battle was an extension of the guerilla 'hit and run' tactics pioneered by Robert I and his companions. As rapid as the Disinherited takeover was, it was also relatively shallow. Despite the installation of the Disinherited in estates throughout Scotland, the power of many of the most influential and ardent Bruce loyalists lay untouched and unbroken. With the victorious army at Halidon Hill long disbanded and Scotland divided between Edward Balliol and Edward III of England, those who had lost out in the redistribution of land that followed the return of the Disinherited or were heavily invested in a Bruce royal government were free to wage a war on two fronts. One was a civil war in the north and west, fought against Edward Balliol, the Disinherited and those Scots nobles who had flocked to Balliol's banner after Halidon Hill. The other was an equally familiar struggle to eject the garrisons of the English king from Scottish land. The Bruce position in both conflicts was greatly improved by the now divided nature of their enemy and the internal fracturing of the Disinherited.

The summer of 1134 saw the large-scale mobilisation of Bruce loyalists throughout Scotland. Most of these uprisings were limited regional affairs but their sheer number soon had Edward Balliol's fledging government on the back foot. The eighteen-year-old Robert Stewart, David II's nephew and eventual successor, launched an impressive series of raids into Balliol-held territory throughout the south-west and central belt.[87] Meanwhile, the surviving members of the extensive Douglas family began challenging Balliol's hold on Argyll, storming castles at Dunoon and Rothesay as well as executing Alan Lyle, the Balliol-aligned sheriff of the region. Stewart was then joined by Earl John Randolph of Moray.[88] The earl, who had only narrowly survived Halidon Hill, fled to France with King David, but returned to Scotland as soon as word of the unfolding rebellion reached him. Determined to strike at the heart of the Balliol regime and Edward's main power base within Scotland, Stewart's and Randolph's combined forces ravaged Galloway.

The now divided Disinherited suddenly found themselves trapped and isolated within enemy territory, allowing them to be picked off one by one. Earl Randolph was able to corner David Strathbogie, the Disinherited Earl of Atholl, and convinced him, practically at sword point, to defect to the Bruce camp.[89] John Campbell, the Bruce-appointed Earl of Atholl, had been killed at Halidon Hill and left no legitimate issue, conveniently allowing the Bruce-aligned Scots to tempt Strathbogie over to their side without triggering any serious internal conflict over the earldom's ownership. Two other members of the Disinherited leadership cadre, John Stirling and Richard Talbot, were captured in Lothian, now nominally English territory, on their way to petition Edward III for help.[90] One of the duo's captors, Godfrey Ross, was actually the Balliol-appointed sheriff of Ayr, a defection reflective of the widespread breakdown of Balliol's fragile royal government. Even Henry de Beaumont, the original mastermind behind the Disinherited's invasion of Scotland and a veteran soldier, succumbed to the onslaught. Isolated and without allies, he was besieged in Dundarg Castle, which he had spent much of the previous year rebuilding.[91] This besieging force was led by the former Guardian Andrew de Moray, who had been released from captivity in England in the months immediately prior to the rebellion's outbreak. Also participating in the siege were Alexander and William Mowbray, former members of the Disinherited who were determined to prevent Henry from forcibly seizing control of the estates of their deceased brother, Robert. Besieged with no hope of rescue, Beaumont was forced to surrender on terms, abandoning Buchan.

With his power in Scotland broken piece by piece over a long summer of guerrilla raids and betrayals, Edward Balliol was forced to flee to the sanctuary of English-held Berwick. David II's supporters had wisely concentrated the majority of their efforts on toppling Balliol and the Disinherited, leaving the English-occupied sections of the kingdom relatively untouched beyond a handful of raids. However, Edward III realised that the long-term security of his new border relied upon the preservation of Balliol kingship in what remained of Scotland. If the Bruce loyalists were allowed to consolidate their position, they would soon turn their attention to reclaiming Edward's newly annexed Scottish territories. He therefore made the unusual decision to embark upon a winter campaign into Scotland.[92]

However, this offensive failed to bring any of the Bruce-aligned Scots to battle and only reached as far as Roxburgh Castle, well within the territories seceded to him by Balliol.[93] Edward Balliol accompanied the expedition and was given command of a small secondary force that pillaged and ransacked the surrounding land on their march west to Carlisle. While these lands were, according to the agreement reached by the two Edwards, legally now part of England, in practice they were very much treated as hostile territory, its truculent and troublesome population viewed as fair game. A disastrously counterproductive result of these English raids was that Patrick of Dunbar, who had agreed to serve the English king after Halidon Hill, changed sides once again after his own estates were robbed and burnt by the soldiers of his new English overlord.[94]

The spring of 1335 saw a series of renewed raids launched by the Bruce Scots against English collaborators and the remaining Balliol supporters, with Earl Thomas Randolph and his Douglas allies rampaging through Lothian.[95] However, struck by a complacency born of success, the various factions of Bruce loyalists began to argue among themselves over the Guardianship and who should lead this renewed war.[96] This lack of leadership was particularly problematic because Edward III, understanding how woefully insufficient his winter campaign had been, re-invaded Scotland with a far larger army, intent on placing Edward Balliol firmly back on the throne.[97] This formidable host was then divided into two, one half commanded by the English king, and the other commanded by Edward Balliol. The two kings then engaged in simultaneous grand military processions up both coastlines, quashing what resistance they came upon, before rendezvousing at Glasgow and proceeding together to Perth.[98] The success of this two-pronged assault and the fractured Bruce leadership's inability to counter it saw large numbers of Scots, including erstwhile Disinherited leader Earl David Strathbogie of Atholl, submit to Balliol.[99] During this troop surge, Earl Thomas Randolph of Moray, one of the Bruce faction's rising stars, was ambushed while on the road and captured.[100] Even the stalwart Stewarts entered into a negotiated truce.[101]

Content in the gains they had made and confident that the tide had once again turned in their favour, the two Edwards dismantled their army and retired to Newcastle for the winter. Before departing they made the rather inexplicable decision to leave notorious turncoat David Strathbogie as their foremost lieutenant in Scotland.[102] While Edward III probably did not know it, his campaigns into Scotland were being hamstrung by the same issues his grandfather, Edward I, had struggled with in his own attempt to subjugate the kingdom. When free to pour the full resources of the English crown into a campaign there was very little that the enemy could do to hinder them, provoking the mass surrender and submission of both Bruce-aligned and effectively neutral Scottish nobles. However, such offensives were by their very nature tidal and the capitulations they forced grudging and half-hearted. Neither Edward had the resources nor political capital to keep such large armies in the field for more than a handful of months. Then, in the absence of this forceful influence, many Scottish nobles recanted their submissions and began aiding the guerrilla campaign against the scattered English garrisons.

With both Robert Stewart and Thomas Randolph temporarily removed from the fight, a truncated parliament of Bruce loyalists once more named Andrew de Moray as Guardian of Scotland.[103] Moray concentrated his remaining forces on confronting Strathbogie, who was attempting to consolidate gains made by the previous English expedition in the north of Balliol-controlled Scotland. French intervention had led to a temporary truce in Scotland between the English king and Bruce supporters; however, this peace did not apply to the forces of the Disinherited who claimed to be subjects of King Edward Balliol. This legal loophole allowed the Guardian to focus on defeating Balliol's Scottish supporters without fear of retaliation from their English allies. Strathbogie's most pressing objective was the capture of Kildrummy Castle, which was being held by Moray's wife, Christina, who was a first cousin of the late King Robert I.[104] Hearing of Moray's rapid approach from the south, Strathbogie broke off the siege and with an army of around three thousand men sought to bring them to battle. In the clash that followed on 30 November, the Disinherited army was lured into making an ill-timed and ill-discipled charge before being enveloped and destroyed by a carefully prepared flanking attack.[105] Strathbogie was killed in the fighting, leaving the remaining Balliol supporters in Scotland effectively leaderless.[106]

Subsequent peace talks stretched into early April 1335 and centred upon the possibility of the childless Edward Balliol naming David II his heir.[107] Such talks came to nothing, and the following campaign season saw the launching of yet another offensive. This English army led by Edward Balliol and Henry of Lancaster faced more concerted resistance than on previous campaigns but nevertheless emerged triumphant, handily defeating ambushes launched by both Wiliam Douglas and Andrew de Moray and reaching Perth, which was quickly captured and re-fortified.[108] This invasion was then supplemented by the arrival of two additional English forces led by Edward III and his brother, the Earl of Cornwall, respectively.[109] After further attempts to intercept these fresh English troops failed, the Bruce commanders reverted to their former tactics and began to raid or besiege the supply lines and garrisons left in the wake of this tripartite expedition. That year's fighting was particularly destructive and costly in human life. The Bruce-aligned Scots adopted a scorched earth policy to deny resources and sanctuary to the invaders, while the English also looted and burnt whatever they could find in an attempt to terrorise the Scots into submission and force the enemy into another decisive battle.

Henry de Beaumont, recently freed from captivity after the paying of a heavy ransom, took part in the early stages of this campaign but then became distracted by the perceived need to avenge the death of David Strathbogie, who had been his son-in-law. This private quest for vengeance saw the lands of several prominent Bruce commanders pillaged and raised but achieved nothing of any real strategic importance. Around this time, Edward III began flirting with a new strategy, in which he aimed to secure Scotland through the building of fortifications. However, the often-rugged terrain of Scotland would have limited the usefulness of such a programme. More to the point, it would have been incredibly expensive. As it was, the few building projects that Edward started were all quickly abandoned and made little difference to the long-term outcome of the war.

As previously noted, the kingdoms of Scotland and France were connected by long-standing ties of friendship and had repeatedly entered into alliances and mutual defence pacts down the centuries. The royal government of Robert I had continued this model by strengthening ties with France throughout the 1320s and made a point of securing French recognition of his family's right to the Scottish crown. This was important, not only for strategic purposes but because the French court had previously provided shelter for John Balliol after his release from imprisonment by the English king. By securing acknowledgement of his kingship, Robert was further unravelling the legacy of Balliol rule and furthering his family's attempt to monopolise Scottish identity. These diplomatic efforts saw significant dividends when David II and several other prominent Scottish nobles needed a safe refuge following their defeat at Halidon Hill and the collapse of the royal government.

King Philip VI, who had a complex relationship with Edward III, made repeated efforts on behalf of his Scottish allies to negotiate a peaceful solution. By bringing to bear severe political pressure, Philip was able to engineer a series of truces, but these ultimately came to nothing because of the Bruce faction's inability to reach a shared agenda around which to negotiate.[110] The war had exacted a heavy toll upon Scotland's aristocracy and people. Consequently, the majority of Bruce commanders were notionally in favour of some form of settled agreement that would end the constant cycle of raids and counter-raids that was bleeding the kingdom dry. The problem lay in the overlapping territorial claims of the Disinherited and the Bruce supporters who had been promoted to replace the formers' banished forebearers. Any long-term peace proposal with any chance of success would require some seceding of territory. No noble or family wanted to be left holding this particular diplomatic short straw. They were therefore motivated to continue to wage war on a personal and regional level upon the Disinherited and their English allies in order to secure and enhance their standing among the other Bruce supporters and thus prevent their interests being sacrificed in a peace treaty by a more powerful faction of Bruce loyalists.

It was also slowly becoming clear to the French king that the hot-headed young Edward's attempts to subjugate Scotland would not be easily assuaged. In 1335, Philip had gone so far as to assemble an expeditionary force of around five or six thousand men that he intended to use to place David II back on the throne of Scotland but had been distracted by the sudden death of his eldest son.[111] This expedition was never launched but Philip did begin to license French captains to attack English shipping as a way of putting pressure upon Edward to end the fighting and even began to make noises about confiscating the English king's remaining holdings in France.[112] In August 1336, with the war in Scotland reaching new heights of barbarity and destruction, Philip VI formally entered the war on the side of David II and his supporters.[113] Philip renewed his piratical attacks on English ships but rather than dispatching an army to Scotland, he instead began to gather a force to conqueror English-controlled Gascony.[114] Edward III who had just concluded another campaigning season in Scotland, returned to London and began preparations for the coming war in France. This war would soon become the defining enterprise of his reign and after several years of intermittent fighting would escalate to see Edward contest the throne of France, resurrecting the long-lapsed claim he held through his maternal grandfather Philip IV.

This profound switch in focus and resources by the hot-headed and glory-hungry young king had a disastrous effect on the English war effort in Scotland. The fighting on the Scottish front never fully ceased but it increasingly became the province of northern marcher lords and second-rate royal officials. To the king, the accolades and the riches were all now to be found in the war in France. What remained in Scotland after the first few years of triumphant Bruce resurgence was a protracted and bitter war over an increasingly sparse network of English-held fortifications within the south of Scotland. What could not survive this change in English royal focus was Balliol Scotland and the Kingdom of the Disinherited. Without the regular appearance of large English armies to relieve the Disinherited's scattered fortresses and intimidate Scotland's regional powerbrokers into submission, however temporarily, Balliol authority within Scotland ebbed away into nothingness over the course of a couple of desperate campaigning seasons. In 1339, with the aid of a substantive French fleet, Bruce forces were able to recapture Perth, the kingdom's capital.[115] This time there would be no further reversals, and the city remained firmly in Bruce hands. The majority of the surviving Disinherited leaders mimicked Edward III in transferring their attention to the war in France, leaving Scotland far behind them. Edward Balliol's remaining Scottish allies were either forced to come to terms with one of the commanders of the now rapidly splintering Bruce war effort or enter the employment of the English garrisons.

The now seventeen-year-old David II returned home to Scotland on 2 June 1141.[116] He arrived to find a Scotland that was largely secure from further English attack but deeply politically divided. In 1338, Andrew de Moray had fallen ill while directing the siege of Edinburgh Castle and died shortly afterwards.[117] He was replaced as Guardian by James Stewart but the appointment was a controversial one.[118]

David II's arrival, signalling as it did an inevitable and major change in the balance of power within Scotland, initially only made this infighting and disorder worse, as each faction fought to secure a position of prominence. Additionally, having been left to their own devices for so many years, the Scottish aristocracy, now separated by a generation from their unification under Robert I, were reluctant to accept any form of outside authority.[119] Despite frequent outbreaks of violence and even forays into open rebellion, over the next five years David II was able to keep the English pinned within the borders while slowly building his authority within Scotland. In the summer of 1346, Philip VI wrote to David asking for his assistance. Deeply concerned by Edward III's renewed invasion of Normandy, Philip called upon his Scottish allies to invade England, thereby forcing Edward to either withdraw from France or capitulate altogether.

David II eagerly agreed to the request, sensing both an opportunity to forge a reputation as a great warrior king in the same mould as his father and to increase his control of the troublesome and independently minded Scottish aristocracy by leading them in victorious war. Spending the summer yoking the Scottish nobility to his cause, David recruited a powerful army of around fifteen thousand men. This army crossed into England on 7 October and burnt and pillaged through the north until they reached the outskirts of Durham, where they encountered a scrambled together six thousand-strong English army led by the Archbishop of York, Ralph Neville and Henry Percy, a former member of the Disinherited.[120] While far harder fought than Dupplin Moor or Halidon Hill, the Battle of Neville's Cross ended in a costly Scottish defeat, in part because they had once again underestimated the difficulty of crossing broken terrain while under fire from English archers.[121] Several thousand Scottish soldiers were killed alongside Earl John Randolph of Moray, Earl Maurice de Moravia of Strathearn, and the Constable, Chamberlain and Marshall of Scotland.[122] Worse, David II, who had twice been struck and wounded by arrow fire, was captured and imprisoned in the Tower of London; a fate he shared with five of his earls and the current patriarch of the Douglas family.[123]

The resultant power vacuum within Scotland made possible a curious and extended postscript to the Disinherited's invasion of Scotland and attempt to restore the Balliol monarchy. The Battle of Neville's Cross had seen almost every major figure within the Bruce royal government either killed or captured. Naturally Edward III, who had just won a spectacular victory of his own at the Battle of Crécy, sought to take advantage of this lack of leadership by invading Scotland. The following May, in 1347, a large English army under the command of none other than Edward Balliol crossed over into Scotland with the goal of subjugating the country and restoring the English garrisons that had been lost over the previous decade of Bruce ascendancy.[124] This army once more ravaged Lothian before sacking Glasgow and raiding deep into Scotland, its apparent goal to frighten and browbeat the Scottish into repudiating their allegiance to the captured David II. Despite the widespread devastation wrought by the army, very little of strategic significance was achieved and there was no upswell of Scottish nobles declaring their loyalty to either Edward Balliol or Edward III of England. What differentiated this campaign from its many predecessors was that in the aftermath, Balliol did not return to England, instead he remained alongside a few diehard supporters in his family's Lordship of Galloway.[125]

Balliol, like his Bruce rivals a descendant of the once autonomous Princes of Galloway, had deep roots within the region, which had maintained a strong sense of its own identity and distinctive culture. When in 1332 the Disinherited had launched their almost foolhardy invasion of Scotland, many Gallodovians rose up in support of his claims to the throne and their lost hereditary lord. Now, rather than contest the centres of royal Scottish power, Balliol decided to establish himself in his family's traditional Scottish power base. From there he hoped to co-ordinate with his English allies, nurse his military assets and gradually extend his authority throughout Scotland. It was a bold plan that exerted a newfound independence from the English crown upon which he had previously relied so heavily.

Unfortunately for Balliol, just as it had a decade earlier in 1336, events in France and the greater priority afforded to the war there by Edward III endangered his position in Scotland. Edward III sought to leverage the extraordinary nature of his victory at Crécy by entering into negotiations with Philip VI and his remaining advisors. These negotiations required the establishment of a truce that extended to Scotland. This curtailed further English efforts to either support Balliol or re-establish themselves in Scotland and allowed the few active Bruce loyalists within the area to concentrate their efforts on containing Balliol. As a result of this and his relative paucity of military resources, Edward's attempts to expand his authority beyond Galloway and into the wider south-west were met with only limited success. Such successes, modest as they were, ended abruptly with the arrival of the bellicose William Douglas from France, who, drawing upon his family's extensive assets, began a relentless series of small-scale tactical offensives that placed Balliol and his English allies firmly on the defensive.

Previous iterations of Bruce royal government had been well aware of the region's Balliol sympathies and the inherent danger in the welding of these alternate allegiances with the region's strong sense of self identity and desire for autonomy. To prevent this, the Bruces, who had power bases of their own in surrounding Carrick and Liddesdale, had taken steps to embed their own followers within Galloway. These Galloway-based, Bruce-aligned nobles such as Alan Stewart and John Kennedy also rose in rebellion against Balliol's rule. While Balliol was himself safe from attack in his stronghold on the small island of Hestan, such rebellions seriously undermined his ability to exercise authority within the lordship. Indeed, while a source of undoubted protection, Balliol's isolation on Hestan was a double-edged sword that saw him become increasingly irrelevant and easy to ignore.[126] Edward Balliol, the one-time King of Scotland, continued on in this manner for the next eight years; maintaining a shaky grip on his ancestral lordship, while the renewed war for the control of Scotland raged around him.

In 1355, Douglas succeeded in finally breaking Balliol power within Galloway, forcing Edward to flee back to England.[127] There would be no more grand adventurers for the former king. In 1356 the now seventy-three-year-old and childless Edward Balliol sold his familial claim to the throne of Scotland, passing it on to his greatest and most inconsistent ally, Edward III, in exchange for a pension.[128] Among the coterie of English nobles who witnessed this transfer was Gilbert de Umfraville, still stubbornly referring to himself as the Earl of Angus, the last of the Disinherited. This final defeat brought an end not only to any hopes of a Balliol restoration but also to the last echoes of the long-vanished Princedom of Galloway. The Disinherited's mad attempt to turn back the clock and restore the families and political establishment that had reigned in the days of Alexander III and John Balliol had ended in failure. Robert I had created a new Scotland in the struggle to resist English overlordship and secure his family's place on the throne. Yet in the same manner, the forces unleashed by the Disinherited in their attempt to resist this change led to the creation of an entirely new Scotland, once again altering the core of the kingdom and how it functioned.

Conclusion

First let us begin with a brief survey of the fates of the victors and vanquished in this exceptionally bitter and bloody extended struggle for control of Scotland. Following his final departure from Galloway and the surrender of his claim to the Scottish throne, a throne once occupied by his father, Edward Balliol retired to England, living comfortably off the income generated by his remaining English estates and the generous pension awarded to him by Edward III. He survived another eight years in exile before dying in January 1364, Scotland's forgotten king. Edward was around eighty-one years old at the time of his death. An unusually long life, for someone of his era, filled with many defeats and many fruitless victories. He also died childless, a strange oversight for a man who had fought so long and so hard to restore his family to the throne of Scotland.

With no children of his own and his brother felled long ago at Annan, it seems that Edward's closest heir at the time of his death was Enguerrand VII de Coucy, the great grandson of his cousin Christine de Lindsay and her husband, the French noble Enguerrand V de Coucy. The charismatic Enguerrand, who had spent time in England as a hostage, was married to Edward III of England's eldest daughter, Isabella, and spent much of his career skilfully negotiating his dual loyalties to France and England, while greatly profiting from the new lands and titles the match brought him in both kingdoms. This meant that Edward's immediate heirs had been loyal retainers of a French monarchy that was, for a substantial period of time, dedicated to preserving the Bruce family's place on the throne of Scotland. Given the complexities of this situation, it seems that the Balliol restoration would have been brief, even in the unlikely eventuality that Edward and his Disinherited had succeeded in fully taking control of the kingdom.

It is possible that Edward Balliol elected to remain unmarried so that he would be free to marry Queen Joan in the event of David II's death or if the ever-capricious fortunes of war rendered his position as King of Scotland untenable. Another possibility is that Edward remained single in an attempt to solicit support from among the Scottish aristocracy, tacitly signalling that he was free to enter into a marriage alliance in exchange for the support of any one of Scotland's prominent aristocratic families. Perhaps the answer is more personal and that Edward, during his long years of exile from Scotland, had become determined only to marry and have children in the event of his ultimate triumph, unwilling to burden his potential offspring with the weight of legacy and familial obligation that he himself had carried since childhood.

A member of an exceptionally well-connected French aristocratic family, who gained a position of prominence through military service to the kings of England and who spent much of his life trying to recover the lost possessions of his Scottish wife, Henry de Beaumont's career attests to the culturally permeable nature of medieval royal government. Adventurer, silver-tongued courtier and veteran soldier, Henry had been integral to the formation and successful organisation of the Disinherited. His drive to recover his wife Alice's lost Earldom of Buchan had seen him quarrel with and befriend kings. The Disinherited's unlikely victories against Scotland and Edward Balliol's subsequent coronation owed much to Beaumont's battlefield expertise and expert understanding of how to employ their army's most potent military asset, its archers, to maximum effect. Yet, upon at last securing some measure of authority and control within Buchan and with a victory over the Bruce loyalists seemingly on the horizon, Beaumont's pride and cupidity played a pivotal role in the political disintegration of the Disinherited, allowing them to be isolated and picked off by their Bruce-aligned rivals.

Following his surrender of Dundarg Castle to an alliance of his mutual enemies, Henry accompanied Edward on his expedition into Scotland in the summer of 1335. In 1336, he took a central role in the English invasion, where he directed the ravaging of Bruce-held lands in vengeance for the death of his son-in-law, David Strathbogie. He also rescued his daughter Kathrine, who had, since her husband's death, been stranded and besieged within Lochindorb. Despite these moderate successes, he made no efforts to reclaim Buchan and resume administration of the earldom. Following the outbreak of war between the Kingdoms of France and England, Henry, seemingly regarding Scotland as a lost cause, turned his attentions to the fresh opportunities created by this conflict. Henry joined Edward III on his subsequent royal expedition to the Low Countries in 1337 and died still on campaign sometime in 1340. While Henry failed to recover his wife's hereditary earldom, the marriage was remarkably fecund, producing around a dozen children. One of the couple's daughters, Isabel, married Henry Grosmont, a royal favourite and the eldest son and successor of the Disinherited's old ally, Earl Henry of Leicester and Lancaster. Their daughter, Blanche, would go on to marry Edward III's fourth son, John of Gaunt. Blanche and John's son, Henry, would eventually overthrow his cousin Richard II and rule England as King Henry IV. It was a turn of events that would probably have delighted his great grandfather, Henry de Beaumont, who was himself descended from a most unlikely king and emperor.

King Edward III's formative experience with the Kingdom of Scotland and its inhabitants was far from auspicious. He had been forced to sign the Treaty of Edinburgh-Northampton by his mother and Mortimer whereby he formally surrendered his claim to overlordship of Scotland; a claim that his royal grandfather and father had both expended considerable efforts attempting to enforce. The young king regarded the peace treaty and the entire surrounding affair as a personal humiliation, hence why he was so open to the idea of providing tacit support for the Disinherited's invasion of Scotland.

Of course, as we have seen, Edward's initial wariness of becoming directly involved in the struggle for Scotland soon gave way to enthusiastic participation, with the king going so far as to move the seat of his administration from London to York in order to better oversee the continued war effort. When Edward's protracted engagement in an increasingly bloody and destructive war for control of Scotland eventually aroused the ire of David II's ally, the French King Philip VI, Edward hurried to the defence of his family's remaining continental domains; at a stroke reducing the war in Scotland to a badly deprioritised second front. In 1340, in order to provide grounds for legally refuting Philip's confiscation of his French lands and to encourage his English subjects to participate in the unfolding war effort, Edward resurrected his long dormant and ignored claim to the French throne. Edward's initial plan for combating the French king, pursued throughout the early 1340s, was to construct a grand alliance of allies drawn from the

Low Countries and Holy Roman Empire. This policy eventually proved to be both strategically ineffective and financially ruinous, with Edward's allies demanding massive sums of money in exchange for half-hearted and fleeting military engagement.

After several years of reorganisation and careful negotiation with the English parliament, Edward III invaded France directly. Despite initial tribulations, the ultimate result of this change to a more direct and aggressive strategy was a string of unexpected and decisive English victories in which English armies, well supported by archers and fighting defensive battles, routed far larger French hosts. Similarly to Scotland and the aftermath of the capture of David II in the parallel English victory won by Edward's subordinates at Neville's Cross, Edward and his lieutenants struggled to fully capitalise upon their battlefield successes. Edward lacked the manpower and resources to forcibly subjugate the entirety of France. He instead hoped to use his string of victories to convince the French nobility to capitulate. As a result, the momentum of his battlefield victories was slowly drained away by a series of peace talks and truces that obfuscated his enemy's reorganisation and recovery. Such reversals worsened as time wore on, exacerbated by the loss of his eldest son, the famed Black Prince, his slide into ill health and the apparent onset of premature senility.

Despite the caveated nature of his achievements and the great difficulty his immediate heirs had in holding onto his hard-won gains in France, Edward's triumphs were widely celebrated by his subjects. Edward's almost all-consuming efforts to take the throne of France ended up having a profound effect upon his extant kingdom. The ongoing war effort inspired profound changes in the purpose, remit and powers of parliament and the English political landscape. Similarly, Edward's military successes and his attempts to co-opt the English nobility as junior partners in a shared martial enterprise through the promotion of the cult of chivalry were formative influences in establishing the English conception of themselves as a great martial people. Edward III died in England in 1377 after an extended period of infirmity. The war in France had become increasingly costly and unpopular as defeats and reversals slowly mounted, a consequence of divided English leadership and the Fabian guerrilla strategy adopted by Charles V of France. Yet for all the bloodshed that Edward's ambitions had unleashed, the memory of the prestige and glories he won continued to shine in the emergent English conscience long after any practical or material gains had faded.

Following his capture at the Battle of Neville's Cross, David II was held in England while his ransom was negotiated. Although David's captivity was relatively comfortable, with the king being housed in a number of traditional English royal centres including Edward III's favoured residence at Windsor Castle, it was also agonisingly protracted. The issue was that neither Edward III nor the remaining Scottish nobility were terribly keen on reaching an agreement. While Edward could certainly use the substantial amount of money the ransoming of a fellow king would undoubtedly raise, he was all too cognisant of the advantages of keeping the Bruce king imprisoned. While David languished in a gilded cage, Edward was directing his northern lieutenants to capitalise upon the Scottish king's absence by recapturing territory lost over the course of the previous decade. Likewise, there were those within the Scottish nobility who were not eager to see David's return, at least at the hefty cost that the English king was demanding.

As previously noted, when David first returned to Scotland from his extended exile in France in 1341, he found the Scottish nobility to be deeply fractured and riven with factionalism, as the various Bruce loyalist commanders competed for influence. While such rivalries did not fade overnight, David succeeded in taking control of the administrative apparatus of the royal government and exercised a measure of authority over the nobility. He was able to do so in part because of his promise to lead Scotland in a unifying campaign against their English enemies that would generate enough spoils to keep the entire nobility sated. With the failure of this campaign, the nobility quickly resumed their rivalries, proving themselves just as eager as their English neighbours to take advantage of the power vacuum created by the severe casualties suffered at Neville's Cross. In the king's absence, his nephew, Robert Stewart, was able to resume his position as Guardian. Robert was the childless David's heir, and the king regarded him as a potential rival for the crown. This fear was seemingly justified when Robert used the power of the Guardianship not to expedite the king's release from English custody but to secure the legitimisation of his brood of illegitimate children.

David, believing that his nephew was attempting to set the stage for the emergence of his own royal dynasty, stripped Robert of the Guardianship.

However, Robert was in short order able to displace David's preferred candidates and resumed the Guardianship regardless of the king's wishes. Considering this struggle for power, it is easy to see why Stewart was not eager to see his uncle return to Scotland. Additionally, behind these political machinations lurked the unvarnished truth that ransoming the king would require raising an enormous amount of money, a task that none of the Scottish nobility truly relished. In 1357, almost eleven years since the start of his captivity, it was finally agreed that David would be released in exchange for the sum of a hundred thousand marks, which was to be paid in instalments over the course of ten years. One of the most important factors in the conclusion of these hideously drawn-out ransom negotiations was that Edward hoped David's release would trigger a conflict between David and Robert.

However, upon returning to Scotland, David quickly re-established his authority within the kingdom, weathering a series of revolts led by his discontented heir. When David encountered difficulties in raising his ransom, he was able to fob Edward III off with a convoluted series of negotiations and a quickly abandoned promise that he would recognise one of Edward's children as his heir. The one area that the Bruce king faltered in was his marriage and the continuation of the Bruce dynasty. In 1370, the still childless David divorced Queen Joan and began looking around for a new wife. However, Joan, who had stood by her husband during his years of exile and imprisonment, did not take this dismissal lightly. The queen appealed to the Papacy and had the divorce overturned. As a result, upon David's premature death from illness at the age of forty-six in 1371, he was succeeded by Robert Stewart. The Bruce dynasty, whose efforts to claim the throne of Scotland had over the past eighty years of intermittent warfare fundamentally altered the composition of the Scottish nobility and their role within the kingdom, had lasted barely two generations. During his long reign, David Bruce had shown himself to be a capable and talented ruler, his legacy unfortunately marred by his enforced absences from the kingdom.

David's successor, Robert Stewart, was another highly talented and capable ruler, but he lacked the legitimacy and charisma Robert I's legacy had bequeathed to the Bruce line. The Second War of Independence waged largely in the king's absence on a regional level by individual families and aristocratic affinities had once again reshaped how the Scottish nobility related to the monarchy and the encompassing kingdom; a process that Robert abetted through his later attempts to evade oversight from his royal uncle. It is in someways fair to say that during his sixteen-year reign, Robert ruled despite the Scottish aristocracy instead of through them. Their now ingrained resistance to authority was to be overridden when practical and skilfully negotiated around when it was not. The Douglas family, once the Stewarts' most stalwart ally and another of the Bruces' traditional supporters, proved themselves to be particularly troublesome subjects, a rivalry that would last generations and play a significant role in shaping the kingdom's future.

This examination of the Disinherited and their attempts to wrestle Scotland away from Bruce rule began all the way back with Galloway, its rule by the Bruce and Balliol's mutual ancestors and the region's grudging, piecemeal, integration into the Kingdom of Scotland. Hopefully, the reasons behind that decision and the extended mediation upon the often-complex relationship between an individual's sense of identity and the polity in which they were born during the medieval period has become increasingly clear. As bold as the Disinherited's decision to invade Scotland with their tiny rag tag army was, and as spectacular as their victories at Dupplin Moor and Halidon Hill were, their campaigns were but the latest iteration of an ongoing struggle between two neighbouring and, distantly related families. Their conflict over the throne of Scotland, from the Bruce family's initial rebellion against the still absent Maid of Norway in 1287 to Edward Balliol's final expulsion from Galloway by Bruce loyalists in 1355, flowed seamlessly into and shaped a larger story. The story of how Scotland, as we now know it, came to be. Of its slow transformation from kingdom to state and how a loose conglomeration of lands held together through an amalgamation of personal relationships blossomed into a shared culture.

This book started with a question posed within its introduction: why are the Wars of Independence, in particularly the first one, regarded as so seminal in the foundation of Scotland and of a sense of Scottish identity? After all, the Kingdom of Scotland had existed in some form or another for centuries before Edward I of England's attempts to conquer it. As the activities of the Bruce and Balliol's ancestors, the Princes of Galloway, reveal in their attempts to resist, negotiate and circumvent the kings of Scotland's attempts to annex the region into their expanding domains, there was a time where the kingdom was undefined and untethered by geographic or cultural boundaries. Similarly, both Alexander II and Alexander III campaigned to annex Argyll and the Hebrides, which retained strong political and cultural connections with Norway and the Norse-Gaels. There was no geographic Scotland; there was a collection of different regions and polities that one by one, and to a varying extent, fell under the influence and authority of a line of aggressive and expansionary kings.

It is fruitless and indeed frustrating to try to map modern understandings of state and nationhood onto such a loose polity, precisely because its fundamental underpinnings were so radically different. The Kingdom of Scotland, as previously stated, was a personal and familial rather than cultural or institutional construct. Yes, its inhabitants recognised that they were living in a kingdom and clearly had some sense of a Scottish identity, but this awareness was far removed from the sort of national identity that came to be lionised in the nineteenth century. It entailed very little sense of engagement, obligation or ownership. Neither was it terribly prescriptive or impermeable, encompassing or resting easily alongside alternative or supplementary identities.

Both the Balliol and Bruce families were descended from Anglo-Norman or English nobles who had at separate points married into rival branches of a family descended from the Princes of Galloway. They had then both married into the Scottish royal family itself, providing them with strong claims to the throne of Scotland. Further, the neighbouring families both held extensive lands in England as well as Scotland. Such mixed heritage and dual loyalties were far from uncommon within Scotland prior to the death of Alexander III and the ensuing succession crisis. Anglo-Norman settlement and involvement with Scotland had under successive Scottish kings greatly strengthened the power and authority of the Scottish monarch, who had harnessed and adapted elements of the newcomers' martial culture and political structure successfully to suit their own needs. As a result of the Scottish kings' willingness to engage and reward the services of such adventurers generously, numerous members of the Scottish nobility had Anglo-Norman or English heritage. Likewise, owing homage for separate lands to multiple kings, while occasionally troublesome during times of conflict, was seen as an issue for individuals to negotiate as best they could rather than an incongruous source of systemic weakness. In this sense, the royal court around which the kingdom was focused and organised was a source of cultural diversity.

Yet somehow the Wars of Independence and the accompanying refutation of English overlordship loom large within public conceptions of Scottish history. It is a conflict that, at first glance at least, provides simple and effective delineations regarding matters of faction and identity. In contrast to the ambiguity and confusion that surrounds the founding of the Kingdom of Scotland, the Wars of Independence are a readily identifiable watershed in Scotland's political and cultural development. They are an event and narrative that fit far better into modern conceptions of nationhood and culture than anything that came before it, the point where the first ragged outlines of state and nation can be glimpsed. Part of this perception is simply due to the proliferation of a broad historical shorthand that smooths the edges off a complex historical process for the sake of expediency and ease of telling. Although, of course, that doesn't stop historians from lamenting and gnashing their teeth, as is our prerogative. On the other hand, and potentially more damagingly, the seeming simplicity and robustness of such narratives are, by defining a culture and polity primarily through its opposition to another, susceptible to excessive mythologisation and wilful misrepresentation through the lens of modern politics.

Rather, it is in exploring the nuances and details of this layered and long-running conflict that we gain a full picture of a struggle between two blocs of Scottish aristocratic families. In examining the breadth of its participants' experience and the numerous shades of grey present throughout this multifaceted struggle, we discover the many ways in which their rivalry fundamentally reshaped the structure of the kingdom. Neither the Comyns, the power behind John Balliol's throne, or their descendants among the Disinherited were, according to contemporary understandings, any less Scottish because of their decision to oppose the rise of Bruce kingship. Indeed, in doing so they were, as the principal supporters and beneficiaries of a rival Scottish king, pursuing their family's best long-term interests.

Robert Bruce and his successors were able to skilfully cultivate support and capitalise upon the parallel struggle to restore English overlordship by pointing to his rival's association with successive kings of England. Yet prior to his coronation and his final break from Edward I, Bruce and his family had also co-operated with, even sworn loyalty to, the King of England. Indeed, in 1296 Robert had fought with the English against a King of Scotland in the hopes that a grateful Edward I would bestow the crown upon his family. Such appeals to anti-English sentiment within Scotland were therefore not so much an articulation of a coherent national identity as they were an expedient and practical reaction to the current political and military situation.

Despite their notional incompatibility, neither the Comyns nor Edward Balliol's supporters thought of themselves as any less Scottish because of their co-operation with the English. Instead, when they were ultimately defeated, the crucible of conflict eventually filtered out their version of what it meant to be Scottish. This was a version of Scottish identity that could sit comfortably within some framework of English overlordship. More importantly though, it was a version of Scottish identity that rested primarily upon membership of a nobility whose composition and role within the kingdom largely resembled what it had been in the 1280s under the Dunkeld kings. This was the version of Scotland that the Comyns were fighting to preserve and that the Disinherited were in their fashion hoping to salvage. In contrast, Robert used the demands of the war to organise and focus both those currently being victimised by the occupying English garrisons and those families who had traditionally lain on the fringe of Scottish politics.

Edward I seized upon the opportunity presented to him by the Scottish nobility in arbitrating the rival Balliol and Bruce claims to the throne of Scotland in an attempt to coerce the Scottish nobility to acknowledge his overlordship. This policy and Edward's later attempts to exercise direct oversight over Scotland and its newly installed Balliol king was a marked departure from established Anglo-Scottish relations. The kings of England had long maintained they held suzerainty over the entirety of the British Isles, a claim that often formed a sticking point in the relationships between English and Scottish kings. However, despite these pretensions, open warfare between the two kingdoms was relatively rare. Indeed, English kings more often made a policy of aiding and empowering their Scottish counterparts, even occasionally intervening militarily on their behalf. It was far more expedient for English kings to attempt to co-opt their northerly neighbours as junior partners and proxies than try to force their submission. It was a policy that spared them the arduous task of having to deal with the Scottish nobility directly. In such a relationship, the practicalities of power and authority trumped the need for clarity of title or position. Both kings were free to present the relationship to their own supporters in the most self-aggrandising terms possible.

Edward I's insistence upon exercising direct and open authority within Scotland, above that of the Balliol king he helped bring to power, was probably the result of his witnessing the steady decline of his own father's once extensive influence in Scotland. Edward's immediate successors, Edward II and Edward III, aspired to follow this new authoritarian and blatantly aggressive model of overlordship, seeking to maintain a network of garrisons across Scotland, occupying its major royal centres and intimidating the Scottish nobility into co-operating with their proxy government. For the rival Scottish factions, the English were at different times both an enemy to overcome and a feature of the political landscape to be carefully negotiated around for maximum advantage. Both the Comyns and Bruces danced in and out of English allegiance as they competed with one another for the support of the Scottish aristocracy. Robert the Bruce's coronation and direct, unconditional opposition to the English, was a bold change of tactic, enacted after it became clear that Edward I valued Comyn support highly and could not be induced to support their replacement by members of the Bruce affinity.

The Comyns found themselves increasingly committed to Edward I and the English almost by default following the Bruce's murder of several of their relatives. Both Edward and the Comyns were implacably opposed to the notion of a Bruce kingship, providing them with a mutual enemy. This left the Comyns, who prior to this had attempted to hold the throne of Scotland for the absent John Balliol and tacitly supported the struggle against the English, politically isolated and vulnerable when Edward I died. Thus, the Wars of Independence, despite their name, also encompassed a civil war between rival Scottish families. The conjoined nature of this war ebbed and flowed but never fully faded.

During the late 1300s and 1310s the majority of fighting occurred between Bruce adherents and those Scottish families disinclined to accept his authority. Even after Robert had secured the Scottish throne and pacified the majority of his domestic enemies, many of his opponents, the ancestors and founders of the Disinherited, continued to serve in English armies in the hope of unseating Robert, who they regarded as a murderer and usurper. Even the Soules Conspiracy, as unsuccessful as it was, showed that at the height of Bruce power and authority, there still existed members of the Scottish nobility who opposed the Bruce regime and were willing to back an alternate Scottish king. Such dissident nobles were not merely English puppets or vassals, and their opposition to the Bruce faction did not entail a forfeiture of Scottish identity. Similarly, while the Disinherited ultimately proved themselves to be dependent upon English intervention, Edward Balliol ruled, or at least aspired to rule, the portions of Scotland remaining to him as King of Scotland. While often overlooked, significant numbers of Scottish nobles had at various points sworn homage and co-operated with him and his English sponsors against the Bruce loyalists. Moreover, although the Disinherited accepted English support, they only did so in the aftermath of the massacre at Annan. Prior to that, foolhardy and optimistic as it may have been, the Disinherited were entirely willing to invade Scotland on their own, with the goal of displacing the Bruces and restoring the Balliols to power.

War has always been a major catalyst for political and social change. During the Second War of Independence, the Disinherited and some Scottish nobles began to declare their loyalty not for the Bruce or Balliol families but 'for the lion', for Scotland itself. In practical terms this may have been little more than a convenient rhetorical device to avoid choosing sides in what was an extremely bloody and contentious civil war. But both the sentiment and the distinction it draws between the kingdom and the parties of the respective royal candidates are incredibly significant and indicative of the cultural change wrought by decades of war and the political upheaval that accompanied the establishment of Bruce rule. Such an abstract declaration of loyalty not for an individual king but a kingdom would have seemed strange and alien within either the twilight years of Dunkeld Scotland or the initial stages of the war with England.

In his efforts to take control of Scotland and expel the English, Robert I radically altered the composition and role of the Scottish aristocracy, displacing his rivals and raising his supporters, many of whom had been regional rivals of members of the former ruling faction, into positions of authority. While Robert went to considerable effort to win over members of the wider Scottish nobility, the needs and circumstances of the ongoing war led him to create a powerful but insular monarchy. In contrast to the consensus and compromise-driven co-operation that had characterised the lead elements of Scottish aristocracy during the succession crisis, Bruce delegated extensive royal authority to a small coterie made up of the trusted lieutenants who had fought by his side throughout the war.

In a similar vein, the war unleashed by the Disinherited's attempts to restore the Balliol monarchy shattered the status quo established by the Bruce monarchy. Despite emerging victorious, the unity of the Bruce's tightly knit alliance of allied families was destroyed. The uncertainty caused by the death of successive Guardians and the lack of royal oversight for much of the war meant that the Bruce-aligned warlords came to see one another as potential rivals. While not opposed to co-ordinated action, the great families of Bruce Scotland were increasingly competitive and wary of one another. In a sense, war with the English and the remains of the Disinherited eventually became the arena in which the principal figures of Scottish politics competed with one another for power and legitimacy. The dynastic failure of the Bruce family further weakened the moral authority and prestige of the monarchy, setting the stage for repeated clashes between the new Stewart kings, soon to be redubbed the Stuarts, and their erstwhile allies. In a sense then, had any of the Disinherited lived to see it, they may have been able to claim something of a pyrrhic victory over the dynasty that had driven them from their homes.

The origins and history of the Disinherited are tangled deep within a process of conflict defined far more by dynastic politics and the ruthless pursuit of power than it was by national sentiment or cultural loyalty. The political revolutions and seismic shifts of this period, as brittle as they were, masked and informed a deeper cultural shift. The lasting lesson of this examination of that extended and layered process is that polities and the cultural identities that formed around them are both far more malleable than we often appreciate, true continuity coming only in the form of constant adaptation and reinvention.

Notes

Introduction

1. Richard D. Oram, *The Lordship of Galloway, C1000 to C1250* (PhD Thesis St Andrews University, 1989), p.97.

Chapter 1: Neighbours and Rivals

1. Christopher Bowles and Ronan Toolis, *The Lost Dark Age Kingdom of Rheged: The Discovery of a Royal Stronghold at Trusty's Hill, Galloway* (Oxbow Books, 2017).
2. K.H. Jackson, 'Angles and Britons in Northumbria and Cumbria', ed. H. Lewis, *Angles and Britons* (Cardiff, 1963), p.72.
3. Andrew McDonald, *The Kingdom of the Isles; Scotland's Western Seaboard C.100–1336* (Scottish Historical Review, 1998), p.22.
4. Clare Downham, *Hiberno-Norwegians and Anglo-Danes: Anachronistic Ethnicities and Viking-Age England* (Mediaeval Scandinavia 19, 2009), p.150.
5. *Cronica Regum Mannie et Insularum: Chronicles of the Kings of Man and the Isles*, trans. G. Broderick (Belfast, 1979), f. 34v., entry for year 1098.
6. *A Scottish Chronicle Known as the Chronicle of Holyrood*, ed. M.O. Anderson (Scottish History Society, 1938), pp.136–7.
7. Oram, *The Lordship of Galloway*, pp.42–43.
8. *Registrum Eyisconatus Glasauensis* (Edinburgh, 1843), No. 3, 9, 10.
9. *A Scottish Chronicle Known as the Chronicle of Holyrood*, pp.136–7.
10. C. Warren Hollister, *Monarchy, Magnates and Institutions in the Anglo-Norman World* (Hambledon Press, 1986); Hugh M. Thompson, *The English and the Normans: Ethnic Hostility, Assimilation, and Identity 1066–c.1220* (Oxford University Press, 2003).
11. John Gillingham, *The English in the Twelfth Century: Imperialism, National Identity, and Political Values* (Boydell Press, 2000).
12. McDonald, *The Kingdom of the Isles*, p.22.
13. Richard D. Oram, *David I: The King Who Made Scotland* (Tempus Publishing, 2004).
14. Roger of Howden, *Chronica*, ed. William Stubbs (London, 1869), ii, p.105.
15. *The Chronicles of Robert of Torigni*, ed. R. Howlett (London, 1889), IV, 229.
16. James Turner, *The Royal Bastards of Twelfth Century England: Blood and Power* (Pen and Sword, 2023).
17. Kathleen Thompson, 'Affairs of State: The Illegitimate Children of Henry I', in *Journal of Medieval History, 29* (2003), p.129.
18. Oram, *David I*, p.59.
19. Richard of Hexham, *De Gestis Regis Stephani*, ed. R. Howlett (London, 1884–89), pp.152–159.
20. Oram, *The Lordship of Galloway*, p.80.
21. *Cronica Regum Mannie et Insularum*, pp.62, 64–66.

22. Russel Andrew McDonald, *Manx Kingship in its Irish Sea Setting, 1187–1229: King Rǫgnvaldr and the Crovan Dynasty* (Dublin: Four Courts Press, 2007).
23. Richard D. Oram, *Domination and Lordship: Scotland, 1070–1230* (Edinburgh University Press, 2011), p.94.
24. *The Chronicle of Melrose*, ed. A.O. Anderson and others (London, 1936), p.83.
25. *The Chronicles of Robert of Torigni*, IV, p.238.
26. Roger of Howden, *Chronica*, pp.ii, p.60.
27. Ibid., p.105.
28. Roger of Howden, *Gesta Regis Henrici Secundi and Gesta Regis Ricardi*, ed. William Stubbs (1867), p.67.
29. Oram, *The Lordship of Galloway*, p.108.
30. A.O. Anderson, *Scottish Annals from English Chroniclers: AD 500 to 1286* (London, 1908), p.258.
31. Ibid., p.258.
32. *The Acts of William I, King of Scots, 1165–1214*, ed. G.W.S Burrow (Edinburgh University, 1971), p.7.
33. Roger of Howden, *Chronica*, pp.ii, 105.
34. *Benedict of Peterborough*, ed. William Stubbs (London, 1867), I, p.336.
35. Oram, *The Lordship of Galloway*, p.121.
36. *The Chronicle of Melrose*, p.45.
37   Johannis de Fordun, *Chronica Gentis Scotorum*, ed. W.F. Skene (Edinburgh, 1872), Vol. I, pp.269–70.
38. *Benedict of Peterborough*, II, p.7.
39. Richard D. Oram, 'Introduction: An Overview of the Reign of Alexander II', in *The Reign of Alexander II, 1214–49. The Northern World: North Europe and the Baltic c. 400–1700 AD. Peoples, Economics and Cultures*, ed. R.D. Oram (Leiden: Brill, 2005), p.8.
40. Keith J. Stringer, 'A New Wife for Alan of Galloway' (PDF) in *Transactions of the Dumfriesshire and Galloway Natural History and Antiquarian Society* (1972), pp.49–55.
41. Keith J. Stringer, 'Periphery and Core in Thirteenth-Century Scotland, Alan Son of Roland, Lord of Galloway and Constable of Scotland', eds. A. Grant & K.J. Stringer, *Medieval Scotland: Crown, Lordship and Community* (Edinburgh: Edinburgh University Press), p.82.
42. C. Veach, 'Conquest and Conquerors', in *The Cambridge History of Ireland. Vol. 1*, ed. B. Smith (Cambridge: Cambridge University Press, 2018).
43. *Calendar of Documents Relating to Scotland*, eds. J.D. Galbraith and G.G. Simpson (Edinburgh, 1881–88), Vol. I, No. 529.
44. R.A. McDonald, *Kings, Usurpers, and Concubines in the Chronicles of the Kings of Man and the Isles* (Palgrave Macmillan, 2019), p.47.
45. *The Chronicle of Melrose*, p.82.
46. Richard D. Oram, 'Quincy, Roger de, Earl of Winchester (c.1195–1264)', *Oxford Dictionary of National Biography* (Oxford University Press, 2004), https://doi:10.1093/ref:odnb/22966 [Accessed May 2023]; Michael Prestwich, *Plantagenet England, 1225–1360. New Oxford History of England* (Oxford: Clarendon Press, 2005), p.246.
47. *Chronicon de Lanercost* (Maitland Club, 1839), p.42.
48. Oram, 'Quincy, Roger de, Earl of Winchester (c.1195–1264)'.
49. Ibid.

50. Thomas Rymer, *Foedera Conventiones, Literae et cujuscunque generis Acta Publica inter Reges Angliae* (London, 1745), p.228.
51. Alice Taylor, *The Shape of the State in Medieval Scotland 1124–1290* (Oxford University Press, 2016), p.114.
52. G.W.S. Barrow, *The Anglo-Norman Era in Scottish History* (Oxford, 1980).
53. Kenji Nishioka, 'Scots and Galwegians in the 'Peoples Address' of Scottish Royal Charters' in *The Scottish Historical Review* (2008), 87 (2): p.206.
54. Oram, *The Lordship of Galloway*, p.252.
55. McDonald, *Kings, Usurpers, and Concubines*, p.249.
56. Susan Marshall, *Illegitimacy in Medieval Scotland 1100–150* (Boydell Press, 2021), p.55.
57. *Chronicon de Lanercost*, p.42.
58. *The Chronicle of Melrose*, p.81.
59. Richard D. Oram, 'Thomas (Thomas of Galloway), earl of Atholl (d. 1231), magnate', Oxford *Dictionary of National Biography* (Oxford University Press, 2004), https://doi.org/10.1093/ref:odnb/49364, [Accessed May 2023].
60. Oram, *The Lordship of Galloway*, p.127.
61. *Chronicon de Lanercost*, p.49.
62. Matthew Paris, *Chronica Majora* (Cambridge), iv, p.563; *Calendar of Documents Relating to Scotland*, Vol. II, No. 1541.
63. Barbara English, 'Forz [Fortibus], William de, count of Aumale', *Oxford Dictionary of National Biography*, (2004). https://doi.org/10.1093/ref:odnb/29480 [Accessed May 2023].
64. *Calendar of Documents Relating to Scotland*, Vol. II, No. 824.
65. Oram, *The Lordship of Galloway*, p.223.
66. E. Acheson, 'Ferrers Family (per. c.1240–1445)', *Oxford Dictionary of National Biography* (Oxford University Press, 2004).
67. Oram, 'Quincy, Roger de, Earl of Winchester (c.1195–1264)'.
68. Oram, *The Lordship of Galloway*, p.224.
69. Ibid., p.171.
70. Matthew Paris, *Chronica Majora*, iv, p.563.
71. Charles O'Mahony, *The Viceroys of Ireland* (1912), p.22.
72. *The Acts of the Parliament of Scotland*, eds. T. Thompson and C. Innes (Edinburgh, 1814–75), I, p.9.
73. *Exchequer Roll* I, p.22.
74. Acheson, 'Ferrers Family'.
75. G.P. Stell, 'Balliol, John de (b. before 1208, d. 1268)', *Oxford Dictionary of National Biography* (Oxford University Press, 2004), https://doi.org/10.1093/ref:odnb/1208 [Accessed May 2023].
76. *Calendar of Documents Relating to Scotland*, Vol. II, No. 1630.
77. Ibid., Vol. I, No. 1338, Vol. II, No. 1578.
78. Ibid., Vol. I, No. 1338, Vol. II, No. 1808.
79. Amanda Beam, *The Balliol Dynasty, 1210–1364* (Edinburgh: John Donald, 2008), p.22.
80. Stell, 'Balliol, John de (b. before 1208, d. 1268)'.
81. Ibid.
82. Ibid.
83. Ibid.

84. *Durham Liber vitae, MS Cotton, Domitian A. VII, Edition and Digital Facsimile with Introduction, Codicological, Prosopographical and Linguistic Commentary, and Indexes, including the Biographical Register of Durham Cathedral Priory (1083–1539) by A J. Piper*, eds. David Rollason & Lynda Rollason (London: British Library, 2007).
85. Beam, *The Balliol Dynasty*, p.123.
86. Ibid., p.125.
87. Stell, 'Balliol, John de (b. before 1208, d. 1268)'.
88. *John of Fordun's Chronicle of the Scottish Nation* (Edinburgh), pp.288–90; Michael Brown, *The Wars of Scotland 1214–1371* (Edinburgh University Press, 2004), p.44.
89. Stell, 'Balliol, John de (b. before 1208, d. 1268)'.
90. Norman H. Ried, *Alexander III, 1249–1286: First Among Equals* (John Donald), p.80.
91. Stell, 'Balliol, John de (b. before 1208, d. 1268)'.
92. Ibid.
93. Beam, *The Balliol Dynasty*, p.180.
94. A.A.M. Duncan, 'Brus, Robert (II) de, lord of Annandale (d. 1194?)', *Oxford Dictionary of National Biography* (Oxford University Press, 2004).
95. Ruth Margaret Blakely, *The Brus Family in England and Scotland: 1100–1295* (Boydell Press, 2005), p.176.
96. G.W.S. Barrow, *Robert Bruce*, (Eyre & Spottiswoode, 1965), pp.34–35, 430, no. 26.
97. Duncan, 'Brus, Robert (II) de, lord of Annandale (d. 1194?)'.

Chapter 2: The Succession Crisis, Factionalism and the Path to Civil War

1. *A Scottish Chronicle Known as the Chronicle of Holyrood*, pp.136–7.
2. Oram, *The Lordship of Galloway*, p.97.
3. Richard D. Oram, 'Fergus, Galloway and the Scots' in *Galloway: Land and Lordship*, ed. G.P. Stell (Edinburgh: The Scottish Society for Northern Studies), p.117.
4. *Chronicon de Lanercost*, p.42.
5. Oram, *Domination and Lordship*, p.75.
6. McDonald, *The Kingdom of the Isles*, p.127.
7. Oram, *David I*, p.59.
8. Judith Green, 'Aristocratic Loyalties on the Northern Frontier of England, 1100–1174,' ed. D. Williams, *England in the Twelfth Century* (Woodbridge, 1990), p.83.
9. Gillingham, *The English in the Twelfth Century*.
10. Taylor, *The Shape of the State*, p.191.
11. Ibid., p.440.
12. Nicholas Vincent, 'Why 1199? Bureaucracy and Enrolment under John and his Contemporaries,' in *English Government in the Thirteenth Century*, ed. Adrian L. Jobson (The Boydell Press, 2004), p.17.
13. G.W.S. Barrow, *Kingship and Unity: Scotland, 1000–1306* (Edinburgh University Press, 1989).
14. Oram, *Domination and Lordship*, p.311.
15. Brown, *The Wars of Scotland*, p.89.
16. John of Fordun, *Chronica Johannes de Fordun, Chronica gentis Scotorum*, Vol. II, ed. W.F. Skene (1876), p.309.
17. Ibid., p.315.
18. Brown, *The Wars of Scotland*, p.208.

19. Norman H Reid, 'Alexander III (1241–1286), king of Scots' in *Oxford Dictionary of National Biography* (online ed.) (Oxford University Press, 2004).

20. John of Fordun, *Chronica Johannes de Fordun*, p.283.

21. Matthew Paris, *English History*, trans. J.A. Giles, (1852), Vol. I, p.36.

22. Keith J. Stringer, 'Marie [née Marie de Coucy] (d. 1284), Queen of Scots, second consort of Alexander II' in *Oxford Dictionary of National Biography* (online ed.). (Oxford University Press, 2004).

23. Ibid.

24. John of Fordun, *Chronica Johannes de Fordun*, Vol. II, (1876), p.288.

25. Alan Young, *Robert the Bruce's Rivals: The Comyns, 1212–1314* (Tuckwell Press, 1997), p.48.

26. Ibid., p.39.

27. *Liber S. Marie de Melros, Munimenta Vetustiora Monasterii Cisterciensis deMelros*, ed. C.N. Innes, (Edinburgh, 1837), I, No. 336.

28. D.E.R. Watt, 'The Minority of Alexander III of Scotland,' in *Transactions of the Royal Historical Society*, 5th Series, Vol. 21, (1971), p.1.

29. Matthew H. Hammond, 'The Durward Family in the Thirteenth Century', in *The Exercise of Power in Medieval Scotland, c.1200–1500*, eds. Steve Boardman and Alasdair Ross (Dublin/Portland, 2003), p.118.

30. G.W.S. Barrow, 'Badenoch and Strathspey, 1130–1312: 1 Secular and Political' in *Northern Scotland*, VIII.

31. *The Chronicle of Melrose*, p.536.

32. Ibid.

33. Walter Bower, *Scotichronicon*, ed. D.E.R. Watt, (Aberdeen, 1989), Vol. V, p.183.

34. Paris, *English History*, Vol. I, p.350.

35. John of Fordun, *Chronica Johannes de Fordun*, Vol. II, (1876), p.292.

36. Watt 'The minority of Alexander III, p.1.

37. Ried, *Alexander III, 1249–1286*, p.80.

38. *Calendar of Documents Relating to Scotland*, Vol. I, Nos. 888, 935, 974.

39. Bower, *Scotichronicon* (1989), Vol. V, p.298.

40. John of Fordun, *Chronica Johannes de Fordun*, Vol. II, (1876), p.297.

41. *Calendar of Documents Relating to Scotland*, Vol. I, Nos 2;077, 2;090, 2;103 2;113 2;116.

42. A.O. Anderson, *Early Sources of Scottish History 500–1286* (Edinburgh, 1922), Vol. I, p.592.

43. Young, *Robert the Bruce's Rivals*, p.71.

44. Bower, *Scotichronicon* (1989), Vol. V, p.346.

45. Anderson, *Early Sources of Scottish History*, p.601.

46. Brown, *The Wars of Scotland*, p.65.

47. David Carpenter, 'The Secret Revolution of 1258', in *Baronial Reform and Revolution in England 1258–1267*, ed. Adrian Jobson (The Boydell Press, 2016).

48. Richard D. Oram, *The Canmores: Kings & Queens of the Scots, 1040–1290* (Tempus, 2002), p.107.

49. Walter Bower, *Scotichronicon* ed. D.E.R. Watt, Vol. V, pp.402, 408.

50. *Chronicon de Lanercost*, p.184.

51. Anderson, *Early Sources of Scottish History*, Vol. I, pp.679–85.

52. Bower, *Scotichronicon*, VI, p.4.

53. A.A.M. Duncan, *The Kingship of the Scots 842–1292: Succession and Independence* (Edinburgh University Press, Edinburgh, 2002), p.321.

54. Ibid.

55. John of Fordun, *Chronica Johannes de Fordun*, Vol. I (1876), p.309.

56. Norman Reid 'The Kingless Kingdom: The Scottish Guardianship of 1286–1306', in *Scottish Historical Review*, 61, (1982), p.105.

57. John of Fordun, *Chronica Johannes de Fordun*, Vol. II, (1876), p.305.

58. Ibid.

59. Ibid.

60. Ibid.

61. Young, *Robert the Bruce's Rivals*, pp.95–96.

62. Knut Helle, 'Norwegian Foreign Policy and the Maid of Norway', *The Scottish Historical Review*, 69 (2002), p.142.

63. Ibid., p.149.

64. *Documents and Records Illustrating the History of Scotland*, ed. F. Palgrave, I, pp.42–3.

65. Richard D. Oram, 'Bruce, Balliol and the lordship of Galloway', in *Dumfries and Galloway Transaction*, 67, (1992), p.29.

66. Blakely, *The Brus Family in England and Scotland*, p.8.

67. C. Warren Hollister, *Henry I*, (Yale University Press, 2003), p.56.

68. Kerrith Davies, 'The Count of the Côtentin: Western Normandy, William of Mortain, and the Career of Henry I', in *The Haskins Society Journal* 22, ed. William L. North, (2010), p.123.

69. Blakely, *The Brus Family in England and Scotland*, p.10.

70. Oram, *Domination and Lordship*, p.75.

71. Ibid.

72. *Scottish Historical Documents*, ed. Gordon Donaldson (Edinburgh, 1970), p.19.

73. Judith A. Green, 'David I and Henry I', in the *Scottish Historical Review*, Vol. 75 (1996), p.18.

74. Richard of Hexham, *Chronicles of Stephen, Henry II and Richard I*, ed. R. Howlett, II (London, 1886), p.145.

75. *Early Yorkshire Charters*, Vol. II, ed. William Farrer (Edinburgh, 1915), p.11.

76. John of Worcester, *The Chronicle of John of Worcester*, III, ed. and trans. P. McGurk (Oxford, 1998), p.196.

77. A.A.M. Duncan, 'Brus, Robert (I) de, lord of Annandale (d. 1142)', in *Oxford Dictionary of National Biography* (Oxford University Press, 2004).

78. Duncan, 'Brus, Robert (II) de, lord of Annandale (d. 1194?)'.

79. *The Brus Family in England and Scotland*, p.1.

80. Sir Bernard Burke, *The Dormant, Abeyant, Forfeited, and Extinct Peerages of the British Empire* (London, 1883), p.80.

81. Duncan, 'Brus, Robert (II) de, lord of Annandale (d. 1194)'.

82. Douglas Richardson, *Magna Carta Ancestry* (2005), p.731.

83. Blakely, *The Brus Family in England and Scotland*, p.87.

84. G.W.S. Barrow, *Robert Bruce and the Community of the Realm of Scotland* (Edinburgh University Press, 1965), p.45.

85. A.A.M. Duncan, 'Brus [Bruce], Robert (VI) de') in *Oxford Dictionary of National Biography* (Oxford University Press, 2004).

86. A.A.M. Duncan, 'The Bruces of Annandale, 1100–1304,' in *Dumfries and Galloway Transactions*, 69, (1994), p.89.

87. Michael Prestwich, 'Edward I and the Maid of Norway,' Vol. 69, No. 188, Part 2: *Studies Commemorative of the Anniversary of the Death of the Maid of Norway* (Oct. 1990), p.156.

88. Michael Prestwich, 'Edward I (1239–1307)' in *Oxford Dictionary of National Biography* (Oxford University Press, 2004).

89. *Calendar of Documents Relating to Scotland*, Vol. II, Nos. 386–92.

90. Alan Young, 'The Comyns and Anglo-Scottish Relations (1286–1314)' in *Thirteenth Century England VII: Proceedings of the Durham Conference*, eds. Michael Prestwich, R.H. Britnell, Robin Frame (Boydell Press, 1997), p.207.

91. *Documents Illustrative of the History of Scotland 1286–1306*, ed. Joseph Stevenson (Edinburgh, 1870), pp.115–116, 126.

92. Ibid.

93. Brown, *The Wars of Scotland*, p.164.

94. *Documents Illustrative of the History of Scotland*, pp.115–116, 126.

95. Ibid.

96. Ibid.

97. *Calendar of Documents Relating to Scotland*, Vol. II, No. 459.

98. *National Manuscripts of Scotland* (1871), I n. L.XX.

99. Ibid.

100. *Documents Illustrative of the History of Scotland*, p.203.

101. Young, *Robert the Bruce's Rivals*, p.110.

102. A.A.M. Duncan, 'Process of Norham', in *Thirteenth Century England V*, ed. P.R. Coss and S.D. Lloyd (Woodbridge, 1999), p.222.

103. E.L.G. Stones and G.G. Simpson, eds., *Edward I and the Throne of Scotland* (1978), I, p.137.

104. E.L.G. Stones, ed. *Anglo-Scottish Relations* (London, 1963), p.89.

105. Young, *Robert the Bruce's Rivals*, p.111.

106. Ibid.

107. G. Stell, 'The Balliol Family and the Great Cause of 1291–2', in *Essays of the Nobility of Medieval Scotland*, ed. K.J. Stringer (Edinburgh University Press, 1985), p.150.

108. Stones and Simpson, *Edward I and the Throne of Scotland*, I, p.141.

109. G.G. Simpson, 'The Claim of Florence, Count of Holland to the Scottish Throne, 1291–2', in *Scottish Historical Review*, XXVI, p.115.

110. Stell, 'The Balliol Family and the Great Cause of 1291–2', p.152.

111. Duncan, *The Kingship of the Scots 842–1292*.

112. Barrow, *Kingship and Unity*.

113. Stones and Simpson, *Edward I and the Throne of Scotland*, I, p.143.

114. Beam, *The Balliol Dynasty*, p.289.

115. Young, 'The Comyns and Anglo-Scottish Relations', p.213.

116. Stones and Simpson. *Edward I and the Throne of Scotland*, I, p.143.

117. Simpson, 'The Claim of Florence, Count of Holland to the Scottish Throne, p.115.

118. Stones, *Anglo-Scottish Relations*, p.17.

119. Ibid.

Chapter 3: Invasion and Civil War
1. Oram, *Domination and Lordship*, p.197.
2. Malcolm Vale, 'St John, Sir John de (d. 1302)'. in *Oxford Dictionary of National Biography* (online ed.) (Oxford University Press, 2008).
3. Ibid.
4. C.M. Fraser, 'Bek, Antony (I) (c.1245–1311)', in *Oxford Dictionary of National Biography* (online ed.) (Oxford University Press, 2008).
5. Ibid.
6. Ibid.
7. Brown, *The Wars of Scotland*, p.169.
8. Stones, *Anglo-Scottish Relations*, No. 20, p.127.
9. The *Annals of Roger de Hoveden: Comprising the History of England and of Other Countries of Europe from A.D. 732 to A.D. 1201*, ed. and trans. Henry T. Riley (London, 1853), p.381.
10. Douglas David Roy Owen, *William the Lion 1143–1214: Kingship and Culture* (Tuckwell, 1997), p.108.
11. Brown, *The Wars of Scotland*, p.169.
12. Duncan, 'Process of Norham', p.222.
13. Alan Young and George Cumming, *The Real Patriots of Early Scottish Independence* (John Donald, 2014), p.111.
14. Oram, 'Bruce, Balliol and the Lordship of Galloway', p.32.
15. *Calendar of Documents Relating to Scotland*, Vol. V, No. 119.
16. *Documents Illustrative of the History of Scotland*, p.393.
17. *Rotuli Scotiae in turri Londinensi et in Domo Capitulari Westmonasteriensi Asservati*, ed. D. Macpherson (London, 1814), I, p.17a.
18. Young & Cumming, *The Real Patriots of Early Scottish Independence*, p.121.
19. Oram, *The Lordship of Galloway*, p.97.
20. Brown, *The Wars of Scotland*, p.169.
21. Stones, *Anglo-Scottish Relations*, p.117.
22. Young, *Robert the Bruce's Rivals*, p.171.
23. *Calendar of Documents Relating to Scotland*, Vol. V, No. 119.
24. *Acts of the Parliaments of Scotland*, Vol. I., p.91.
25. Ibid., p.447.
26. *Calendar of Documents Relating to Scotland*, Vol. II, No. 1631.
27. Young & Cumming, *The Real Patriots of Early Scottish Independence*, p.61.
28. *Acts of the Parliaments of Scotland*, Vol. I, p.448.
29. W.D.H. Sellar, 'MacDougall, John, Lord of Argyll (d. 1316)', *Oxford Dictionary of National Biography* (online ed.). (Oxford University Press, 2004).
30. *Calendar of Documents Relating to Scotland*, Vol. II, No. 1631.
31. G.W.S. Barrow and Ann Royan, 'James Stewart, Fifth Steward of Scotland, 1260–1309', in *Essays on the Nobility of Medieval Scotland*, ed. Keith Stringer (Edinburgh: John Donald, 1985), p.166.
32. Brown, *The Wars of Scotland*, p.171.
33. *Calendar of Documents Relating to Scotland*, Vol. II, No. 1541, p.184.
34. *Register of John de Halton*, ed. William Thompson (London, 1913), pp.i, 84.
35. Young, *Robert the Bruce's Rivals*, p.125.
36. *Foedera*, ed. T. Rhymer, (Record Commission, London, 1816), i, II, 823.

37. *Rotuli Scotiae in turri*, I, 8, 12,17; *Acts of the Parliaments of Scotland*, Vol. I, p.89.
38. *Register of John le Romeyn*, ed. William Brown (Durham, 1913), ii, No. 1389.
39. Brown, *The Wars of Scotland*, p.171.
40. *Acts of the Parliaments of Scotland*, Vol. I, p.91; *Calendar of Documents Relating to Scotland*, Vol. II, Nos. 1631, 1737.
41. Young, *Robert the Bruce's Rivals*, p.135.
42. Ibid.
43. John Bannerman, 'MacDuff of Fife,' in *Medieval Scotland: Crown, Lordship and Community, Essays Presented to G.W.S. Barrow*, eds. A. Grant & K. Stringer (Edinburgh, 1993), p.20.
44. Ibid., pp.20–38.
45. G.W.S. Barrow, *Robert Bruce*, (Edinburgh, 1988), p.57; *Rotuli Scotiae in turri Londinensi*, I, 8, 12, 17–20.
46. Stones, *Anglo-Scottish Relations*, No. 20, p.131.
47. *Rotuli Scotiae in turri Londinensi*, I, 19, 20; *Documents Illustrative of the History of Scotland*, Nos. 317, 319, 320.
48. Barrow, *Robert Bruce* (1988), p.58; Stones, *Anglo-Scottish Relations*, No. 21, p.131.
49. Stones, *Anglo-Scottish Relations*, No. 21, p.131.
50. Robin Studd, 'Reconfiguring the Angevin Empire' in *England and Europe in the Reign of Henry III*, eds. Ifor W. Rowlands and Björn K.U. Weiler (Taylor and Francis, 2017), p.42.
51. Michael Prestwich, *Edward I* (Yale University Press, 1988), p.376.
52. *Calendar of Documents Relating to Scotland*, Vol. V, No. 129.
53. David Simpkin, *The English Aristocracy at War: From the Welsh Wars of Edward I to the Battle of Bannockburn* (Boydell Press, 2008), p.122.
54. *Chronicle of Lanercost 1272–1346*, trans. Sir Herbet Maxell (Glasgow, 1913), p.115.
55. Young & Cumming, *The Real Patriots of Early Scottish Independence*, p.119.
56. *Acts of the Parliaments of Scotland*, Vol. I, p.453.
57. G.W.S. Barrow, 'The Scottish Clergy and the War of Independence,' in *Scottish Historical Review 43* (1963), p.17.
58. Brown, *The Wars of Scotland*, p.192.
59. *Calendar of Documents Relating to Scotland*, Vol. II No. 718, 723 Vol. V, No. 135.
60. Ibid., No. 716; Barrow, *Robert Bruce* (1988), p.63.
61. *Chronicle of Lanercost*, p.115.
62. *Chronicle of Guisborough*, ed. H. Rothwell, p.270.
63. Stones, *Anglo-Scottish Relations*, p.137; Young, *Robert the Bruce's Rivals*, p.141.
64. Brown, *The Wars of Scotland*, p.175.
65. Fiona Watson, *Under the Hammer: Edward I and Scotland, 1286–1307* (John Donald, 2008).
66. *Chronicle of Lanercost*, pp.115, 124.
67. Brown, *The Wars of Scotland*, p.175.
68. *Calendar of Documents Relating to Scotland*, Vol. II, No. 737; *Rotuli Scotiae in turri Londinensi*, I, 22, 23, 29, 30.
69. *Documents Illustrative of the History of Scotland*, II. No. 152; *Chronicle of Fordun*, ed. W.F. Skene (Edinburgh, 1872), II, p.317.
70. 'Foedera' (1816), i, II, p.909.
71. Andrew Fisher, 'Murray, Andrew (d. 1297)' *Oxford Dictionary of National Biography* (Oxford University Press, 2004) (online edition); *Calendar of Documents Relating to Scotland*, Vol. II, No. 376.

72. Anderew Fisher, 'Wallace, Sir William (d. 1305)', *Oxford Dictionary of National Biography* (Oxford University Press, 2004) (online edition).
73. Alexander Grant, 'Bravehearts and Coronets: Images of William Wallace and the Scottish Nobility', in *The Wallace Book*, ed. E.J. Cowan (Edinburgh, 2007).
74. *Documents Illustrative of the History of Scotland*, II, p.167.
75. Ibid., pp.202, 212.
76. *Chronicle of Guisborough*, p.297.
77. Young, *Robert the Bruce's Rivals*, p.167.
78. Chronicle of Guisborough, ed. H. Rothwell, p.294; Chronicle of Fordun (1872), II, p.321.
79. Calendar of Documents Relating to Scotland, Vol. II, No. 853, p.224; G.W.S. Barrow, *Robert Bruce & the Community of the Realm of Scotland* (4th ed.) (Edinburgh, 2005).
80. Brown, *The Wars of Scotland*, p.185; Michael Prestwich, 'The Battle of Stirling Bridge: An English Perspective', in *The Wallace Book*, ed. Edward J. Cowan (Edinburgh: John Donald, 2007), p.64.
81. Young & Cumming, *The Real Patriots of Early Scottish Independence*, p.137.
82. *Chronicle of Guisborough*, p.299; *Chronicle of Lanercost*, p.163.
83. Watson, *Under the Hammer*, p.61.
84. *Chronicle of Fordun* (1872), Vol. II, 324.
85. *Calendar of Documents Relating to Scotland*, Vol. II, Nos. 1017, 1978.
86. M. Ash, 'William Lamberton, Bishop of St Andrews, 1297–1328', in *The Scottish Tradition Essays in Honour of R.G. Cant*, ed. G.W.S. Barrow (Edinburgh, 1974).
87. *Chronicle of Fordun* (1872), Vol. II, p.324.
88. Sir Thomas Gray, *Scalacronica*, trans. and ed. A. King (Durham, 2005), p.45.
89. Young & Cumming, *The Real Patriots of Early Scottish Independence*, p.163.
90. Ibid., p.181.
91. John Barbour, *The Bruce* (Edinburgh, 1997), p.78; Walter Bower, *Scotichronicon*, ed. D.E.R. Watt (Aberdeen, 1982), Vol. VI, p.309.
92. Gray, *Scalacronica* (2005), p.29.
93. *Flores Historiarum*, ed. Henry Richard Luard (London, 1890), Vol. III, p.323.
94. *Chronicle of Guisborough*, p.367; Brown, *The Wars of Scotland*, p.200.
95. *Chronicle of Lanercost*, p.176; Stones, *Anglo-Scottish Relations*, p.261.
96. *Calendar of Documents Relating to Scotland*, Vol. II, No. 1,926; Prestwich, *Edward I*, p.556.
97. Brown, *The Wars of Scotland*, p.203.
98. *Chronicle of Fordun* (1872), Vol. II, p.336; Barrow, *Robert Bruce*, p.176.
99. P. Barnes and G.W.S Barrow, 'The Movements of Robert Bruce between September 1307 and May 1308', in *Scottish Historical Review*, 69 (1970), p.58.

Chapter 4: A New Scotland and the Fate of the Exiles

1. M. Haskell, 'Breaking the Stalemate; The Scottish Campaign of Edward I, 1303–4', in *Thirteenth-Century England, VII*, eds. Michael C. Prestwich, Richard Britnell and Robin Frame (Boydell Press, 1997), p.223.
2. Fiona Watson, 'Settling the Stalemate: Edward I's Peace in Scotland, 1303–1305', in *Thirteenth-Century England VI*, eds. Michael C. Prestwich, Richard Britnell and Robin Frame (Boydell Press, 1997), p.127.
3. C. McNamee, 'William Wallace's Invasion of Northern England, 1297', in *Northern History*, 26 (1990), p.40.

4. Fisher, 'Wallace, Sir William (d. 1305)'; Alexander Falconer Murison, *William Wallace: Guardian of Scotland* (New York, 2003), p.43.

5. Young, *Robert the Bruce's Rivals*, p.188.

6. Brown, *The Wars of Scotland*, p.200.

7. Barrow, *Robert Bruce and the Community of the Realm*, p.100.

8. Fiona Watson, 'The Enigmatic Lion: Scotland, Kingship and National Identity in the Wars of Independence' in *Image and Identity: The Making and Remaking of Scotland through the Ages*, eds. D. Broun, R. Finlay and M. Lynch (Edinburgh, 1998), p.18.

9. E.L.G. Stones, 'The Submission of Robert Bruce to Edward I, 1301–2' in *Scottish Historical Review*, 34 (1955), p.122.

10. G.W.S. Barrow, 'Elizabeth [née Elizabeth de Burgh] (d. 1327), Queen of Scots', in *Oxford Dictionary of National Biography* (online ed.) (Oxford University Press, 2004); Rosalind K. Marshall, *Scottish Queens, 1034–1714* (Tuckwell Press, 2003), p.34.

11. Chronicle of Guisborough, p.367; Brown, *The Wars of Scotland*, p.200.

12. *Calendar of Documents Relating to Scotland*, Vol. II, No. 1,926; Prestwich, *Edward I*, p.556.

13. Roy Martin Haines, *King Edward II: Edward of Caernarfon, His Life, His Reign, and Its Aftermath, 1284–1330* (London, 2003), p.49; Jochen Burgtorf, 'With My Life, His Joyes Began and Ended: Piers Gaveston and King Edward II of England Revisited', in *Fourteenth Century England*. Vol. V. ed. Nigel Saul (Woodbridge, UK: The Boydell Press, 2008), p.31.

14. M. Prestwich, 'Colonial Scotland: The English in Scotland under Edward I,' in *Scotland and England 1286–1815*, ed. R.A. Mason (Edinburgh, 1987).

15. Dauvit Broun, 'Defining Scotland and the Scots before the Wars of Independence,' in D. Broun, R. Rinlay and M. Lynch, *Image and Identity: The Making and Remaking of Scotland through the Ages, Edinburgh* (1998), p.4.

16. Alan Young, 'Buchan in the 13th Century', in *Medieval Scotland: Crown, Lordship and Community Essays Presented to G.W.S. Barrow*, eds. Alexander Grant & Keith J. Stringer (Edinburgh, 1993).

17. Bower, *Scotichronicon* (1882), Vol. VI, p.224.

18. Barbour, *The Bruce*, p.360.

19. *The Records of the Parliaments of Scotland to 1707*, eds. K.M. Brown et al (St Andrews, 2007), 1308/1.

20. Brown, *The Wars of Scotland*, p.169.

21. A.D.M. Barrell, 'The Papacy and the Regular Clergy in Scotland in the Fourteenth Century', in *Scottish Church History Society Records*, 24:2 (1991), p.103.

22. G.W.S. Barrow, 'The Scottish Clergy in the War of Independence,' in *Scottish Historical Review*, 41 (1962), p.1.

23. The Acts of the Parliament of Scotland, Vol. I, 289, 459.

24. Ibid.

25. Ibid.

26. Ibid.

27. *Calendar of Documents Relating to Scotland*, Vol. III, No. 3337; *Rotuli Scotiae in turri Londinensi*, p.113.

28. *Chronicle of Fordun* (1872), Vol. II, 337; Thomas Gray, *Scalacronica*, trans. H. Maxwell (Glasgow, 1907), p.51.

29. Barrow, *Robert Bruce and the Community of the Realm*, p.231.

30. Ibid., p.242.

31. Ibid.

32. *Chronicle of Fordun* (1872), Vol. II, p.339; Gray, *Scalacronica* (1907), p.51.

33. Alfred Hiatt, 'Beyond a Border: The Maps of Scotland in John Hardyng's Chronicle', in *The Lancastrian Court Proceedings of the 2001 Harlaxton Symposium,* ed. J. Stratford (2003).

34. Barbour, *The Bruce*, p.377.

35. Ibid., p.410.

36. David Cornell, *Bannockburn: The Triumph of Robert the Bruce* (Yale University Press, 2003), p.156.

37. Jennifer C. Ward, 'Joan, Countess of Hertford and Gloucester (1272–1307)', *Oxford Dictionary of National Biography* (Oxford: Oxford University Press, 2004).

38. Michael Altschul, 'Clare, Gilbert de, Eighth Earl of Gloucester and Seventh Earl of Hertford (1291–1314)', *Oxford Dictionary of National Biography* (Oxford: Oxford University Press, 2004); Michael Altschul, *A Baronial Family in Medieval England: The Clares 1217–1314* (Baltimore, 1965), pp.132–3.

39. Ibid.

40. J.S. Hamilton, 'Bohun, Humphrey de, Fourth Earl of Hereford and Ninth Earl of Essex, 1276–1332', *Oxford Dictionary of National Biography* (Oxford: Oxford University Press, 2004).

41. Ibid.

42. Andrew M. Spencer, *Nobility and Kingship in Medieval England: The Earls and Edward I 1272–1307* (Cambridge University press, 2013), p.251.

43. *Calendar of Documents Relating to Scotland*, Vol. II, No. 1842.

44. Barrow, *Robert Bruce and the Community of the Realm of Scotland* (1988), p.226.

45. Henry Summerson, 'Clifford, Robert, First Lord Clifford, (1274–1314), *Oxford Dictionary of National Biography* (Oxford: Oxford University Press, 2004).

46. Ibid.

47. I.J. Sanders, *English Baronies: A Study of their Origin and Descent 1086–1327* (Oxford, 1960), p.143.

48. J.R. Maddicott, 'Beaumont, Henry de, First Lord Beaumont (c.1280–1340), Baron', *Oxford Dictionary of National Biography* (Oxford: Oxford University Press, 2004).

49. *Calendar of Documents Relating to Scotland*, Vol. III, No. 184.

50. Maddicott, 'Beaumont, Henry de, First Lord Beaumont.

51. Fiona Watson, 'Comyn, John, Seventh Earl of Buchan, (c.1250–1308)', *Oxford Dictionary of National Biography* (Oxford: Oxford University Press, 2004).

52. Barbour, *The Bruce*, p.450.

53. J.R. Maddicott, 'Thomas of Lancaster, Second Earl of Lancaster', *Oxford Dictionary of National Biography* (online ed.) (Oxford University Press, 2008).

54. Brown, *The Wars of Scotland*, p.208.

55. H.W. Ridgeway, 'Valence [Lusignan], William de, Earl of Pembroke William de, Earl of Pembroke (d. 1296), Magnate', *Oxford Dictionary of National Biography* (online ed.) (Oxford University Press, 2004).

56. J.R.S. Phillips, *Aymer de Valence, Earl of Pembroke, 1307–1324: Baronial Politics in the Reign of Edward II* (Clarendon Press, 1972), p.75.

57. Prestwich, *Plantagenet England*, p.257.

58. *Calendar of Documents Relating to Scotland,* Vol. II, No. 1811a.

59. Fiona Watson, 'Dunbar, Patrick, 8th Earl of Dunbar or of March, and Earl of Moray (1285–1369), *Dictionary of National Biography* (Oxford University Press, 2004).

60. *Regesta Regum Scotorum, V, The Acts of Robert I*, ed. A.A.M Duncan (Edinburgh, 1988), No. 41.

61. Brown, *The Wars of Scotland*, p.226.

62. Stephen Boardman, *The Campbells, 1250–1513* (Edinburgh, 2006), p.21.

63. *Regesta Regum Scotorum, V*, No. 389.

64   67 *Regesta Regum Scotorum, V*, No. 7.

65. Micheal Penman, *David II* (Edinburgh, 2004), p.25.

66. Alexander Grant, *Independence and Nationhood 1306–1469* (Edinburgh, 1991), p.26.

67. *Registrum Magni Sigilli Regum Scotorum: The register of the Great seal of Scotland, A.D. 1306–1668*, ed. J.M. Thompson (Edinburgh, 1882), i, App.1, No. 8.

68. Ibid., i, App.1, No. 68.

69. Ibid., i, App.1, No. 38, No. 123.

70. *Regesta Regum Scotorum, V*, No. 35.

71. Ibid., No. 194.

72. Cynthia J. Neville, *Native Lordship in Medieval Scotland: The Earldoms of Strathearn and Lennox, c.1140–1365* (Portland & Dublin, 2005), p.124.

73. *Regesta Regum Scotorum*, Nos. 24, 28, 35, 101.

74. G.W.S. Barrow, 'Lothian in the First War of Independence, 1296–1328', in *The Scottish Historical Review*, Vol. 55, No. 160, Part 2 (October 1976), p.151.

75. J. Scammel, 'Robert I and the North of England', in *The English Historical Review*, 73 (1958), p.385.

76. Scammel, 'Robert I and the North of England', p.385; Michael Penman, *Robert the Bruce, King of the Scots* (Yale University Press, 2014), p.149.

77. *Regesta Regum Scotorum, V*, No. 424; *Chronicle of Lanercost*, p.313.

78. S. Duffy, *Robert the Bruce's Irish Wars* (Stroud, 2002).

79. Gillian Kenny, 'The Wife's Tale: Isabel Marshal and Ireland', in *William Marshal and Ireland*, ed. J. Bradley (Dublin, 2017), p.315.

80. M.T. Flanagan, 'Clare, Richard fitz Gilbert de [called Strongbow], Second Earl of Pembroke', *Dictionary of National Biography* (Oxford University Press, 2004).

81. Emmett O'Byrne, *War, Politics and the Irish of Leinster 1156–1160* (Dublin, 2003), p.15.

82. A.A.M. Duncan, 'The Scots' Invasion of Ireland, 1315', ed. R.R. Davies, *The British Isles, 1100–1500* (Edinburgh: J. Donald, 1988).

83. *Rotuli Scotiae in turri Londinensi*, I, pp.118, 143.

84. Barrow, 'Elizabeth [née Elizabeth de Burgh] (d. 1327), Queen of Scots'.

85. R. Frame, 'The Bruces, in Ireland', in *Irish Historical Review*, 24 (1974), p.3.

86. Francis John Byrne, *Irish Kings and High Kings* (London, 1973), p.40.

87. *Regesta Regum Scotorum, V*, Nos. 58, 301; Bower, *Scotichronicon* (1882), Vol. VI, p.383.

88. Colm McNamee, *Wars of the Bruces: Scotland, England and Ireland 1306–1328* (Edinburgh, 2002), p.166.

89. Philip Slavin, *Experiencing Famine in Fourteenth-century Britain* (Montreal, 2022).

90. Frame, 'The Bruces, in Ireland', p.30.

91. McNamee, *Wars of the Bruces*, p.201.

92. *Regesta Regum Scotorum, V*, No. 139.

93. Bruce Webster, 'Balliol, Edward, (b. in or after 1281, d. 1364), *Oxford Dictionary of National Biography* (Oxford University Press, 2004).

94. Ibid.

95. *Calendar of Documents Relating to Scotland*, Vol. II, No. 593.

96. Michael Penman, 'A fell coniuracioun agayn Robert the douchty king: The Soules Conspiracy of 1318–1320', in *Innes Review*, 50 (1999), p.25.

97. Thomas McMichael, 'The Feudal Family of de Soulis', in *Dumfriesshire and Galloway Natural History & Antiquarian Society: Transactions and Journal of Proceedings*, 3rd series, Vol. 26, (1947–48), p.163.

98. *Regesta Regum Scotorum, V*, No. 392.

99. Oram, 'Bruce, Balliol, and the Lordship of Galloway', p.35.

100. Neville, *Native Lordship in Medieval Scotland*, p.83.

101. Penman, 'A fell coniuracioun agayn Robert the douchty king', p.27.

102. Ibid.

103. Ibid., p.29.

104. Ibid., p.27.

105. Ibid.

106. Ibid., p.25.

107. Ibid., p.38.

108. Fiona Watson, 'Sir Robert, lord of Liddesdale (c. 1293–1332), royal bastard', *Oxford Dictionary of National Biography* (online ed.) (Oxford University Press, 2004).

109. Phillips, 'Aymer de Valence', p.204.

110. Kathryn Warner, *Isabella of France: The Rebel Queen* (Amberley Publishing, 2012), p.55.

111. Clifford J. Rogers, *War Cruel and Sharp: English Strategy Under Edward III, 1327–1360* (Boydell Press, 2000), p.20.

112. Ibid., p.21.

113. McNamee, *The Wars of the Bruces*, p.245.

114. Prestwich, 'Colonial Scotland'.

115. Brown, *The Wars of Scotland*, p.217.

116. McNamee, *The Wars of the Bruces*, p.276.

117. Penman, *David II* (2004), p.6.

118. Stephen Boardman, *The Early Stewart Kings: Robert II and Robert III* (Edinburgh, 1996), p.12.

119. Elizabeth Van Houts, *Married Life in the Middle Ages* (Oxford, 2019), p.64.

Chapter 5: The Great Gamble of the Disinherited

1. S. Cameron and A. Ross, 'The Treaty of Edinburgh and the Disinherited (1328–32)', *History*, 84 (1999), p.237.

2. *Regesta Regum Scotorum*, V, No. 345.

3. Ibid., No. 342.

4. Stones, *Anglo-Scottish Relations*, Document 42; Gray, *Scalacronica* (1907), p.156.

5. Maddicott, 'Thomas of Lancaster, Second Earl of Lancaster'.

6. Ibid.

7. Ibid.

8. Maddicott, 'Beaumont, Henry de, First Lord Beaumont.

9. Guy Perry, *The Briennes: The Rise and Fall of a Champenois Dynasty in the Age of the Crusades, c. 950–1356* (Cambridge University Press, 2018), p.75.

10. Ibid., p.140.

11. Maddicott, 'Beaumont, Henry de, First Lord Beaumont.

12. Ibid.
13. Barbour, *The Bruce*, p.450.
14. Maddicott, 'Beaumont, Henry de, First Lord Beaumont.
15. Ibid.
16. Alison Weir, *Queen Isabella: She-Wolf of France, Queen of England* (London: Pimlico Books, 2006), p.307.
17. Scott L. Waugh, 'Edmund, first earl of Kent (1301–1330)', *Oxford Dictionary of National Biography* (Oxford: Oxford University Press, 2004).
18. *Calendar of Documents Relating to Scotland,* Vol. III, No. 201.
19. Young, 'The Comyns and Anglo-Scottish Relations', p.207.
20. Watson, 'Comyn, John, seventh earl of Buchan'.
21. Helen M. Jewell, 'Latimer, William, first Lord Latimer (d. 1304), baron and soldier', *Oxford Dictionary of National Biography* (Oxford: Oxford University Press, 2004).
22. Ibid.
23. Beam, *The Balliol Dynasty*, p.288.
24. Ibid., p.297.
25. *The Brut or the Chronicle of England*, ed. F.W. Brie (London, 1906), I, p.274.
26. Webster, 'Balliol, Edward (b. in or after 1281, d. 1364)'.
27. Fiona Watson, 'Strathbogie, David, styled tenth earl of Athol' *Oxford Dictionary of National Biography* (Oxford University Press, 2004).
28. *Chronicle of Guisborough*, p.367.
29. A. Ross, 'Men for All seasons? The Strathbogie Earls of Atholl and the Wars of Independence, C. 1290–1335, 2,' *Northern Scotland*, 21, (2001), p.1.
30. Ibid.
31. *Calendar of Documents Relating to Scotland*, Vol. III, No. 5.
32. *Registrum Magni Sigilli Regum Scotorum*, i, App.1, No. 71.
33. Watson, 'Strathbogie, David, styled tenth earl of Athol'.
34. Ibid.
35. Henry Summerson, 'Umfraville, de, family', *Oxford Dictionary of National Biography* (online ed.), (Oxford University Press, 2008).
36. Ibid.
37. *Foedera* (1816) ii, I, p.51.
38. David Cornell, 'Bannockburn: The Triumph of Robert the Bruce', in *The Historian*, 73(2), (New Haven, Conn.: Yale University Press, 2009), pp.378–379.
39. Fiona Watson, 'Umfraville, Gilbert de, seventh earl of Angus', *Oxford Dictionary of National Biography* (online ed.). (Oxford University Press, 2004).
40. Summerson, 'Umfraville, de, family'.
41. Scott L. Waugh, 'Talbot, Richard, second Lord Talbot (c.1306–1356), soldier and administrator', *Oxford Dictionary of National Biography* (online ed.), (Oxford University Press, 2004).
42. Scott L. Waugh, 'Talbot, Gilbert, first Lord Talbot', *Oxford Dictionary of National Biography* (online ed.). (Oxford University Press, 2004).
43. Ibid.
44. Ibid.
45. Waugh, 'Talbot, Richard, second Lord Talbot'.
46. Natalie Fryde, *The Tyranny and Fall of Edward II 1321–1326* (Cambridge: Cambridge University Press 2003), p.115.

47. Waugh, 'Talbot, Richard, second Lord Talbot'.
48. Acheson, 'Ferrers family'.
49. Acheson, 'Ferrers family'.
50. Ibid.
51. Ibid.
52. Penman, 'A fell coniuracioun agayn Robert the douchty king', p.25.
53. J.M.W. Bean, 'Percy, Henry, third Lord Percy (c.1321–1368)', *Oxford Dictionary of National Biography* (online ed.). (Oxford University Press, 2004).
54. W.M. Ormrod, 'Wake, Thomas, second Lord Wake (1298–1349), nobleman', *Oxford Dictionary of National Biography* (online ed.), (Oxford University Press, 2004).
55. Ibid.
56. Andrew Ayton, 'Ughtred, Thomas, first Lord Ughtred', *Oxford Dictionary of National Biography* (online ed.). (Oxford University Press, 2004).
57. Bruce Webster, 'Scotland Without a King, 1329–1341', in *Medieval Scotland: Crown, Lordship and Community*, eds. A. Grant and K.J. Stringer (1993).
58. Michael A. Penman, *David II* (Edinburgh, 2005), p.37.
59. David R. Ross, *James the Good: The Black Douglas* (Glasgow: Luath Press, 2020), p.213.
60. Sonja Cameron, 'Sir James Douglas, Spain and the Holy Land' in *Freedom and Authority – Scotland 1050–1650*. eds. Brotherstone & Ditchwell, (Edinburgh, 2000), p.116.
61. Ian Mortimer, *The Greatest Traitor: The Life of Sir Roger Mortimer, 1st Earl of March, Ruler of England, 1327–1330* (London, 2002), p.219.
62. J. Campbell, 'England, Scotland and the Hundred Years War in the Fourteenth Century,' in *Europe in the late Middle Ages*, eds. J.R. Hale, J.R.L. Highfield and B. Smalley (London, 1965), p.155.
63. Robert Knecht, *The Valois Kings of France 1328–1589* (London, 2007), p.2.
64. Rogers, *War Cruel and Sharp*, p.24.
65. *Foedera, conventions, litterae* etc, eds. Thomas Rhymer, edit A. Clarke, F. Holbrooke and J. Coley (London, 1869), II, 2, 813.
66. Les *Grandes Chroniques de France*, ed. Jules Viard (Paris, 1953), 9, 121.
67. *Foedera, conventions, litterae* (1869), II, 2,833.
68. Stephen Porter, *Edward III's Faithful Knight: Walter Mauny and His Legacy* (Stroud, 2022), p.48.
69. *Calendar of the Patent Rolls* (London 1942), 1330–4, 270.
70. Ibid., 1330–4, 260, 283, 305, 306, 308, 326, 367, 385, 397, 461.
71. Simpkin, *The English Aristocracy at War*, p.7.
72. Michael Prestwich, *War, Politics and Finance under Edward I* (London, 2007), p.67.
73. Jim Bradbury, *The Medieval Archer* (Woodbridge, 1985), p.71.
74. Michael Powicke, *Military Obligation in Medieval England* (Oxford, 1962), p.88.
75. Ibid.
76. Iain A. Macinnes, *Scotland's Second War of Independence 1332–1357* (Woodbridge, 2016), p.72.
77. Ibid.
78. Bower, *Scotichronicon* (1882), Vol. VII, p.72; *Chronicle of Lanercost*, p.268.
79. 'Gesta EdwardI Tertii Auctore Canonico Bridlingtoniensi' in *Chronicles of the Reigns of Edward I and Edward II*, V II ed. William Stubbs (London, 1883), p.104.
80. Johannis de Fordun, p.ii, p.346; Andrew of Wyntoun, *The Orgynale Cronykil of Scotland*, ed. D. Laig (Edinburgh 1879), ii, p.384.

81. *Chronicle of Lanercost*, p.268; 'Gesta EdwardI Tertii Auctore Canonico Bridlingtoniensi', p.104.
82. Penman, *David II* (2005), p.47.
83. R. Nicholson, *Edward II and the Scots: The Formative Years of a Military Career* (Oxford, 1965), p.81.
84. Rogers, *War Cruel and Sharp*, p.36; Watson, 'Sir Robert, lord of Liddesdale'.
85. Rogers, *War Cruel and Sharp*, p.36.
86. *Chronicle of Guisborough*, p.270.
87. *Chronicle of Lanercost*, pp.115, 124.
88. Watson, 'Dunbar, Patrick, 8th Earl of Dunbar or of March'.
89. 'Gesta EdwardI Tertii Auctore Canonico Bridlingtoniensi', p.149.
90. Ibid.
91. *Chronicle of Lanercost*, p.269.
92. *The Brut, I*, p.275.
93. Gray, *Scalacronica* (1907), p.159.
94. Nicholson, *Edward II and the Scots*, p.42.
95. *The Anonimalle Chronicle 1307 to 1334* from *Brotherton Collection* MS. 29, eds. W.R. Childs and J. Taylor (Leeds, 1991), p.148.
96. MacInnes, *Scotland's Second War of Independence*, p.60.
97. G.W.S. Barrow, 'The Army of Alexander III's Scotland,' in *Scotland in the Reign of Alexander III*, ed. N.H. Reid (Edinburgh, 1990), p.132.
98. Matthew Strickland, 'Kings of Scots at War', in *Military History of Scotland*, eds. E.M. Spiers, J.A. Craig and M. Strickland (Edinburgh, 2012), p.96.
99. *The Records of the Parliaments of Scotland to 1707*, 1318/29.
100. *Calendar of Patent Rolls* (London, 1891), 1343, 1344 1345, 1393.
101. The Records of the Parliaments of Scotland to 1707, 1318/29.
102. D.H. Cadwell, 'Scottish Spearmen 1298–1314: An Answer to Cavalry', in *War in History*, Vol. 19(3) (2012), p.270.
103. Andrew of Wyntoun, ii, p.386.
104. *Johannis de Fordun* (1872), Vol. II, 347; Andrew of Wyntoun, ii, p.395.
105. *The Brut*, I, 277.
106. *The Anonimalle Chronicle*, p.54.
107. *The Brut*, I, 276.
108. Walter Bower, *Scotichronicon*, ed. D.E.R. Watt (Edinburgh, 1998), Vol. VII, 77.
109. *Chronicle of Lanercost*, p.268.
110. 'Gesta EdwardI Tertii Auctore Canonico Bridlingtoniensi', p.106.
111. Andrew of Wyntoun, ii, p.388
112. Andrew of Wyntoun, ii, p.388; 'Gesta EdwardI Tertii Auctore Canonico Bridlingtoniensi', p.160.
113. Bower, *Scotichronicon* (1998), Vol. VII, p.81; *The Anonimalle Chronicle*, p.153.

Chapter 6: Once More Under the Yolk

1. Helen. J. Nicholson, *Theory and Practice of War in Europe, 300–1500* (New York, 2003), p.14; Scott Moynihan, 'Miracles, Divine Agency, And Christian Muslim Diplomacy During the Crusades', *Miracles, Political Authority and Violence in Medieval and Early Modern History*, eds. Matthew Rowley, Natasha Hodgson (Abingdon, 2022), p.50.
2. *The Chronicle of Lanercost*, p.269; *Foedera, conventions, litterae* (1869), II, 2,876.

3. Andrew of Wyntoun, ii, p.389.

4. Johannis de Fordun (1872), Vol. II, p.355.

5. I.A. MacInnes, 'Who's Afraid of the Big Bad Bruce? Balliol Scots and "English Scots" during the Second War of Independence', in *The Soldier Experience in the Fourteenth Century*, eds. A.R. Bell, A. Curry, A. Chapman, A. King and D. Simpkin (Woodbridge, 2011), p.129.

6. Michael Penman, *The Scottish Civil War: The Bruces & the Balliols & the War for Control of Scotland, 1286–1356* (Edinburgh, 2002).

7. *Documents Illustrative of the History of Scotland*, II. No. 152; *Chronicle of Fordun* (1872), Vol. II, p.317.

8. *Chronicle of Lanercost*, p.269.

9. Rogers, *War Cruel and Sharp*, p.49.

10. Gray, *Scalacronica* (1907), p.159.

11. Andrew of Wyntoun, ii, p.393.

12. A.A.M. Duncan 'Bruce, Alexander, earl of Carrick (d. 1333)', *Oxford Dictionary of National Biography* (online ed.) (Oxford University Press, 2004).

13. Gray, *Scalacronica* (1907), p.161.

14. M.H. Brown, 'Douglas, Sir Archibald, lord of Liddesdale (1294–1333), magnate', *Oxford Dictionary of National Biography* (online ed.) (Oxford University Press, 2004).

15. Rogers, *War Cruel and Sharp*, p.49.

16. *Calendar of Documents Relating to Scotland*, Vol. I, No. 1480, p.269.

17. *Chronicle of Lanercost*, p.270.

18. A.A.M. Duncan, 'Murray [Moray], Sir Andrew, of Bothwell (1298–1338), soldier and administrator', *Oxford Dictionary of National Biography* (online ed.) (Oxford University Press, 2004).

19. Ibid.

20. Webster, 'Scotland without a King', p.223.

21. *Chronicle of Lanercost*, p.270.

22. Gray, *Scalacronica* (1907), p.161.

23. *Chronicle of Lanercost*, p.270.

24. *Calendar of Documents Relating to Scotland*, Vol. I, No. 1086, p.196.

25. Rémy Ambühl, *Prisoners of War in the Hundred Years War: Ransom Culture in the Late Middle Ages* (Cambridge, 2013).

26. H.S. Lucas, 'John Crabbe: Flemish Pirate, Merchant and Adventurer', in *Speculum* 20 (1956), p.12.

27. 'Gesta EdwardI Tertii Auctore Canonico Bridlingtoniensi', p.109; Bower, *Scotichronicon* (1998), Vol. VII, p.89.

28. *Foedera, conventions* (1869), II, 2,847.

29. Rogers, *War Cruel and Sharp*, pp.51–52.

30. Ibid.

31. Ibid.

32. Ibid.

33. Henry Knighton, *Chronicon*, ed. J.R. Lumby (London 1895), 1:465; *The Anonimalle Chronicle*, p.152.

34. *Chronicle of Lanercost*, p.271; Bower, *Scotichronicon* (1998), Vol. VII, p.83.

35. Knighton, *Chronicon*, 1:465; Beam, *The Balliol Dynasty: 1210–1364*, p.387.

36. *Liber Pluscardensis Historians of Scotland*, Vol. VII, ed. Felix H. Skene (Edinburgh, 1877), p.267.
37. *Chronicle of Lanercost*, p.271.
38. *Rotuli Parliamentorum*, Vol. II, ed. J. Strachey (London, 1783), p.69.
39. Rogers, *War Cruel and Sharp*, p.58.
40. *Calendar of the Patent Rolls 1330–34* (Her Majesty's Stationery Office: London, 1920), p.400.
41. Ibid., p.18.
42. Knighton, *Chronicon*, 1:486; *The Anonimalle Chronicle*, p.154.
43. Andrew of Wyntoun, ii, p.398; Liber Pluscardensis, p.268.
44. H.J. Hewitt, *The Organization of War Under Edward III* (Manchester, 1966), p.91.
45. Ibid., p.93.
46. R. Cox, 'A Law of War? English Protection and Destruction of Ecclesiastical Property during the Fourteenth Century', in *English Historical Review*, 128 (2013), p.1381.
47. Barnes & Barrow, 'The Movements of Robert Bruce', p.58.
48. Scammel, 'Robert I and the North of England', p.385.
49. W. Stanford Reid, 'Sea-Power in the Anglo-Scottish War, 1296–1328', in *Mariner's Mirror*, 46 (1960) p.7; *Chronicle of Lanercost*, p.272.
50. *Chronicle of Lanercost*, p.277; *The Anonimalle Chronicle*, p.157.
51. Andrew of Wyntoun, ii, p.397; Bower, *Scotichronicon* (1998), Vol. VII, p.89.
52. *The Anonimalle Chronicle*, p.159.
53. Nicholson, *Edward II and the Scots*, p.121.
54. Thomas Burton, *Chronica Monasterii de Melsa*, ed. E.A. Bond (London 1866), 2:368.
55. 'Gesta EdwardI Tertii Auctore Canonico Bridlingtoniensi', p.111.
56. Gray, *Scalacronica* (1907), p.162.
57. Ibid.
58. Gesta EdwardI Tertii Auctore Canonico Bridlingtoniensi', p.113.
59. Burton, *Chronica Monasterii de Melsa*, 2:369.
60. *The Brut*, p.282.
61. Ibid., p.283.
62. *Foedera, conventions, litterae* (1869), II:2:864.
63. Gesta EdwardI Tertii Auctore Canonico Bridlingtoniensi', p.113.
64. Burton, *Chronica Monasterii de Melsa*, 2:370.
65. Nicholson, *Edward II and the Scots*, p.131.
66. *Chronicon Domini Walteri de Hemingburgh*, ed. H.C. Hamilton (London, 1849), II, p.308.
67. Rogers, *War Cruel and Sharp*, p.69.
68. Ibid., p.58.
69. Gesta Edwardi Tertii Auctore Canonico bridlingtonensi, p.114.
70. Ibid., p.113.
71. *The Brut*, p.283.
72. *The Anonimalle Chronicle*, p.166.
73. Gesta EdwardI Tertii Auctore Canonico Bridlingtoniensi', p.16.
74. Burton, *Chronica Monasterii de Melsa*, 2:370; *The Brut*, p.285.
75. Rogers, *War Cruel and Sharp*, p.74.
76. A.J. Macdonald, 'Triumph and Disaster: Scottish Military Leadership in the later Middle Ages' in *England and Scotland at War 1296–1513*, eds. A King and D. Simpkin (Leiden, 2012), p.282.

77. Iain A. MacInnes, '"Shock and Awe" the Use of Terror as a Psychological Weapon in The Bruce-Balliol Civil War, 1332–8' in *England and Scotland in the Fourteenth Century: New Perspectives*, eds. A King and M.A. Penman (Woodbridge, 2007), p.40.

78. A.J. Macdonald, 'Kings of the Wild Frontier? The Earls of Dunbar or March 1070–1435' in *The Exercise of Power in Medieval Scotland 1200–1500*, eds. S. Boardman and A. Ross (Dublin, 2003), p.150.

79. Penman, *David I* (2005), p.51.

80. Rogers, *War Cruel and Sharp*, p.75.

81. Beam, *The Balliol Dynasty*, p.280.

82. Iain A. MacInnes, '"To be Annexed forever to the English Crown" The English occupation of Southern Scotland, 1334–1337,' in *England and Scotland at War 1296–1513*, eds. A. King and D. Simpkin (Leiden, 2012), p.183.

83. Ibid.

84. *The Brut*, I, p.274.

85. Rogers, *War Cruel and Sharp*, p.80.

86. *Liber Pluscardensis*, p.276.

87. Andrew of Wyntoun, ii, p.414; Bower, *Scotichronicon* (1998), Vol. VII, p.107.

88. Andrew of Wyntoun, ii, p.414; Bower, *Scotichronicon* (1998), Vol. VII, p.89.

89. Burton, *Chronica Monasterii de Melsa*, 2:372; Ross, Men for all Seasons, p.8.

90. Johannis de Fordun (1872), Vol. II, p.349; Gesta EdwardI Tertii Auctore Canonico Bridlingtoniensi, p.119.

91. Bower, *Scotichronicon* (1998), Vol. VII, p.119; Gesta EdwardI Tertii Auctore Canonico Bridlingtoniensi', p.120.

92. *Chronicle of Lanercost*, p.288.

93. Ibid., p.269.

94. Gray, *Scalacronica* (1907), p.119.

95. Bower, *Scotichronicon* (1998), Vol. VII, p.107.

96. Ibid., p.109; A.J. Macdonald, 'Profit, Politics and Personality: War and the Later Medieval Scottish Nobility,' in *Freedom and Authority, Scotland 1050–1650: Historical and Historiographical Essays Presented to Grant G. Simpson*, eds. T. Brotherstone and D. Ditchburn (East Linton, 2000), p.118.

97. *Chronicle of Lanercost*, p.292.

98. Knighton, *Chronicon*, 1:475; Bower, *Scotichronicon* (1998), Vol. VII, p.109.

99. *Chronicle of Lanercost*, p.294; Burton, *Chronica Monasterii de Melsa*, 2:372.

100. Bower, *Scotichronicon* (1998), Vol. VII, p.115.

101. *Adae Murimuth Continuatio Chronicarum, Robertus de Avesbury de Gestis Mirabibius regis Edwardi tertii*, ed. E.M. Thompson (London, 1889), p.302.

102. Bower, *Scotichronicon* (1998), Vol. VII, p.115; Andrew of Wyntoun, ii, p.422.

103. MacInnes, *Scotland's Second War of Independence*, p.23.

104. W. Douglas Simpson, 'The Campaign and Battle of Culbean, A.D. 1335' in *Proceeding of the Society of Antiquaries of Scotland*, 64 (1930), p.201.

105. *Chronicle of Lanercost*, p.294.

106. Ibid.

107. *Foedera, conventions, litterae* (1869), II, 2, p.930.

108. 'Gesta EdwardI Tertii Auctore Canonico Bridlingtoniensi', p.128.

109. MacInnes, *Scotland's Second War of Independence*, p.26.

110. *Foedera, conventions, litterae* (1869), II, 2, p.930.

111. *Original Letters Illustrative of English History*, ed. H. Ellis (London, 1846), 30.
112. James Campbell, 'England Scotland and the Hundred Years War in the Fourteenth Century', in *The Wars of Edward III*, ed. Clifford J. Rogers (Woodbridge, 1999), p.208.
113. Campbell, 'England Scotland and the Hundred Years War', p.208.
114. Ibid.
115. Bower, *Scotichronicon* (1998), Vol. VII, p.141; Andrew of Wyntoun, ii, p.451.
116. Andrew of Wyntoun, ii, p.466.
117. *Chronicle of Lanercost*, p.313.
118. Penman, *David II* (2005), p.67.
119. Bower, *Scotichronicon* (1998), Vol. VII, p.155.
120. *Chronicle of Lanercost*, p.337; Bower, *Scotichronicon* (1998), Vol. VII, p.259.
121. R. Hardy, 'The Military Archery at Neville's Cross 1346' in *The Battle of Neville's Cross 1346*, eds. D.W. Rollason and M.C. Prestwich, (Stamford, 1998), p.112.
122. *Chronicle of Lanercost*, p.337; Bower, *Scotichronicon* (1998), Vol. VII, p.259.
123. *Chronicle of Lanercost*, p.259.
124. *Calendar of Documents Relating to Scotland*, Vol. II, No. 1479.
125. MacInnes, *Scotland's Second War of Independence*, p.50.
126. C.A. Raleigh Radford, 'Balliol's Manor House on Hestan Island', in *Transaction of the Dumfriesshire and Galloway Natural History and Antiquarian Society*, 35, (1957), p.33.
127. *Adae Murimuth Continuatio Chronicarum*, p.454; Johannis de Fordun (1872), Vol. II, p.363.
128. *Foedera, conventions, litterae* (1869), III, i, pp.321–2.

Bibliography

Primary Sources

Adae Murimuth Continuatio Chronicarum, Robertus de Avesbury de Gestis Mirabibius regis Edwardi tertii, ed. E.M. Thompson (London, 1889).

Andrew of Wyntoun, *The Orgynale Cronykil of Scotland*, ed. D. Laig (Edinburgh, 1879).

A Scottish Chronicle Known as the Chronicle of Holyrood, ed. M.O. Anderson (Scottish History Society, 1938).

Benedict of Peterborough, ed. William Stubbs (London, 1867).

Calendar of Documents Relating to Scotland, eds. J.D. Galbraith and G.G. Simpson (Edinburgh, 1881–8).

Calendar of the Patent Rolls 1330–34 (Her Majesty's Stationery Office: London, 1920).

Calendar of the Patent Rolls (London, 1891).

Calendar of the Patent Rolls, 1330–4 (London, 1942).

Cronica Regum Mannie et Insularum: Chronicles of the Kings of Man and the Isles, trans. G. Broderick (Belfast, 1979).

Chronicle of Fordun, ed. W.F. Skene (Edinburgh, 1872).

Chronicle of Guisborough, ed. H. Rothwell.

Chronicon de Lanercost (Maitland Club, 1839).

Chronicle of Lanercost 1272–1346, trans. Sir Herbet Maxell (Glasgow, 1913).

Chronicon Domini Walteri de Hemingburgh, ed. H.C. Hamilton (London, 1849)

Documents And Records Illustrating the History of Scotland, ed. F. Palgrave.

Documents Illustrative of the History of Scotland 1286–1306, ed. Joseph Stevenson (Edinburgh, 1870).

Durham Liber vitae, MS Cotton, Domitian A. VII, Edition and Digital Facsimile with Introduction, Codicological, Prosopographical and Linguistic Commentary, and Indexes, including the Biographical Register of Durham Cathedral Priory (1083–1539) by A.J. Piper, eds. David Rollason & Lynda Rollason (London: British Library, 2007).

Early Yorkshire Charters, Vol. II, ed. William Farrer (Edinburgh, 1915).

Exchequer Roll.

Flores Historiarum, ed. Henry Richard Luard (London, 1890).

Foedera, ed. T. Rhymer (Record Commission, London, 1816).

Foedera, conventions, litterae etc, eds. Thomas Rhymer, edit A. Clarke, F. Holbrooke and J. Coley (London, 1869).

'Gesta EdwardI Tertii Auctore Canonico Bridlingtoniensi' in *Chronicles of the Reigns of Edward I and Edward II*, V II, ed. William Stubbs (London, 1883).

Gray, Sir Thomas, *Scalacronica*, trans. H. Maxwell (Glasgow, 1907).

Gray, Sir Thomas, *Scalacronica*, trans. and ed. A. King (Durham, 2005).

Henry Knighton, *Chronicon*, ed. J.R. Lumby (London 1895).

Johannis de Fordun, *Chronica Gentis Scotorum*, ed. W.F. Skene (Edinburgh, 1872).

John of Fordun, *Chronica Johannes de Fordun, Chronica gentis Scotorum*, ed. W.F. Skene (1876).
John of Fordun's Chronicle of the Scottish Nation (Edinburgh).
John of Worcester, *The Chronicle of John of Worcester*, III, ed. and trans. P. McGurk (Oxford, 1998).
Les *Grandes Chroniques de France*, ed. Jules Viard (Paris, 1953).
Liber S. Marie de Melros, Munimenta Vetustiora Monasterii Cisterciensis deMelros, ed. C.N. Innes, (Edinburgh, 1837).
Liber Pluscardensis Historians of Scotland, Vol. VII, ed. Felix H. Skene (Edinburgh, 1877).
Matthew Paris, *Chronica Majora* (Cambridge).
Matthew Paris, *English History*, trans. J.A. Giles (1852).
National Manuscripts of Scotland (1871).
Original Letters Illustrative of English History, ed. H. Ellis (London, 1846).
Registrum Eyisconatus Glasauensis (Edinburgh, 1843).
Registrum Magni Sigilli Regum Scotorum: The register of the Great seal of Scotland, A.D. 1306–1668, ed. J.M. Thompson (Edinburgh, 1882).
Regesta Regum Scotorum, V, The Acts of Robert I, ed. A.A.M Duncan (Edinburgh, 1988).
Register of John de Halton, ed. William Thompson (London, 1913).
Register of John le Romeyn, ed. William Brown (Durham, 1913).
Richard of Hexham, *Chronicles of Stephen, Henry II and Richard I*, ed. R. Howlett, II (London, 1886).
Richard of Hexham, *De Gestis Regis Stephani*, ed. R. Howlett (London, 1884–89).
Roger of Howden, *Chronica*, ed. William Stubbs (London, 1869).
Roger of Howden, *Gesta Regis Henrici Secundi and Gesta Regis Ricardi*, ed. William Stubbs (1867).
Rotuli Parliamentorum, Vol. II, ed. J. Strachey (London, 1783).
Rotuli Scotiae in turri Londinensi et in Domo Capitulari Westmonasteriensi Asservati, ed. D. Macpherson (London, 1814).
Scottish Historical Documents, ed. Gordon Donaldson (Edinburgh, 1970).
The Acts of the Parliament of Scotland, eds. T. Thompson and C. Innes (Edinburgh, 1814–75).
The Acts of William I, King of Scots, 1165–1214, ed. G.W.S Burrow (Edinburgh University, 1971).
The *Annals of Roger de Hoveden: Comprising the History of England and of Other Countries of Europe from A.D. 732 to A.D. 1201*, ed. and trans. Henry T. Riley (London, 1853).
The Anonimalle Chronicle 1307 to 1334 from *Brotherton Collection* MS. 29, eds. W.R. Childs and J. Taylor (Leeds, 1991).
The Brut or the Chronicle of England, ed. F.W. Brie (London, 1906).
The Chronicle of Melrose, ed. A.O. Anderson and others (London, 1936).
The Chronicles of Robert of Torigni, ed. R. Howlett (London, 1889).
The Records of the Parliaments of Scotland to 1707, eds. K.M. Brown et al (St Andrews, 2007).
Thomas Burton, *Chronica Monasterii de Melsa*, ed. E.A. Bond (London, 1866).
Walter Bower, *Scotichronicon*, ed. D.E.R. Watt (Aberdeen, 1982).
Walter Bower, *Scotichronicon*, ed. D.E.R. Watt, (Aberdeen, 1989).
Walter Bower, *Scotichronicon*, ed. D.E.R. Watt, (Edinburgh, 1998).

Secondary Sources

Acheson, E., 'Ferrers Family (per. c.1240–1445)', *Oxford Dictionary of National Biography* (Oxford University Press, 2004).

Altschul, Michael, *A Baronial Family in Medieval England: The Clares 1217–1314* (Baltimore, 1965).

Altschul, Michael, 'Clare, Gilbert de, Eighth Earl of Gloucester and Seventh Earl of Hertford (1291–1314)', *Oxford Dictionary of National Biography* (Oxford: Oxford University Press, 2004).

Ambühl, Rémy, *Prisoners of War in the Hundred Years War: Ransom Culture in the Late Middle Ages* (Cambridge, 2013).

Anderson, A.O., *Early Sources of Scottish History 500–1286* (Edinburgh, 1922).

Anderson, A.O., *Scottish Annals from English Chroniclers: AD 500 to 1286* (London, 1908).

Ash, M., 'William Lamberton, Bishop of St Andrews, 1297–1328', in *The Scottish Tradition Essays in Honour of R.G. Cant*, ed. G.W.S. Barrow (Edinburgh 1974).

Ayton, Andrew, 'Ughtred, Thomas, first Lord Ughtred', *Oxford Dictionary of National Biography* (online ed.). (Oxford University Press, 2004).

Bannerman, John, 'MacDuff of Fife,' in *Medieval Scotland: Crown, Lordship and Community, Essays Presented to G.W.S. Barrow*, eds. A. Grant & K. Stringer (Edinburgh, 1993).

Barbour, John, *The Bruce* (Edinburgh, 1997).

Barnes, P. and G.W.S Barrow, 'The Movements of Robert Bruce between September 1307 and May 1308', in *Scottish Historical Review*, 69.

Barrell, A.D.M., 'The Papacy and the Regular Clergy in Scotland in the Fourteenth Century', in *Scottish Church History Society Records*, 24:2, (1991).

Barrow, G.W.S., 'Badenoch and Strathspey, 1130–1312: 1 Secular and Political' in *Northern Scotland*.

Barrow, G.W.S., 'Elizabeth [née Elizabeth de Burgh] (d. 1327), Queen of Scots', in *Oxford Dictionary of National Biography* (online ed.) (Oxford University Press, 2004).

Barrow, G.W.S., *Kingship and Unity: Scotland, 1000–1306* (Edinburgh University Press, 1989).

Barrow, G.W.S., 'Lothian in the First War of Independence, 1296–1328', in *The Scottish Historical Review*, Vol. 55, No. 160, Part 2 (October 1976).

Barrow, G.W.S., *Robert Bruce* (Eyre & Spottiswoode, 1965).

Barrow, G.W.S., *Robert Bruce* (Edinburgh, 1988).

Barrow, G.W.S., *Robert Bruce and the Community of the Realm of Scotland* (Edinburgh University Press, 1965).

Barrow, G.W.S., *Robert Bruce & the Community of the Realm of Scotland* (4th ed.) (Edinburgh, 2005).

Barrow, G.W.S., *The Anglo-Norman Era in Scottish History* (Oxford, 1980).

Barrow, G.W.S., 'The Army of Alexander III's Scotland,' in *Scotland in the Reign of Alexander III*, ed. N.H. Reid (Edinburgh, 1990).

Barrow, G.W.S., 'The Scottish Clergy in the War of Independence,' in *Scottish Historical Review*, 41 (1962).

Barrow, G.W.S., 'The Scottish Clergy and the War of Independence', in *Scottish Historical Review 43* (1963).

Barrow G.W.S., and Ann Royan, 'James Stewart, Fifth Steward of Scotland, 1260–1309', in *Essays on the Nobility of Medieval Scotland*, ed. Keith Stringer (Edinburgh: John Donald, 1985).

Beam, Amanda, *The Balliol Dynasty, 1210–1364* (Edinburgh: John Donald, 2008).

Bean, J.M.W., 'Percy, Henry, third Lord Percy (c.1321–1368)', *Oxford Dictionary of National Biography* (online ed.). (Oxford University Press, 2004).

Blakely, Ruth Margaret, *The Brus Family in England and Scotland: 1100–1295* (Boydell Press, 2005).

Boardman, Stephen, *The Campbells, 1250–1513* (Edinburgh, 2006).

Boardman, Stephen, *The Early Stewart Kings: Robert II and Robert III* (Edinburgh, 1996).

Bowles, Christopher, and Ronan Toolis, *The Lost Dark Age Kingdom of Rheged: The Discovery of a Royal Stronghold at Trusty's Hill, Galloway* (Oxbow Books, 2017).

Bradbury, Jim, *The Medieval Archer* (Woodbridge, 1985).

Broun, Dauvit, 'Defining Scotland and the Scots before the Wars of Independence,' in D. Broun, R. Rinlay and M. Lynch, *Image and Identity: The Making and Remaking of Scotland through the Ages, Edinburgh* (1998).

Brown, M.H., 'Douglas, Sir Archibald, lord of Liddesdale (1294–1333), magnate', *Oxford Dictionary of National Biography* (online ed.) (Oxford University Press, 2004).

Brown, Michael, *The Wars of Scotland 1214–1371* (Edinburgh University Press, 2004).

Burgtorf, Jochen, 'With My Life, His Joyes Began and Ended: Piers Gaveston and King Edward II of England Revisited', in *Fourteenth Century England*. Vol. V. ed. Nigel Saul (Woodbridge, UK: The Boydell Press, 2008).

Burke, Sir Bernard, *The Dormant, Abeyant, Forfeited, and Extinct Peerages of the British Empire*, (London, 1883).

Byrne, Francis John, *Irish Kings and High Kings* (London, 1973).

Cadwell, D.H., 'Scottish Spearmen 1298–1314: An Answer to Cavalry', in *War in History*, Vol. 19(3) (2012).

Cameron, Sonja, 'Sir James Douglas, Spain and the Holy Land' in *Freedom and Authority – Scotland 1050–1650*. eds. Brotherstone & Ditchwell (Edinburgh, 2000).

Cameron, S., and A. Ross, 'The Treaty of Edinburgh and the Disinherited (1328–32)', *History*, 84, (1999).

Campbell, J., 'England, Scotland and the Hundred Years War in the Fourteenth Century,' in *Europe in the late Middle Ages*, eds. J.R. Hale, J.R.L. Highfield and B. Smalley (London, 1965).

Campbell, James, 'England Scotland and the Hundred Years War in the Fourteenth Century', in *The Wars of Edward III*, ed. Clifford J. Rogers (Woodbridge, 1999).

Carpenter, David, 'The Secret Revolution of 1258', in *Baronial Reform and Revolution in England 1258–1267*, ed. Adrian Jobson (The Boydell Press, 2016).

Cornell, David, *Bannockburn: The Triumph of Robert the Bruce* (Yale University Press, 2003).

Cornell, David, 'Bannockburn: The Triumph of Robert the Bruce', in *The Historian*, 73(2), (New Haven, Conn.: Yale University Press, 2009).

Cox, R., 'A Law of War? English Protection and Destruction of Ecclesiastical Property during the Fourteenth Century', in *English Historical Review*, 128 (2013).

Davies, Kerrith, 'The Count of the Côtentin: Western Normandy, William of Mortain, and the Career of Henry I', in *The Haskins Society Journal* 22, ed. William L. North, (2010).

Downham, Clare, *Hiberno-Norwegians and Anglo-Danes: Anachronistic Ethnicities and Viking-Age England* (Mediaeval Scandinavia 19, 2009).

Duncan, A.A.M., 'Bruce, Alexander, earl of Carrick (d. 1333)', *Oxford Dictionary of National Biography* (online ed.) (Oxford University Press, 2004).

Duncan, A.A.M., 'Brus, Robert (I) de, lord of Annandale (d. 1142)', in *Oxford Dictionary of National Biography* (Oxford University Press, 2004).

Duncan, A.A.M., 'Brus, Robert (II) de, lord of Annandale (d. 1194?)', *Oxford Dictionary of National Biography* (Oxford University Press, 2004).

Duncan, A.A.M., 'Brus [Bruce], Robert (VI) de') in *Oxford Dictionary of National Biography* (Oxford University Press, 2004.

Duncan, A.A.M., 'Murray [Moray], Sir Andrew, of Bothwell (1298–1338), soldier and administrator', *Oxford Dictionary of National Biography* (online ed.) (Oxford University Press, 2004).

Duncan, A.A.M., 'Process of Norham', in *Thirteenth Century England* V, ed. P.R. Coss and S.D. Lloyd (Woodbridge, 1999).

Duncan, A.A.M., 'The Bruces of Annandale, 1100–1304,' in *Dumfries and Galloway Transactions*, 69 (1994).

Duncan, A.A.M., *The Kingship of the Scots 842–1292: Succession and Independence* (Edinburgh University Press, Edinburgh, 2002).

Duncan, A.A.M., 'The Scots' Invasion of Ireland, 1315', ed. R.R. Davies, *The British Isles, 1100–1500* (Edinburgh: J. Donald. 1988).

English, Barbara, 'Forz [Fortibus], William de, count of Aumale', *Oxford Dictionary of National Biography* (2004). https://doi.org/10.1093/ref:odnb/29480 [Accessed May 2023].

Fisher, Andrew, 'Murray, Andrew (d. 1297)' *Oxford Dictionary of National Biography* (Oxford University Press, 2004) (online edition).

Fisher, Anderew, 'Wallace, Sir William (d. 1305)', *Oxford Dictionary of National Biography* (Oxford University Press, 2004) (online edition).

Flanagan, M.T., 'Clare, Richard fitz Gilbert de [called Strongbow], Second Earl of Pembroke', *Dictionary of National Biography* (Oxford University Press, 2004).

Frame, R., 'The Bruces, in Ireland', in *Irish Historical Review*, 24 (1974).

Fraser, C.M., 'Bek, Antony (I) (c.1245–1311)', in *Oxford Dictionary of National Biography* (online ed.) (Oxford University Press, 2008).

Fryde, Natalie, *The Tyranny and Fall of Edward II 1321–1326* (Cambridge: Cambridge University Press 2003).

Grant, Alexander, 'Bravehearts and Coronets: Images of William Wallace and the Scottish Nobility', in *The Wallace Book*, ed. E.J. Cowan (Edinburgh, 2007).

Grant, Alexander, *Independence and Nationhood 1306–1469* (Edinburgh, 1991).

Green, Judith A., 'Aristocratic Loyalties on the Northern Frontier of England, 1100–1174,' ed. D. Williams, *England in the Twelfth Century* (Woodbridge, 1990).

Green, Judith A., 'David I and Henry I', in the *Scottish Historical Review*. Vol. 75 (1996).

Gillingham, John, *The English in the Twelfth Century: Imperialism, National Identity, and Political Values* (Boydell Press, 2000).

Haines, Roy Martin, *King Edward II: Edward of Caernarfon, His Life, His Reign, and Its Aftermath, 1284–1330* (London, 2003).

Hamilton, J.S., 'Bohun, Humphrey de, Fourth Earl of Hereford and Ninth Earl of Essex, 1276–1332', *Oxford Dictionary of National Biography* (Oxford: Oxford University Press, 2004).

Hammond, Matthew H., 'The Durward Family in the Thirteenth Century', in *The Exercise of Power in Medieval Scotland, c.1200–1500*, eds. Steve Boardman and Alasdair Ross (Dublin/Portland, 2003).

Hardy, R., 'The Military Archery at Neville's Cross 1346' in *The Battle of Neville's Cross 1346*, eds. D.W. Rollason and M.C. Prestwich (Stamford, 1998).

Haskell, M., 'Breaking the Stalemate; The Scottish Campaign of Edward I, 1303–4', in *Thirteenth-Century England, VII*, eds. Michael C. Prestwich, Richard Britnell and Robin Frame (Boydell Press, 1997).

Helle, Knut, 'Norwegian Foreign Policy and the Maid of Norway', *The Scottish Historical Review*, 69 (2002).

Hewitt, H.J., *The Organisation of War Under Edward III* (Manchester, 1966).

Hiatt, Alfred, 'Beyond a Border: The Maps of Scotland in John Hardyng's Chronicle', in *The Lancastrian Court Proceedings of the 2001 Harlaxton Symposium*, ed. J. Stratford (2003).

Hollister, C. Warren, *Henry I* (Yale University Press, 2003).

Hollister, C. Warren, *Monarchy, Magnates and Institutions in the Anglo-Norman World* (Hambledon Press, 1986).

Houts, Elizabeth van, *Married Life in the Middle Ages* (Oxford, 2019).

Jackson, K.H., 'Angles and Britons in Northumbria and Cumbria', ed. H. Lewis, *Angles and Britons* (Cardiff, 1963).

Jewell, Helen M., 'Latimer, William, first Lord Latimer (d. 1304), baron and soldier', *Oxford Dictionary of National Biography* (Oxford: Oxford University Press, 2004).

Kenny, Gillian, 'The Wife's Tale: Isabel Marshal and Ireland', in *William Marshal and Ireland*, ed. J. Bradley (Dublin, 2017).

Knecht, Robert, *The Valois Kings of France 1328–1589* (London, 2007).

Lucas, H.S., 'John Crabbe: Flemish Pirate, Merchant and Adventurer', in *Speculum* 20 (1956).

Macdonald, A.J., 'Kings of the Wild Frontier? The Earls of Dunbar or March 1070–1435' in *The Exercise of Power in Medieval Scotland 1200–1500*, eds. S. Boardman and A. Ross (Dublin, 2003).

Macdonald, A.J., 'Profit, Politics and Personality: War and the Later Medieval Scottish Nobility', in *Freedom and Authority, Scotland 1050–1650: Historical and Historiographical Essays Presented to Grant G. Simpson*, eds. T. Brotherstone and D. Ditchburn (East Linton, 2000).

Macdonald, A.J., 'Triumph and Disaster: Scottish Military Leadership in the later Middle Ages' in *England and Scotland at War 1296–1513*, eds. A. King and D. Simpkin (Leiden, 2012).

MacInnes, Iain A., *Scotland's Second War of Independence 1332–1357* (Woodbridge, 2016).

MacInnes, Iain A., '"Shock and Awe" the Use of Terror as a Psychological Weapon in The Bruce-Balliol Civil War, 1332–8' in *England and Scotland in the Fourteenth Century: New Perspectives*, eds. A. King and M.A. Penman (Woodbridge, 2007).

MacInnes, Iain A., '"To be Annexed forever to the English Crown" The English occupation of Southern Scotland, 1334-1337,' in *England and Scotland at War 1296–1513*, eds. A. King and D. Simpkin (Leiden, 2012).

MacInnes, I.A., 'Who's Afraid of the Big Bad Bruce? Balliol Scots and "English Scots" during the Second War of Independence', in *The Soldier Experience in the Fourteenth Century*, eds. A.R. Bell, A. Curry, A. Chapman, A. King and D. Simpkin (Woodbridge, 2011).

Maddicott, J.R., 'Beaumont, Henry de, First Lord Beaumont (c. 1280–1340), Baron', *Oxford Dictionary of National Biography* (Oxford: Oxford University Press, 2004).

Maddicott, J.R., 'Thomas of Lancaster, Second Earl of Lancaster', *Oxford Dictionary of National Biography* (online ed.) (Oxford University Press, 2008).

Marshall, Rosalind K., *Scottish Queens, 1034–1714* (Tuckwell Press, 2003).

Marshall, Susan, *Illegitimacy in Medieval Scotland 1100–150* (Boydell Press, 2021).

McDonald, Russel Andrew, *Kings, Usurpers, and Concubines in the Chronicles of the Kings of Man and the Isles* (Palgrave Macmillan, 2019).

McDonald, Russel Andrew, *Manx Kingship in its Irish Sea Setting, 1187–1229: King Rǫgnvaldr and the Crovan Dynasty* (Dublin: Four Courts Press, 2007).

McDonald, Andrew, *The Kingdom of the Isles; Scotland's Western Seaboard C.100–1336* (Scottish Historical Review, 1998).

McNamee, Colm, *Wars of the Bruces: Scotland, England and Ireland 1306–1328* (Edinburgh, 2002).

McNamee, Colm, 'William Wallace's Invasion of Northern England, 1297', in *Northern History*, 26 (1990).

McMichael, Thomas, 'The Feudal Family of de Soulis', in *Dumfriesshire and Galloway Natural History & Antiquarian Society: Transactions and Journal of Proceedings*, 3rd series, Vol. 26 (1947–48).

Mortimer, Ian, *The Greatest Traitor: The Life of Sir Roger Mortimer, 1st Earl of March, Ruler of England, 1327–1330* (London, 2002).

Moynihan, Scott, 'Miracles, Divine Agency, And Christian Muslim Diplomacy During the Crusades', *Miracles, Political Authority and Violence in Medieval and Early Modern History*, eds. Matthew Rowley, Natasha Hodgson (Abingdon, 2022).

Murison, Alexander Falconer, *William Wallace: Guardian of Scotland* (New York, 2003).

Neville, Cynthia J., *Native Lordship in Medieval Scotland: The Earldoms of Strathearn and Lennox, c. 1140–1365* (Portland & Dublin, 2005).

Nicholson, Helen. J., *Theory and Practice of War in Europe, 300–1500* (New York, 2003).

Nicholson, R., *Edward II and the Scots: The Formative Years of a Military Career* (Oxford, 1965).

Nishioka, Kenji, 'Scots and Galwegians in the 'Peoples Address' of Scottish Royal Charters' in *The Scottish Historical Review* (2008).

O'Byrne, Emmett, *War, Politics and the Irish of Leinster 1156–1160* (Dublin, 2003).

O'Mahony, Charles, *The Viceroys of Ireland* (1912).

Oram, Richard D., 'Bruce, Balliol and the lordship of Galloway', in *Dumfries and Galloway Transaction*, 67 (1992).

Oram, Richard D., *David I: The King Who Made Scotland* (Tempus Publishing, 2004).

Oram, Richard D., *Domination and Lordship: Scotland, 1070–1230* (Edinburgh University Press, 2011.

Oram, Richard D., 'Fergus, Galloway and the Scots' in *Galloway: Land and Lordship*, ed. G.P. Stell (Edinburgh: The Scottish Society for Northern Studies).

Oram, Richard D., 'Introduction: An Overview of the Reign of Alexander II', in *The Reign of Alexander II, 1214–49. The Northern World: North Europe and the Baltic c. 400–1700 AD. Peoples, Economics and Cultures*, ed. R.D. Oram (Leiden: Brill, 2005).

Oram, Richard D., 'Quincy, Roger de, Earl of Winchester (c.1195–1264)', *Oxford Dictionary of National Biography* (Oxford University Press, 2004), https://doi:10.1093/ref:odnb/22966 [Accessed May 2023].

Oram, Richard D., *The Lordship of Galloway, C1000 to C1250* (PhD Thesis St Andrews University, 1989).

Oram, Richard D., *The Canmores: Kings & Queens of the Scots, 1040–1290* (Tempus, 2002).

Oram, Richard D., 'Thomas (Thomas of Galloway), earl of Atholl (d. 1231), magnate', Oxford *Dictionary of National Biography* (Oxford University Press, 2004), https://doi.org/10.1093/ref:odnb/49364 [Accessed May 2023].

Ormrod, W.M., 'Wake, Thomas, second Lord Wake (1298–1349), nobleman', *Oxford Dictionary of National Biography* (online ed.), (Oxford University Press, 2004).

Owen, Douglas David Roy, *William the Lion 1143–1214: Kingship and Culture* (Tuckwell, 1997).

Penman, Michael, 'A fell coniuracioun agayn Robert the douchty king: The Soules Conspiracy of 1318–1320', in *Innes Review*, 50 (1999).

Penman, Micheal, *David II* (Edinburgh, 2004).

Penman, Michael, *David II* (Edinburgh, 2005).

Penman, Michael, *Robert the Bruce, King of the Scots* (Yale University Press, 2014).

Penman, Michael, *The Scottish Civil War: The Bruces & the Balliols & the War for Control of Scotland, 1286–1356* (Edinburgh, 2002).

Perry, Guy, *The Briennes: The Rise and Fall of a Champenois Dynasty in the Age of the Crusades, c. 950–1356* (Cambridge University Press, 2018).

Phillips, J.R.S., *Aymer de Valence, Earl of Pembroke, 1307–1324: Baronial Politics in the Reign of Edward II* (Clarendon Press, 1972).

Porter, Stephen, *Edward III's Faithful Knight: Walter Mauny and His Legacy* (Stroud, 2022).

Powicke, Michael, *Military Obligation in Medieval England* (Oxford, 1962).

Prestwich, Michael, 'Colonial Scotland: The English in Scotland under Edward I,' in *Scotland and England 1286–1815*, ed. R.A. Mason (Edinburgh, 1987).

Prestwich, Michael, *Edward I* (Yale University Press, 1988).

Prestwich, Michael, 'Edward I (1239–1307)' in *Oxford Dictionary of National Biography* (Oxford University Press, 2004).

Prestwich, Michael, 'Edward I and the Maid of Norway,' Vol. 69, No. 188, Part 2: *Studies Commemorative of the Anniversary of the Death of the Maid of Norway* (Oct. 1990).

Prestwich, Michael, *Plantagenet England, 1225–1360. New Oxford History of England* (Oxford: Clarendon Press, 2005).

Prestwich, Michael, 'The Battle of Stirling Bridge: An English Perspective', in *The Wallace Book*, ed. Edward J. Cowan (Edinburgh: John Donald, 2007).

Prestwich, Michael, *War, Politics and Finance under Edward I* (London, 2007).

Raleigh Radford, C.A., 'Balliol's Manor House on Hestan Island', in *Transaction of the Dumfriesshire and Galloway Natural History and Antiquarian Society*, 35 (1957).

Ried, Norman H., *Alexander III, 1249–1286: First Among Equals* (John Donald).

Reid, Norman H., 'Alexander III (1241–1286), king of Scots' in *Oxford Dictionary of National Biography* (online ed.) (Oxford University Press, 2004).

Reid Norman H., 'The Kingless Kingdom: The Scottish Guardianship of 1286–1306,' in *Scottish Historical Review* (1982).

Reid, W. Stanford, 'Sea-Power in the Anglo-Scottish War, 1296–1328', in *Mariner's Mirror*, 46 (1960).

Richardson, Douglas, *Magna Carta Ancestry* (2005).

Ridgeway, H.W., 'Valence [Lusignan], William de, Earl of Pembroke William de, Earl of Pembroke (d. 1296), Magnate', *Oxford Dictionary of National Biography* (online ed.) (Oxford University Press, 2004).

Rogers, Clifford J., *War Cruel and Sharp: English Strategy Under Edward III, 1327–136* (Boydell Press, 2000).

Ross, A., 'Men for All seasons? The Strathbogie Earls of Atholl and the Wars of Independence, C. 1290–1335, 2', *Northern Scotland*, 21 (2001).

Ross, David R., *James the Good: The Black Douglas* (Glasgow: Luath Press, 2020).

Rymer, Thomas, *Foedera Conventiones, Literae et cujuscunque generis Acta Publica inter Reges Angliae* (London, 1745).

Sanders, I.J., *English Baronies: A Study of their Origin and Descent 1086–1327* (Oxford, 1960).

Scammel, J., 'Robert I and the North of England', in *The English Historical Review*, 73 (1958).

Sellar, W.D.H., 'MacDougall, John, Lord of Argyll (d. 1316)', *Oxford Dictionary of National Biography* (online ed.). (Oxford University Press, 2004).

Simpkin, David, *The English Aristocracy at War: From the Welsh Wars of Edward I to the Battle of Bannockburn* (Boydell Press, 2008).

Simpson, G.G., 'The Claim of Florence, Count of Holland to the Scottish Throne, 1291–2', in *Scottish Historical Review*, XXVI.

Simpson, W. Douglas, 'The Campaign and Battle of Culbean, A.D. 1335' in *Proceeding of the Society of Antiquaries of Scotland*, 64 (1930).

Slavin, Philip, *Experiencing Famine in Fourteenth-century Britain* (Montreal, 2022).

Spencer, Andrew M., *Nobility and Kingship in Medieval England: The Earls and Edward I 1272–1307* (Cambridge University press, 2013).

Stell, G.P., 'Balliol, John de (b. before 1208, d. 1268)', *Oxford Dictionary of National Biography* (Oxford University Press, 2004), https://doi.org/10.1093/ref:odnb/1208 [Accessed May 2023].

Stell, G.P., 'The Balliol Family and the Great Cause of 1291–2', in *Essays of the Nobility of Medieval Scotland*, ed. K.J. Stringer (Edinburgh University Press, 1985).

Strickland, Matthew, 'Kings of Scots at War', in *Military History of Scotland*, eds. E.M. Spiers, J.A. Craig and M. Strickland (Edinburgh, 2012).

Stringer, Keith J., 'A New Wife for Alan of Galloway' (PDF) in *Transactions of the Dumfriesshire and Galloway Natural History and Antiquarian Society* (1972).

Stringer, Keith J., 'Marie [née Marie de Coucy] (d. 1284), Queen of Scots, second consort of Alexander II' in *Oxford Dictionary of National Biography* (online ed.). (Oxford University Press, 2004).

Stringer, Keith J., 'Periphery and Core in Thirteenth-Century Scotland, Alan Son of Roland, Lord of Galloway and Constable of Scotland', eds. A. Grant & K.J. Stringer, *Medieval Scotland: Crown, Lordship and Community* (Edinburgh: Edinburgh University Press).

Stones, E.L.G., ed. *Anglo-Scottish Relations* (London, 1963).

Stones, E.L.G., 'The Submission of Robert Bruce to Edward I, 1301–2' in *Scottish Historical Review*, 34.

Stones E.L.G., and G.G. Simpson, eds., *Edward I and the Throne of Scotland* (1978).

Studd, Robin, 'Reconfiguring the Angevin Empire' in *England and Europe in the Reign of Henry III*, eds. Ifor W. Rowlands and Björn K.U. Weiler (Taylor and Francis, 2017).

Summerson, Henry, 'Clifford, Robert, First Lord Clifford (1274–1314), *Oxford Dictionary of National Biography* (Oxford: Oxford University Press, 2004).

Summerson, Henry, 'Umfraville, de, family', *Oxford Dictionary of National Biography* (online ed.), (Oxford University Press, 2008).

Taylor, Alice, *The Shape of the State in Medieval Scotland 1124–1290* (Oxford University Press, 2016).

Thomspon, Hugh M., *The English and the Normans: Ethnic Hostility, Assimilation, and Identity 1066–c.1220* (Oxford University Press, 2003).

Thompson, Kathleen, 'Affairs of State: The Illegitimate Children of Henry I', in *Journal of Medieval History*, 29 (2003).

Turner, James, *The Royal Bastards of Twelfth Century England: Blood and Power* (Pen and Sword, 2023).

Vale, Malcolm, 'St John, Sir John de (d. 1302)'. in *Oxford Dictionary of National Biography* (online ed.) (Oxford University Press, 2008).

Veach, C., 'Conquest and Conquerors', in *The Cambridge History of Ireland. Vol. 1*, ed. B. Smith (Cambridge: Cambridge University Press, 2018).

Vincent, Nicholas, 'Why 1199? Bureaucracy and Enrolment under John and his Contemporaries,' in *English Government in the Thirteenth Century*, ed. Adrian L. Jobson (The Boydell Press, 2004).

Ward, Jennifer C., 'Joan, Countess of Hertford and Gloucester (1272–1307)', *Oxford Dictionary of National Biography* (Oxford: Oxford University Press, 2004).

Warner, Kathryn, *Isabella of France: The Rebel Queen* (Amberley Publishing, 2012).

Watson, Fiona, 'Comyn, John, Seventh Earl of Buchan, (c. 1250–1308)', *Oxford Dictionary of National Biography* (Oxford: Oxford University Press, 2004).

Watson, Fiona, 'Dunbar, Patrick, 8th Earl of Dunbar or of March, and Earl of Moray (1285–1369), *Dictionary of National Biography* (Oxford University Press, 2004).

Watson, Fiona, 'Settling the Stalemate: Edward I's Peace in Scotland, 1303–1305,' in *Thirteenth- Century England VI*, eds. Michael C. Prestwich, Richard Britnell and Robin Frame (Boydell Press, 1997).

Watson, Fiona, 'Sir Robert, lord of Liddesdale (c. 1293–1332), royal bastard', *Oxford Dictionary of National Biography* (online ed.) (Oxford University Press, 2004).

Watson, Fiona, 'Strathbogie, David, styled tenth earl of Athol' *Oxford Dictionary of National Biography* (Oxford University Press, 2004).

Watson, Fiona, 'The Enigmatic Lion: Scotland, Kingship and National Identity in the Wars of Independence' in *Image and Identity: The Making and Remaking of Scotland through the Ages*, eds. D. Broun, R. Finlay and M. Lynch (Edinburgh, 1998).

Watson, Fiona, 'Umfraville, Gilbert de, seventh earl of Angus', *Oxford Dictionary of National Biography* (online ed.). (Oxford University Press, 2004).

Watson, Fiona, *Under the Hammer: Edward I and Scotland, 1286–1307* (John Donald, 2008).

Watt, D.E.R., 'The Minority of Alexander III of Scotland,' in *Transactions of the Royal Historical Society*, 5th Series, Vol. 21 (1971).

Waugh, Scott L., 'Edmund, first earl of Kent (1301–1330)', *Oxford Dictionary of National Biography* (Oxford: Oxford University Press, 2004).

Waugh, Scott L., 'Talbot, Gilbert, first Lord Talbot', *Oxford Dictionary of National Biography* (online ed.). (Oxford University Press, 2004).

Waugh, Scott L., 'Talbot, Richard, second Lord Talbot (c. 1306–1356), soldier and administrator', *Oxford Dictionary of National Biography* (online ed.), (Oxford University Press, 2004).

Webster, Bruce, 'Balliol, Edward, (b. in or after 1281, d. 1364), *Oxford Dictionary of National Biography* (Oxford University Press, 2004).

Webster, Bruce, 'Scotland Without a King, 1329–1341', in *Medieval Scotland: Crown, Lordship and Community*, eds. A. Grant and K.J. Stringer (1993).

Weir, Alison, *Queen Isabella: She-Wolf of France, Queen of England* (London: Pimlico Books, 2006).

Young, Alan, 'Buchan in the 13th Century', in *Medieval Scotland: Crown, Lordship and Community Essays Presented to G.W.S. Barrow*, eds. Alexander Grant & Keith J. Stringer (Edinburgh, 1993).

Young, Alan, *Robert the Bruce's Rivals: The Comyns, 1212–1314* (Tuckwell Press, 1997).

Young, Alan, 'The Comyns and Anglo-Scottish Relations (1286–1314)' in *Thirteenth Century England VII: Proceedings of the Durham Conference*, eds. Michael Prestwich, R.H. Britnell, Robin Frame (Boydell Press, 1997).

Young, Alan and George Cumming, *The Real Patriots of Early Scottish Independence* (John Donald, 2014).

Index

Dear Reader,

We hope you have enjoyed this book, but why not share your views on social media? You can also follow our pages to see more about our other products: facebook.com/penandswordbooks or follow us on X @penswordbooks

You can also view our products at www.pen-and-sword.co.uk (UK and ROW) or www.penandswordbooks.com (North America).

To keep up to date with our latest releases and online catalogues, please sign up to our newsletter at: www.pen-and-sword.co.uk/newsletter

If you would like a printed catalogue with our latest books, then please email: enquiries@pen-and-sword.co.uk or telephone: 01226 734555 (UK and ROW) or email: uspen-and-sword@casematepublishers.com or telephone: (610) 853-9131 (North America).

We respect your privacy and we will only use personal information to send you information about our products.

Thank you!